TEETH MARKS ON MY CHOPSTICKS

A Knucklehead Goes to Wall Street

BY MATTHEW CONNOLLY

Edited by Bill Summers

—Unpolished Press—

Teeth Marks on My Chopsticks
Copyright © 2018 by Matthew Connolly All rights reserved.
First Edition: 2019

ISBN 13: 978-0-9997572-1-5
ISBN 10: 0-9997572-1-0

Editor: Bill Summers
Formatting: Streetlight Graphics

No part of this book may be reproduced, scanned, or distributed in any printed or electronic form without permission. Please do not participate in or encourage piracy of copyrighted materials in violation of the author's rights. Thank you for respecting the hard work of this author.

This is a work of fiction. Names, characters, places, and incidents either are the product of the author's imagination or are used fictitiously, and any resemblance to locales, events, business establishments, or actual persons—living or dead—is entirely coincidental.

PART I
AND SO IT BEGINS

1

ALL MY MEMORIES ARE STILL pictures. No video memories for me. I still remember this picture. It does not feel good, makes me queasy even today. Why am I on the floor, and why is there a strange pain where my family jewels are purported to be? Those were my first thoughts before my senses came back. I am on my knees, my head is turned to see a pair of stockinged legs sauntering away from me. I prop myself up on a padded green chair and my nuts are starting to burn and I am starting to feel like I'm going to puke. What the hell just happened?

Shockingly enough, I am on a Wall Street trading floor at JP Morgan and it's 7:30 on an October morning of 1987. I just had the audacity to notify an options trader that she had made a basic adding mistake the day before on some trades she did and that basic adding mistake just cost the bank and herself $75,000. I guess she was not thrilled. She had a phone in her hand and she whipped it like a Nolan Ryan fastball and walked away. The problem was, said phone ricocheted off the green chair and zapped me right in my peaches. I dropped to the floor. She just walked away. Freaking harsh. OK Matt, regroup and scurry off to your cubicle in the back office.

I was a clerk. My first job after I barely graduated college was as a file clerk for JP Morgan Securities in New York. For the first year of my working life, here is what I did all day, every day. I reconciled a computer printout of 100 pages of trades with another group within the bank who had a similar 100-page printout with different information. Let me explain.

My subsidiary of JP Morgan was the bond trading arm called "JP Morgan Securities" and they traded boatloads of futures contracts on government bonds on a daily basis. Most of those trades were done with another subsidiary of JP Morgan called, surprisingly enough, "JP Morgan Futures." Most of JPM Futures was based in Chicago where the bond futures pits were located, and that is where the bulk of trades were executed. JPM Securities would do their trades with JPM Futures in Chicago over the phone, write a ticket of the trade, then that ticket would make its way to us where we would input it into our IBM XT or AT computers. In those days, they were state of the art. Nowadays, the computing power would be like a $2 calculator. A solar powered calculator, no less!

Anyway, someone in Chicago was also inputting their side of the trade into some similar type of state-of-the-art machinery. Every trade would result in a positive or negative P&L (profit or loss) and a risk position. A risk position was the net position of the trade. For instance, if JPM Securities started with zero and bought five contracts and sold five contracts and made $5,000, their risk position would be zero and P&L would be $5,000, and JPMorgan Futures would also have a risk position of zero, but a P&L of $-5,000. Then, if JPM Securities bought ten contracts and sold five and made $1,000, they would be "long" five contracts and JPMorgan futures would be -$1,000 and "short" five contracts. Since we traded with each other, our gains and losses and theirs should always offset and vice versa on our trading positions. Get it? It's basic accounting, and a "T" account for any of you accounting dinosaurs should suffice to run the whole god-damn thing, right? Not so fast....

TEETH (2) MARKS

The trading floor runs 100 miles per hour and people are inherently stupid (me especially) so guess what? Shit was wrong every god-damn day and sometimes in a big way. I found that many times "brilliant" people with advanced degrees would add 2+2 and come up with 5. That is where I came in. Basically, I would have to check the addition and subtraction of people who actually graduated on time and had 4.0 grade point averages. Sometimes, they were not terribly thrilled to be told that they added wrong by a guy who could barely break the 2.0 GPA threshold. Add in that those mistakes may cost the bank upwards of $50,000 or many times more, as well as make them look bad or be fired, and it was sometimes a very emotional environment.

Anyway. After all the trades were input on both sides every day, the computer reports would run on overnight batches and print out at 4 a.m. the next day. It usually took a good five hours to do all the computer processing and run the reports, so we had to have it done overnight. Today it would take 5 minutes. And please remember, that in the 12-hour cycle of reconciliation, the markets were moving around all the time. Nowadays, it may take an hour to find a mistake and correct it, but it was a good 16 hours back then. I would get into work at 8 a.m. and immediately start going through the reports. My counterpart at JPMorgan Futures would come in at 8 a.m. and start going through his/her reports. In a perfect world, my reports and their reports would all mirror each other. It never happened this way. We would spend all morning comparing all 100 pages of the reports and noting our differences. We would then compare the actual trade tickets to the reports to see if input errors caused the discrepancies. If the input was good, we would have to check with the trading floor clerks to see if they could figure out the issue. If they had no luck it was stage time. I was on…I'd have to go contact the trader and get to the bottom of it. Sometimes they would know immediately they made a mistake and not be angry. Usually the "angry factor" increased if the loss the error caused them was pretty big. When they fucked up and it was in their favor... guess what? They usually didn't yell at me. Shocking, huh? Yes, sometimes a mistake was made and my trader actually made money, rather than lost money. Those were the times I did not have to cover my balls.

Other times, they would insist they were correct and the other side was wrong. The trader would pick up the phone and start bitching at the person at JPMorgan futures they had transacted with. When the other side insisted they were right, it would be fun to eavesdrop:

> My trader: You fucking idiot, I told you to SELL 50, not BUY 50 yesterday!
>
> Their trader: I know you said BUY!
>
> My trader: I said SELL!

On and on it went...

Finally one of the traders would hang up on the other one, and my trader would say to me:

"Check the goddamn tape!"

I hated this. My life just became a pain in the ass.

The tape room. Where good days go to die. First off, I'd be lucky if the time stamp on the ticket of the trade was correct within an hour. Secondly, it was tape. Like reel tape, not the digital computer stuff we have now. There was usually some cigarette-smoking troll in charge of the tape room. Let's just say cigarette smells were the best smells coming out of that room. We would sit in the room with the troll, tell the troll the phone line the trade was done on and the approximate time...Then start listening and hopefully find out what really happened before I passed out from toxic fumes. It could take 10 minutes, it could take 3 hours.

When we finally found the tape of the trade, it was always pretty easy to decipher. We would then take a "tape of the tape"... I would record the offending transaction on a portable tape player then play it back to my trader if they were wrong, or to the other side's trader if they were wrong. Someone was always pissed and it sucked and I was usually at the wrong end of a tirade. Oh, by the way, did you know that if I had "half a fucking brain I would have sorted this problem four hours ago before the market moved?" Here was another popular one: "Why did it take you so fucking long to find this trade on the tape?" Fun. Fun. Fun. Oh, did I mention I was working from 8 a.m. to 8 p.m. and making $16,500 a year?

Actually, I was very happy. I loved my job and was just happy I was lucky enough to work in New York in a $99 summer suit (I had two $99 summer suits from Sears) and say I worked on Wall Street.

Before I finish the whole first chapter of recounting a typical day of my job, let me tell you how I got my first job.

Total. 100%. Luck.

During my senior year in college, one of my housemates invited me to a party at his family's home. I was chubby and broke so I never turned down free food. It was just an added benefit that I enjoyed his parents on the periodic visits I made to his house. At this party, my friend introduced me to his brother in law, who worked on Wall Street. Nice guy, five-minute conversation, just the basics. Whatever. When is the food coming out?

Anyway, that was probably in April of 1987. A few months later, after graduation my friend calls me and tells me his brother-in-law's firm may be hiring clerks. Do I want an interview? You're god-damn right I want an interview! At that point, I had done nothing to find a job, and I was still 3 credits short of my diploma.

My friend lends me a suit (it was tight), and on a Thursday in late June I head into New York City, 15 Broad Street to be exact. Nervous? You're damn right. I sweat like a gorilla in

65 degree weather and had never worn a suit before. I was interviewing on Wall Street (15 Broad is only steps away) and it was 85 degrees. I probably smelled worse than the tape room troll at that point!

I get buzzed up and am met at the elevator by a guy who looks only a few years older than me. He shakes my hand and says, "Follow me." We walk through the corridors and his first question is, "What's your favorite football team?" I tell him I am a Giants fan and he shakes his head in disgust. Uh-oh, strike one! He then asks me what my favorite baseball team is... I hesitate then answer: "I am a die-hard Yankees fan." He nods and says, "We will get along just fine." Whew! Who the fuck is this guy, anyway?

Not another word was said on our way to the offices in the back. He drops me off in an office and ends with: "Talk to the VP and don't fuck it up and you will be starting Monday. Can you come back in and see Human Resources tomorrow?"

Me: "I'm pretty sure my schedule is clear."

I think I shit a rainbow right about that point.

I had a quick, basic interview with the VP in charge of the group who just wanted to make sure I was not a serial killer, I guess. I saw HR the next day and started Monday.

It ends up that the guy who brought me from the elevator to the office was my new co-boss. My first interview consisted of me being asked my favorite sports teams. I guess he figured all Yankee fans had their heads screwed on straight. I'm not so sure...

OK, back to brass tacks. So all day long I would track down differences in my report to the report generated in Chicago. Every time we found a difference, we would take a pencil and update the numbers. Every trader account would be updated, and then those risk and P&L numbers would fold up into bigger numbers that would eventually account for the whole firm's risk position in futures & options and also a daily Profit & Loss report. When all the adjustments were made, I and my counterpart supporting the Chicago office would use an adding machine to update the numbers, then make the changes needed in the computer. The last thing we did at about 2 p.m. before we started on today's trades (for tomorrow) was re-run the batch reports for all the updated numbers. We would then check the reports to "prove" we were in sync. When we "proved," we could start the next day's work. Rinse and repeat. Rinse and repeat. Day in and day out.

The guy I started out talking to every day was a junior clerk like me. We became close and moved up together at JPMorgan, and later, into jobs at different firms. We'd speak on the phone for 4 to 5 hours a day, so we were destined to become friends. We knew what booze we liked, we knew what we had for breakfast (he was bran muffin and a coffee), and we also became familiar with our timing preferences for our morning constitutional. I guess that was the idea of the bran muffin and coffee. He is still a great friend to this day and lives in the same town as I do. But I digress...

Back to the story. For about two months after I started, I just watched and learned and didn't know enough to do any interacting with the traders. It was September of 1987 before I was able to add any real value or even function at a low level. I was just starting to figure things out when things got crazy.

It was October 19, 1987. Just another typical day in back-office land. Being stuck in the back, we were in our own little world and didn't pay a lot of attention to what was happening in the markets, or anywhere else for that matter. My world consisted of the following:

> 1) Where were we going for happy hour Thursday night?
>
> 2) Oh shit, it's October and I still have only two summer suits. Am I really gonna have to shell out

$200 for a real suit? (Did I mention I'm a cheap shit?)

3) I wonder when I can get a car loan so I don't have to borrow money from my future in-laws to pay for repairs?

October 19 was just like any other day. We left work at 8 p.m. not having a clue that the market had crashed that day. I wonder if I went to happy hour? Anyway, the next morning I got in at 7 a.m. and the shit had hit the fan. I had tons of messages, tons of overnight faxes of futures trades that London and Tokyo had done. I knew within five minutes that it was going to be a crazy day, but I had no idea how crazy. Ignorance is bliss.

Basically, all the futures and options I was responsible for reconciling were for US Government Notes and Bonds. Pretty safe investments.

On October 19 at 8:30 a.m., the government had released its report on the nation's employment picture. The stronger the report (the more jobs created), the higher interest rates would go. It was a strong report and the interest rate market was starting to price in the Federal Reserve raising rates, so prices on US government Treasury notes and bonds were tanking (prices move lower as interest rates move higher). As interest rates became more attractive, many accounts were selling their equity holdings and moving into the more attractive rates of US Government Treasury notes and bonds. As the day went on this trend just kept going and going. By the end of the day, Treasury prices had stabilized but equity (stocks) had shit the bed and were down a lot. From what I found out later, most traders were pretty much paralyzed. The move was so big and so strange that no one knew what to do. The economy was strong and employment was good, so why did interest rates stop going up and why did equity prices start crashing? For the most part, traders were just shocked and unprepared.

Over the next week, the markets were insane and moving in massive amounts day after day, both up and down. In the futures markets on government bonds, there were limits on how far a future could move in a certain trading session. The future on US government bonds was "limit up" two or three days in a row as equities crashed. Then as equities recovered, those same futures would be limit down. I'm telling you, it was bedlam. I saw a few careers made and lost in that week, and it stuck in my mind for the rest of my career.

On the afternoon of the 19th, one trader who had a very marginal trading reputation decided to "go long" short-term futures (a bet that interest rates would go lower as equities crashed). She carried that position overnight and when she walked into work the next morning the market had moved so much that she made her whole profit target for the year in one night! I wonder if she went to happy hour?

There were also another three traders who lost so much money on October 19 or the next few days that their jobs were threatened. One options trader lost so much that when I went out to his desk to check on a trading discrepancy, his partner told me, "I think he's in the bathroom throwing up." She was not kidding, and that is indeed where he was. He actually slept under his desk on the trading floor a few days during that week. It was pretty nasty. I'm pretty sure there was no shower involved so it was literally "nasty." No one had ever seen anything like it before so it was all new ground for everyone. I thought it was fun and just wanted to know where happy hour was...

Looking back now, this was exactly the moment that I got the urge and ambition to be a trader. I LOVED the chaos, the bedlam, the unpredictability of it all. I thrived on it and I really thought that I had the tools needed to survive over a long period of time in this business. You have to check your ego at the door, you have to prioritize your actions very quickly, you have to have common sense. Above all, you have to have a sense of human psychology and what drives people to trade the way they trade. This will allow you to be in sync with what is happening in the markets.

For a month or so the markets were crazy, but they slowly crept back to normal as equities stabilized and the Federal Reserve actually lowered interest rates instead of raising them. I was hooked on trading and there was no turning back. At the time, the people who ran the back office operations were sensitive to the fact that many of their employees might want to move out to the trading floor. Most of these back-office supervisors wanted their good people to stay and have careers in the back office, not deplete their talent pool by moving along. You always had to be careful of how you broached the subject and who you confided in, because certain people took offense when a person's ambitions strayed from their plan for you. Besides where my next beer was being poured, this was the first time I ever had any plans or ambitions career-wise. Hallafreakinlullah?

2

THE WAY I SEE IT, back in those days I had two things going for me. I worked like a dog in my current job to make everything perfect, because I was naive enough at the time to think that doing that would help me move forward. In actuality, there were some bosses who rewarded that and some bosses who would NEVER want to lose you because of how easy you made their life and would actually sabotage you so they could keep you under their thumb. I saw both those scenarios play out in my career. The second thing I had going for me was my connection to the guy who ran it all on the trading floor at JP Morgan Securities. I just did not know at the time that I had that going for me. Let me explain how this works:

Reality: The guy who ran it all and got me my job didn't know me from the bottom of his shoe except that he knew I was looking for a job and they needed good clerks and I hadn't made a fool of myself when I met him. That would come later but I was IN by that point so there was no turning back! I will explain that later, back to the story.

How my bosses saw it: Holy shit, this guy is close to the big boss so we need to keep that in mind going forward. This guy (me) is not that bright but he does work hard and get the job done so we have to be careful with him. The truth was, I was told that besides getting me my interview, there would be no contact or favors done for me by the big guy again. He got me an interview, the rest was 100% me and that is exactly how I wanted it. Pass or fail on my own. But my bosses did not know that. Since I have only half a brain, I really should have had no chance but I got lucky again.

I was probably a year into my first duties and had very subtly let a few people know I would love to get onto the trading floor when my opening occurred. Let me back up and explain a little bit about the desk I would end up on next and its role. I was currently in a back office role as a clerk, off the trading floor. There was, however, a desk called the "Edit desk" that was on the trading floor but reported to the back office operations group. It was basically a middle office desk, run by operations but located on the trading floor. This desk was responsible for real time reconciliation of cash bond trades between JP Morgan Securities traders and all the five broker firms (Cantor, Garvin, Chapdelaine, etc), as well as trades done directly with other banks (Goldman, Chase etc). There were probably eight people on the desk, with each person assigned to a high profile trader, as well as a few other traders who did less volume (more on this later). Basically, this was a desk of Trader Assistants. Each clerk would be responsible for every part of their main trader's day, from set up, to trade checks, profit and loss statements and reconciliation. It was a much more stressful job, with more responsibilities, a much higher profile, and more pay due to more overtime. Did someone say more pay? Does that mean I can start buying Pabst instead of Old Milwaukee? Talk about incentive!

Okay, back to the story. So the people at the Edit desk are assigned traders to watch over. There were about five very high profile traders on the whole floor and then maybe fifty much lower volume and profile traders. If you had one of the top five, you had better be prepared for huge amounts of stress and responsibility because a lot more was at stake. The highest profile trader, even though he was not the highest volume trader, was the big guy, the guy who got me the job in the first place. He traded all the products, took a ton of risk, and made or lost a boatload of money. Are you starting to see where this might be going? Apparently when I was gleefully filling out my new $200 winter suit in the back office, someone on the Edit desk made a massive mistake in the big guy's risk/profit statement and it became such a big problem that there was very bad blood between the big guy (remember he ran everything at the Securities unit) and the operations group management. I was the solution to the problem (can you imagine that?). The operations group thought that if they put me out on the Edit desk responsible for the big guy and I did great, problem solved. If I totally fucked it up, I was the guy he brought in so it was his fault and not theirs. They also thought he might be a little easier on me than on some stranger. That explains how I got my move from the back office to the trading floor. Funny how the world works. This move was probably the biggest break I ever got and exposed me to all kinds of things in the trading world that fascinated me. But more importantly: Screw Pabst, maybe I'm going straight to Budweiser!

My new boss was the guy who co-managed the group, the Jets/Yankees fan who gave me an interview during our thirty steps to the VP's office. He managed the Edit desk on the trading floor. At the time I was probably twenty three, he might have been twenty six or so. I was making around $22,000 after overtime and had no title. My new boss was an Associate, I think (I was never big on titles). The trading floor at 15 Broad was a regular floor of the building with no walls around it. There were a few offices with walls, the little Generals' room and little Princesses' room (restrooms) had walls, as well as the cafeteria. Other than that, pretty flat real estate with a bunch of desks pushed together. In those days, traders had little green cathode ray screens that each broker supplied. The most senior and important traders had maybe five or six little screens, with junior traders having one or two. In 1989, JP Morgan Securities was a struggling new trading unit, an offshoot of the iconic and powerful Morgan Guaranty Trust Company. That meant the trading floor was packed together with old stuff. Not nearly as glamorous as nowadays. In addition, people still smoked right on the trading floor so the smell and the smoke lingered and there was a brownish tint on everything. Don't get too depressed, because there was a bright shining part of the whole operation which made it the greatest place on earth. Ready? There was a bar in the basement and the elevator took you right there!! Are you kidding me? And I'm getting paid to work here? ... Sadly, this bar shut down right around my being able to access it. I was not a happy camper, but in hindsight this bar closing probably saved my career. Some things are just not made to be that easy.

For a struggling rookie like myself, more interested in saving his extra cash for social purposes, the cafeteria at JP Morgan was a godsend. As the story goes, JP Morgan himself put into the corporate charter that the company would provide meals to workers during working hours. There were many theories as to why, from great generosity to an ingenious way to get more productivity from workers since there were no seats in the cafeteria. You slopped your food on your tray and brought it back to your desk, eating and working, eating and working. Over the years the cafeteria was cut back until it went away totally. I was not a big coffee drinker in those days, but the coffee was notorious for being high test and very nasty. We used to call it "swill." As in: "Hey asshole, get me a cup of swill while your in the cafeteria." If you let a cup of swill sit overnight in a Styrofoam cup, by the morning the nasty swill would have broken down the molecular structure of the cup and it would be sprouting leaks and sagging like the leaning tower of Pisa. I shit you not!

As a side note, before I get back to my new job, this was 1989ish and right outside our building they were filming the movie "Ghost" on Wall Street. It was interesting for a few reasons. We all knew who Patrick Swayze was and everybody wanted to get a glimpse of him. Nobody really knew who Whoopi Goldberg was, and she spent time filming there also. I caught a glimpse of Patrick Swayze taking a break and hanging out and my thought was: "Holy crap, he is a wee little man." I could not believe how small he was. That aside, it was interesting how they filmed the scenes on the street with all the people and the traffic. As I remember, they let regular workers walk up and down the street along with the extras and the actors. They had people with little headsets in business attire walking along and telling people not to stare, keep walking as normal, and "you might get into a movie." It was actually pretty cool how they did it. Okay, back to my new job.

Let's start with the mechanics of a typical day on my new job and then I'm sure I will lose track and start talking about all kinds of other things that probably will bore the hair off you. Anyway, I was basically an offsite trading assistant. I sat on the other side of the trading floor but I was responsible for all the real time reconciliation of my trader (the big guy, if you remember). Once the trading in New York started at 9 a.m., there was so much happening that I would liken the Edit desk to a MASH (Mobile Army Surgical Hospital) unit. Basically, we did triage on the risk and profit/loss position during the day, until the final reconciliation happened in the back office over night and the next morning. In a perfect world we'd get it 90% perfect and the other 10% would hopefully not cause us to lose our jobs or our traders to lose theirs. First thing in the morning, I'd pull my trader's reports out of a two-inch thick stack of reports. Each trader had a portfolio name that was attached to their account and during the day we would be screaming out portfolio names instead of trader names. The portfolios were only two characters so it was much more efficient. My trader's portfolio was OW (if I remember), so I'd sort through the reports until I found the reports under OW. These reports had all the trading from the previous day and if all went well it would match the previous day's closing position. Remember, rinse and repeat?

Bear with me and you will understand the cycle. If I was lucky and the reports matched, I would go to my trader's seat and make sure that laid out in front of him were all his current positions so he could start his day. Let me explain. These were all traders who traded government bonds and they all had specific bonds within the US government bond universe they were responsible for. If each trader had ten bonds in their universe, every query from a salesperson or a broker to our firm must go through the trader responsible for that specific bond. Each day they had a starting position in each bond (long or short) and every trade they did would change the position and therefore the risk profile. It would be my job to double check their trading and adding in real time to make sure if they thought they were "long 300 million" of a bond, which made money if the market went higher, that they hadn't made a mistake and were actually "short 300 million" which made money if the market went down. That could and did happen and was almost never pretty. In reality my new job was just an extended version of my starting job except that there was ten times more going on, ten times more risk if I made a mistake, and fewer traders I was responsible for.

So once I was pretty sure the starting number was correct, as long as I kept track of every trade my trader did during the day and how he added or subtracted from the cumulative position, theoretically at day's end his final risk position would match and the profit or loss would match. Easier said than done, I assure you! Each trader had a sheet of paper called a trading blotter with the current position in each bond on the sheet. As each trade was done, the trader would update the trading blotter and then write a trade ticket for each trade. There were generally four types of trades. The first was a trade done over the phone with a broker as the intermediary. The second was a trade done with a salesperson who worked for JP Morgan. These salespeople sat either around the trading floor or in another office and spoke to clients such as other banks, hedge funds, corporations, etc. If a client had a bond to buy or sell, they would call our salesperson and the salesperson would relay the details to the correct trader for that bond, and they would execute a trade. The trader would update the blotter in front of him and then the salesperson would be responsible for writing the ticket.

The third trade would be a direct trade the trader executed with another bank's trader over the phone. The last type would be an internal trade, where one trader sitting next to another would trade with each other to offset or to share risk. In summary, besides a trade with a salesperson, each trader would have to write a ticket as well as update their blotter. These green tickets with yellow and pink copies would find their way to us fine assistants on the Edit desk and we would then go to work. A ticket runner would accumulate all the green tickets from the traders and bring them to the Edit desk. Each ticket had the trader's portfolio on it so it would be sorted by portfolio and passed to each trader's assistant. You with me so far? If not, don't worry about it, this is just fill for the funny stories and weird situations anyway.

Theoretically, every trade done has a ticket associated with it. Each assistant would check every single ticket for accuracy. The broker tickets would be checked with the brokers, sales tickets checked with salespeople, direct bank trades with the other banks...and finally, internal trades would be checked by one assistant yelling over to another assistant to check the details. It went something like this: "Hey jerkoff, do you know OW selling ON 100 million of 2 year notes at 100-8/32nds?" ON and OW were the portfolios. If I knew the exact other side of the trade, I'd respond with something like, "That's a check, shit-for-brains." If I knew different details, I'd say, "I know 100-9" or "I know 80 million." Then we would check our trader's paper blotters or with the traders themselves to see if we could sort it out. Let's talk for a moment about how insane most traders were.

In the example above, we have an internal trade where each side knows different details. That would be called a "break." A position break was when the amounts were not agreed upon, or a buy should have been a sell, etc. A P/L break (profit/loss) was when the price was not agreed. We would have to sort this out. In a normal world, sorting this out would take about five seconds. We could walk over and look at the trader's blotter and see if the details of the blotter matched the ticket, or if he just wrote the ticket wrong. If he wrote the ticket wrong but his blotter matched the other trader's info, we could just modify the ticket and send it through. Conversely, the trader could take five seconds out of their life to help us sort THEIR issue! Here was the problem. Traders are freakin' psychos! There, I said it and now I feel much better. If the traders saw us snooping around their blotters, they would freak out many times for many reasons. Our desk took a lot of the brunt of hangovers, marital fights, or just bad trading days. Here is how we remedied that. We would send each other on missions. I would go sneak a peek at my colleague's trader's blotter to find a discrepancy and they would do the same for me. That way, they would not see their own assistant snooping around, so would not associate any problem with their own account. If you think that is sneaky, how about this one. When a trader with an account problem got up to hit the little Generals room or run to the cafeteria, we would go into spy mode. When said trader vacated, someone would run over to the desk and try to sort out the problem and adjust the trading blotter so the trader would not have to be directly told about it or asked. When you ran over with a big problem that might take some time, you just hoped they were taking a crap, not just a leak. That extra five minutes might be crucial to you getting screamed at or fired! Gross? Yes, but just the facts of life back then. So rinse and repeat. If you start the day with the right numbers, check that every single trade was correct and inputted correctly and reflected correctly on the blotter during the day and at the end of the night, all would be happy and blissful and easy. It never worked like that.

If you think about it, this job was just an "on steroids" version of my first job and just a natural progression as a person would get more comfortable with the business. That is as long as the quicker pace and multi-tasking escalation could be handled. We worked our butts off at that desk, but guess what? We loved every minute of it, we had guys and gals that got along like family, fought like family, and covered each other's backs like family. We also hoped that doing a good job here would help us take the next step forward. Some of us wanted to just have a few years in New York City, some wanted to move up in the Operations world, some wanted to stay at that desk forever, and some wanted to get a sniff at the trading side.

Okay, let's keep moving. Where were we? We had 8-10 people at this desk and say, 40 traders. Each of us would have a main trader, then maybe a few less work-intensive traders. Then there were the twenty or so traders who had no assistant assigned to them, but would sporadically have issues that we would have to sort out. We were so busy and crazed with our main responsibilities that when these traders came over with problems, no one wanted to step up and help them. It was a source of frustration to the traders and our own desk. Just like anywhere you work, it was always the same assistants coming to the rescue, and the others would put their heads down and act busy. Someone on our desk finally got so frustrated with the lack of enthusiasm to help these traders out that a great idea was born. It was nuts, and funny to think about now. This person actually made a cheap, shitty wheel like the one on the show Wheel of Fortune. Only this wheel had on it all the names of the assistants working on the Edit desk. When a trader with no assistant came over to get help with a problem, we would point to the wheel on the wall and make that trader spin it. Whoever it landed on HAD to help out that trader. Can you imagine a gaggle of 25-year-old knuckleheads making a grizzled trading veteran with an MBA from Wharton or University of Chicago spin a god-damn wheel to get some help? The wheel had a name. The Wheel of Responsibility. At first we had to explain what the wheel was, but after a month or two if a desperate trader came over we would just point to the wheel. We had them well trained. There were a few times when we pointed at the wheel and the trader was incensed at the whole thing. At one point, an enraged trader ripped the wheel off the wall. Unfortunate. I think that incident is what led to a few traders having personal on-site assistants on the trading floor. The Edit desk still existed, but certain assistants were cleared space to sit next to their main trader and help out those in the area. Since my responsibility was the big guy, I was moved out onto the trading desk to be his specific assistant on the desk. I was the happiest guy in the world about this because I felt it got me one step closer to the major leagues and it opened up a whole new level of responsibilities. I could hear the Heineken chilling!

JP Morgan had a reputation as a stodgy, stuffed shirt type of place. It really was an uptight place and the culture was snobby, blue blood, and for the most part, very arrogant. Those of us black sheep on the Edit desk used to have a lot of fun with some of the people who took themselves so seriously. The one thing I will say about stodgy, boring, stuffed shirt boorish people? Holy crap, did they let loose at the holiday party every year. In my view, people are people, we are all the same for the most part. Maybe 15% of each of us is different, the rest all the same. In that vein, it must take a hell of a lot of energy for these arrogant Ivy league people who think they are smarter than everyone else to keep up their fronts all day long at work. At the party, it was always fun to watch the walls break down and see some of them become human for a few hours.

There were two different holiday parties every year at JP Morgan. One was the typical boring, boorish, pinky-sticking-out fancy parties. Once a year the iconic office at 23 Wall was closed to banking and became the setting for the official holiday party for staff and spouses. I'm not sure when I was finally allowed into my first one, but it may have been after my first promotion. This was an incredibly fancy party, people whispering, no music, mostly champagne and shrimp cocktail. Oh, the shrimp cocktail. These freaking shrimp must have been flown in from the The Three Mile Island nuclear accident site, they were that massive. The shrimp was the only redeeming quality of these parties, as far as I was concerned. I can only remember one time at this yearly snobfest that it was fun and that was when someone's wife got loaded and started yelling crazy shit at the guy who was the number two guy on the trading floor. What made it so funny was that the woman's husband was in a fairly junior support role and here she is yelling delusional stuff at the deputy of the whole trading floor. I love alcohol, it always makes things fun. So that was the "official" party.

The real party, however, was what was called the "kick the dog party." This was a very dangerous party to go to for the following reasons. Firstly, it was held during the holiday season which put people in a frolicking mood. Secondly, it was always held on the night that people were told what their yearly bonuses were going to be. Since 90% of the stuffed-shirts, self involved, egotistical, over-educated people were never happy with their bonuses....well, add booze to those emotions and lots of it, and it became a very fun potion for crazy shit to happen. Oh yeah, and the dregs of the JP Morgan society (us at the Edit desk) were actually invited to this one. Another added element of craziness, ten immature knuckleheads with a three-hour open bar. Can you see where this is going?

For the first few of these parties, I made a drunken fool of myself. For the most part, I'm either a happy drunk or just sit there with a stupid dumbass grin on my face. I was extremely grateful and happy to be doing something I enjoyed so much. I was already over my head as far as career aspirations and was looking forward to the future. I was also working for the big guy, but during the day it was all business and I was scared shitless of him just like everyone else. I don't think I ever once saw him treat anyone poorly and he was always very fair with me...but we were all still scared of him anyway. The problem was, you add about 15 free beers to a happy Matt who owes his job and future to the guy he works for but never really gets to talk to and put them together at a party, and guess what? I would babble and thank him 100 times at about three of these parties in a row and he must have hated it and thought I was stalking him. To his credit, he was always understanding about the emotions that came out at these parties.

Anyway, in the four or five years the kick the dog party happened, so many great stories came out of them. Before the stories start, a quick summary of the structure of this party. This was a non-sanctioned party, which meant the bank did not pay for it. The rules were that someone would pick a good half dive bar (translation: a good drinking bar) for the party and the big guy would spring for the first three hours of open bar. After that, it would turn into a cash bar but most years one of the few traders who was actually happy with his/her bonus would quietly keep the bar open a few more hours under his/her tab. The bank would always pay for cars home after these parties but even the cab vouchers would have to be handled carefully so the bank would take care of the bill. That means we were always warned to make sure we carpooled and tried to share rides to keep the bill down. For us in operations, we were always scared to abuse the car privilege so we would try to get a ride share from more senior people so they would hand in the car voucher.

Once again, this led to some very uncomfortable moments, especially for a drunk like me! One year I randomly found a salesperson who was pretty senior and my apartment in New Jersey was on the way to the fancy town he lived in. So he took the drunken rookie in his car and was very sorry he did it. At that point I had probably been in that apartment (actually I was rooming at my sister's apartment) for a year and had no excuse for what happened next. I was so drunk that I could not give our driver directions to my apartment, or even my address. Hey, don't judge me, I was able to mumble out the town I lived in and we proceeded to drive around my town for over an hour before we stumbled onto the street. Let's recap: Drunken rookie in a car with a senior salesperson. Drunken rookie can't find his way home. Said rookie delays senior salesman over an hour. Not a good situation. Then I puked in the car. That's right. Technicolor yawn with full splash on senior salesman. I cringe at the thought.

Actually I don't really remember any of this. What I remember is a guy I didn't know coming over to the desk the next day saying my name and looking for me. He was still not happy, but was at least half-smiling about the incident. He proceeded to yell the story out on the trading floor in full detail. Matt mumbling, Matt lost, Matt puking. Not good. He was trying to teach me a lesson and it was embarrassing for about half a day. Did I learn my lesson? Yes and no. I still got drunk as a skunk at future parties, but I did make one change that I thought was pretty smart. I would write my address and basic directions on a sheet of paper. That paper would find its way into my suit pocket before the party. When it came time to jockeying for a car home and giving directions, the paper would come out. In subsequent years, I would actually lick the paper with my address on it and stick it on my ample forehead so there was no way it could be missed. I shit you not.

3

In addition to the daily duties of taking care of the traders, the desk had a few other functions that were more generic in support of the business as a whole. In those days, US government bonds were probably 80% of our (JP Morgan Securities) business. We were what was called a "Primary Dealer" in US government debt. There were roughly twenty or so banks that were primary dealers at the time. Basically that meant that the US Treasury department, which is in charge of issuing the country's bonds, would appoint banks to deal with them in a special capacity to make sure the bonds they issued would find their way into the market in a reasonable way. A big part of that job was the auction process, or how the billions of dollars worth of bonds would find their way into investors' hands through the primary dealer network. At least once a week the US Treasury would hold auctions of certain bonds they were trying to issue. These issues could be 1 day to 360 days (called Treasury Bills) all the way out to 30 years (Treasury Bonds). Bonds with starting maturities of 2 years to 10 years were generally called Notes. You paying attention? Bills, Notes and Bonds. Please stay awake as it gets less boring now.

At the time (1989ish), computers were just starting to make their way on the scene so many things were completely manual at the bank. As normal, government technology is always ten years behind the private sector, so the Treasury and the Federal Reserve were 100% manual. Let me explain to you this process in all its glory for the two years I was involved. The Treasury Department decides how much money they need to raise and then the auction process was done in person at the Federal Reserve banks. I am not sure if it was done at all the Federal Reserve banks around the country, or just the New York Branch. Either way, the New York branch was where all the action took place.

Before I start, here is a little anecdote that may or may not be true but it could be. Before my time on the Edit desk, it was mostly staffed with older clerks who had been there for many, many years. During and after my time, turnover at the desk became greater as they hired staff that looked at it as a starting point and a phenomenal way to learn the nuts and bolts of the system. Remember that before I started there was a bar in the basement that a person could take an elevator to from any floor? It still boggles my mind; I'd have never survived. Anyway... the story was that the person responsible for the auction process spent a lot of time in this basement bar, and not enough time at his desk. Dude, no judgment here, I'm more envious of you if it's true. Apparently, a few auctions were missed entirely because our person in charge of the auctions was sitting on a bar stool in the basement, rather than taking the three-block walk over to the Federal Reserve. Considering the bond market was getting more popular and our firm was trying to grow, this was not looked upon favorably by The Federal Reserve or bank management. Once you were appointed a Primary Dealer, you would be expected to participate at every auction (by buying the bonds). Guess what? It's tough to participate when you don't even show up. So that had to end.

The manager running the desk (Yankee/Jet fan, remember?) took over the process when it became a problem. That could only be a temporary fix because he was too busy to do that all the time, so he started to train us knuckleheads that worked for him to get the job done.

When I first got involved, I'd spend the morning talking to the trading desk and the sales force and they would communicate to me what they and their customers wanted to buy of that day's offerings and at what price. I filled out a sheet of paper (tender) per bid with all the relevant details. Each tender would have issue, amount, rate and customer on it. For instance:

Issue: 10 year note

Amount: $10,000,000

Rate: 4.07% yield

Customer: JP Morgan Sec (for our own account)

For each auction, there could be five to forty of these tenders that had to be filled out correctly before I left to make the three-block trip to the Federal Reserve. Sounds pretty basic so far, right? OK, now let's add in the ingredients that always make life stupid: Ego, greed and arrogance. Every auction day, I would get my tenders done and leave for the Federal Reserve at 12:30 p.m. (most auctions closed at 1 p.m.), enter the Fed building, find the auction room, and stick my paper tenders into a big locked box with an opening in it. Simple, right? In and out by 12:45 p.m. and back drinking free swill in the office by 1 p.m.. After the auction closed at 1 p.m., the Fed/Treasury would take the tenders and calculate the auction results. A few hours later, they would call each bank's trading desk direct and let you know what bonds you ended up with in the process. That information would be relayed to traders and customers.

Probably after about six pints of beer at a happy hour, one of the traders got the bright idea that our firm would do better in the auctions if we decided our auction prices closer toward the 1 p.m. auction close, rather than throughout the morning. How could we still do that and make the trip to the

Fed and get our tenders in on time? Fucking pay phones! Yup, we went out and found the closest pay phones to the Federal Reserve. We would leave the office with some filled out tenders and some blank ones also. After we found a pay phone that was free, we would drop in a few quarters and call the trading desk. Can you imagine the panic when I went to two or three scoped out phones and they were being used? I would be crapping myself. Okay, where were we? So I get the trading desk on the phone and it's probably 12:45 or so. Then traders and customers start to yell their new bids to the trading desk and I have to write it all down and find a way to run it all in and stuff the god-damn box before the guy at the Fed slams his hand over the box opening and screams, "Auction closed!" That really is how it ended. After a few shitshows at the beginning, we fine-tuned the process so it was more manageable. Two people would make the journey to the Fed and the batch of tenders that we filled out in the morning would be stuffed in the box at 12:45 while knucklehead #2 was trying to find a pay phone that worked and was not TOO sticky. This was New York in the 1980's, after all.

The problem is that the more we fine-tuned the process, the more crazy the demands became. Add that to the fact that now multiple banks were looking for the extra edge of a pay phone and the whole thing was just a big...crazy... pile of crap. The traders would wait until 12:58 p.m. to give us a bid and someone would have to go screaming up the Fed's steps to crash in the tender before the hand went over the god-damn box! Not only was it insanity, but we were just kids whose jobs depended on getting this done, and we were responsible for helping to underwrite billions of dollars in US debt so the economy could function smoothly. How scary is that?

Around this time, the big guy in charge of the trading floor got one of the first cell phones. It was one of those big Motorola things that was about 18" inches tall and weighed three pounds. We were on the cutting edge. As pay phones for the auction process were becoming scarce, and other banks would send their staff out at 8 a.m. on auction days to sit on the phone for five hours so they had a "close to the Fed" phone, a great use of this new technology was uncovered. Take the cell phone to the entrance of the Federal Reserve on auction day, fill out your tenders and smash them in the god-damn box (that box was the bane of my existence, and it gets worse) right at the end. This worked out well for a few months until every bank got cell phones. Then you had fifteen people with three-pound cell phones outside the Federal Reserve screaming bids and trying to find a piece of cement to put their clipboards on to write. Not only was the Fed not happy about the debacle outside their stodgy old building every auction day, but can you imagine the stress on us holding a three-pound cell phone to our ears for an hour? I probably got more radiation in my head than a million x-rays from those god-damn auctions.

As I said, the Fed needed to put an end to this craziness, and the obvious solution was to internalize the craziness. They created a dedicated room within the Fed building for the auction process. This room was enclosed by steel grates and had a linoleum floor that must have been 50 years old and very worn. In the middle of the room was that freaking box that I still have nightmares about (I still see a picture in my mind of the hand over the opening as I'm trying to put our tenders in). Around the outside of the room were 20-25 little cubicles, each with a phone and a shelf. The Fed made each bank pay for an auction line from that room up to their trading desk. The shelf was used to put your tenders on so you could fill them out. From 12:45 p.m. to 1:01 p.m. roughly fifty people would crowd that room and be filling out tenders and rushing to the box. It was mayhem. Now add in a slippery 50 year old linoleum floor and 25 people scurrying to a box in the middle of the floor and it was instant comedy. People yelling at each other, slipping and sliding, accusing each other of blocking the other bank's access to the god-damn box!! It was hilarious, but not a great shining moment for all of humanity, I'll say that.

My last story before we move on is my first brush with being fired and also my first brush with backwards government mentality. It was a normal auction day. As time went on, to save time at the end of the auction, we would pre-fill out tenders so we would just have to add in the amount and the price and then slip and slide ourselves to the box before that prick's hand came over the hole. Anyway, as is human nature, as this process went further along and we got better at it and streamlined it, the traders would immediately exploit that by waiting until the last possible second to decide on their bids in the auctions. By the end of my tenure doing this, we would still be getting bids with less than a minute to go. My boss would scream at the traders that any bid communicated after 12:58 p.m. was on a "best efforts" basis and not guaranteed to get in. The reality was that every god-damn bid that was given better find its way into that box or else a shitstorm would occur. There was just too much money at stake. In the streamlining process, my tenders would have the zeros filled out already. For example, my blank tenders would have ",000,000,000" for tenders that would be for billions of bonds and ",000,000" for tenders meant for millions. I would just have to fill in whatever the small number, an "8" for 8 billion on the first one or an "8" for 8 million on the second one. The problem was that it was always a guess on how many six-zero and how many nine-zero tenders to fill out. No one on the trading floor knew in advance what they were going to want to bid. Then you had to find the right ones in the last-minute panic. Fun, fun, fun.

On a particularly busy auction day, I was on the phone with the trading desk from the Fed. It was a frantic auction, screaming and yelling, slipping and sliding. With ten seconds left, I get a bid from the desk for 30,000,000 bonds. That is a decent sized bid; at the time the total amounts of each bond might be 8,000,000,000 between 20 banks. There was also some type of limit on the total each bank could buy. Maybe around 3,000,000,000 max, or 1/3 of an issue. The trader screams 30 million at 4.02% into the phone and I rifle through my blank tenders. Lo and behold I have NO six zero tenders left, only nine zero tenders for billions. OK, Matt, think fast, your job is on the line, you have to try to get this bid in. No time to think. I take a "billions" tender, fill in 30, fill in 4.02%, then ingeniously cross out three of the zeros. Voila! Problem solved. My partner scrambles the tender over to the bin and I am feeling like a hero. Someone owes me a drink at happy hour tonight! Not so fast, kimosabee...

Roughly an hour after the auction ends, I am tucked into my desk on the trading floor checking tickets when the number two guy on the floor comes marching over, screaming, "Who did the fucking auction today, we have a major problem!" Holy crap, I wished I could have made him spin the *wheel of responsibility* for this one. I look around and three of my cohorts are pointing at me. Bitches. I raise my hand and he says "Office, now!" Uh oh... I knew it was too good to last. I was just getting used to Budweiser too! We sit down and he is steaming. Steaming.

> #2: We are screwed. You fucked up!
>
> Me: What happened?
>
> #2: I'll tell you what happened. You put a goddamn bid in for 30 BILLION dollars and not 30 MILLION dollars!
>
> #2: The Fed says we broke the law by doing that because any bank that bids for over 3 billion at one price is in violation. They threatened to throw us out of the primary dealership. How could this happen?

Me: There is no way I put a bid in for 30 billion. No way.

#2: Who else submitted bids for us today?

Me: Just me.

#2 picks up the auction line and calls the Federal reserve:

#2 (to Fed): My guy is sitting right here, he says no way we put a bid in for 30 Billion.

#2 (to Fed): uh-huh.

#2 (to Fed): OK, I'll send him over… (he hangs up)

#2 (to me): Go over to the Fed and figure this out. Don't plan on coming back if you can't explain it.

Me: (to myself): Okay, nice knowin' ya!

So for the second time that day, I took the three-block stroll over to the Federal Reserve. This time I had jelly legs and a creeping nausea in my stomach. The truth was that the whole incident happened so quick that I just reacted and got the job done. On my walk over, I was still trying to figure out in my head exactly what happened and how I screwed this one up. I checked in through the information desk and was told what floor the auction operations were handled on. I went up to the window in auction operations and introduced myself and asked for the person in charge of the auctions. At first they would not even speak to me. Not at all. Even after I explained I needed to see what the mistake was that I made in the auction, they still refused. What a bunch of government assholes. So I begged. I said that if I did not come back with at least an explanation of my error, I would be fired that day. I think it must have been my cheap fraying suit lapels from Sears that evoked pity in them for this chubby guy with the big forehead. They said the best they could do was take a photostat (a copy, yes I know I'm old) of the offending tender and give it to me. I was happy to get that, just to solve the mystery. When I got the copy and looked at it I did the following:

1) Looked at the tender

2) Looked at the people behind the counter confused

3) Looked at the tender

4) Cocked my head in confusion

5) Looked up at them and said, "This tender says 30,000,000 not 30,000,000,000!!?"

They actually closed the window of the counter and walked away. It was insane. Here was the problem with the tender:

The last three zeros were crossed out. So my good friends at the Fed decide to bust my small little Irish peaches just to get their kicks. I bet the fuckers were laughing at me behind the counter.

The amount on the tender read: 30,000,000,--- with a line through the last three zeros. Clearly 30 million to anyone with a set of eyes. What's the big deal? I was pissed.

I was still unsure of what would happen back at the office when I showed #2 the copy of the tender. I guess it depended on whether the Federal Reserve would really follow through on their threats. I walked over to #2's desk on the trading floor, handed him the copy, and said, "No explanation, this is all they would give me." He took one look at the tender and steam started coming from his ears. He turned bright red and said something along the lines of, "Those dumb fucks!" He then marches me to the office and picks up the auction line and starts SCREAMING at the unlucky person who answered from the Fed. He 100% backed me up and told them they were absolutely wrong, clearly it was "million" and not "billion" and they should be ashamed of themselves.

The conversation ended with him saying, "Don't embarrass yourselves by having this come up again."...then he hung up. The Fed agreed to the $30 million dollar ticket. I was impressed, the guy had a set of iron nuts talking to the Fed like that. He looked up at me and said, "Not your fault, back to your desk." Holy crap. What the hell business have I gotten myself into?

Another responsibility of the Edit desk during this time was month-end pricing. In those days, 90% of everything was manual and not electronic. Computers barely existed, and certainly there were no computers talking to each other. At the end of every day, each trader would have to try to guess the closing price for each security under their sector. Once they figured an estimate for the prices, they would input manually into their little green Cathode Ray Tubes the prices and then a master price list for all securities was put together by our desk for use in the overnight computer runs. These prices would be used to calculate the daily profit/loss (p/l) statement for each account. Remember, each trader's profit/loss statement for the year was used to determine the amount of the bonus they received or did not receive. There was a lot of money at stake, and each trader was in charge of putting their own prices in? That's a little like asking the fox to guard the hen house, right? That would be like allowing a person who owned a bunch of shares of Apple stock to set their own closing price on a daily basis, instead of the exchange doing it. A recipe for disaster.

To counter this, on the last day of the month the US Treasury compiled a master list of all their securities with average prices of each bond. They got the prices by calling around each bank during the last day and getting what they thought the price was. The US Treasury then compiled a complete list and sent messengers to each bank with a pouch full of long yellow sheets. The name of these sheets was (of course) The Yellow Sheet. After the Yellow Sheet was delivered with the end-of-the-month average prices, the Edit desk would be responsible for inputting these prices into each trader's system. The Yellow sheet was delivered by 6 p.m. and we would usually have all the prices into the system by 8 p.m.. Then we would find a cheap bar and go have a few beers and bitch and moan about the traders. Just like any other job, right? Anyway, if this system worked correctly, at the end of every month the books and records of the bank would be reflected as accurately as possible for official documents. In addition, if any traders were hiding losses in their books, it would theoretically become apparent in this process. By changing the traders' prices to the "real" prices, major discrepancies would show up after every month end. Our desk had minimal contact with this process after the Yellow Sheet prices were input but we did see the results the next morning when we ripped our traders' positions and profit/loss report off the printer. Management would get a detailed report comparing each trader's prices to the average prices from the Yellow Sheet and if the difference was big enough, the trader would be called into the office to explain to management why the prices were off. Every once in a while a difference would be caused because one of us knuckleheads who just wanted to hit happy hour screwed up inputting a price. That is why we checked each input three times and it took us two hours to do it. Mistakes happened very rarely.

There was one trader in this process who always had large differences. He was also the trader who had the most securities in his sector and also the most "off the run" securities. These were the oldest and least traded securities of the whole US Treasury market. The differences were massive but they were always somehow explained away. Every month for two years these differences would show up at month's end. As it turns out, after I left the Edit desk it finally came to light that the account was under water and the trader had been hiding losses. I'm not sure how it was finally disclosed, but our month-end process should have caught it much sooner. It just goes to prove that every process has to be tight and not have loopholes involved, it's just too easy to believe what you want to believe and not understand the numbers. As it turned out, this trader got paid at least three big bonuses before his game was figured out. He lost his job but kept all his money. The bank ate all the losses. It just never seemed right to me.

4

Working as the big guy's assistant was great for many reasons. He traded large positions in all the different products on the trading floor. Cash US Treasuries, Futures on US Treasuries, Eurodollar futures, mortgage-backed securities, municipal bonds, municipal bond futures, US government Agencies, Repurchase Agreements, among others. I got exposure to these products, as well as to the other traders who traded them. Often times, the big guy's trades were executed with the other traders on the floor who were responsible for those products, so I would get a chance to check the trades with them and also get an idea of the strategy behind each trade. Unfortunately, figuring out all these products and making sure his account was perfect every day took a major toll on my happy hour attendance. While not volume-intensive, the big guy's trades were complex and let's just say he was not the most complete record keeper in the world. Often times I would get two or three words on his blotter, maybe a grunt from him as he was walking to his office...and I'd have to track down the trades and sort everything out. Still, I really did enjoy the challenge of making sense out of chaos.

One of the pieces of chaos in that job I did not enjoy had me out of the office for a half day at a time running around New York City. The big guy was in demand. Three or four times a week, traders or salespeople had him out with clients. He would get asked all the time and it seemed like he never said no. The guy was all over the place. Let's just say between cocktail hour(s), dinner with wine and then the after-bar...he rarely drove home. He would leave his car wherever he parked it, and take a black car home and then back to work the next morning. He was a good role model, no drinking and driving! Here's the problem. He would arrive in the office at promptly 6 a.m., do a few things in his office, then sit down at his trading desk, get his wallet out, grab a white stub and a $20 bill, hand me both, and say, "Find my car, have it here by 4 p.m.." In those days, parking stubs did not have the address on them. If I was lucky, it would have the parking company name on the ticket. I could start there with the track-down process. By the third instance of this happening, I had become smart enough to ask him to recreate as much of his night for me as he could.

    Me: Where did you have cocktail hour?

    The big guy: We started at Morgan's, then I think we ate at Carmine's.

So that gave me an idea of where in the city I might find his car. Since he was trading, I also had to time my search correctly because I still had to get all his trading stuff done. Usually I'd wait until he went into meetings at noon, then I'd start the process of trying to track down his car and drive it back to his garage in the city so he could drive home. The more confident I was that I had figured out the part of the city the car might be in, the later in the day I could wait to venture out. After I retrieved the car, I'd head back to the office to finish my day out. None of that was stressful. You want to know what stress is? Being 24 years old and having to drive your boss's new Mercedes from some parking garage in mid town, through city traffic, then down to his garage downtown. Talk about pressure. My personal car at the time was a 1983 Chevy Chevette I had bought from a friend's parents for $300. Who the fuck would trust me with a new Mercedes? Maybe the big guy was not so smart after all. The Mercedes fun would not end there, either.

Once a year, the heads of all the primary dealers would get together for a dinner. At this dinner, each of the roughly 20 "big guys" would take a survey and fill out their predictions on where certain markets would be one year forward. So if the dinner was taking place in January of 1988, the questions would all center on where the markets would end up on December 31, 1988. Then the next dinner would be January of 1989 where the winner would be crowned. The winner would be the person whose guesses were the closest to where the markets actually finished. The big guy at JPM Securities was responsible for the survey, the results and the payout. The payout was always a case of Crystal champagne. At the time, the big guy at Goldman Sachs was Jon Corzine, future Governor of NJ and future destroyer of the brokerage where I held my trading account in 2011 when said brokerage collapsed and my money got frozen. That's another book. Where was I? Oh yes, the yearly competition. One year Jon Corzine won the competition while he was at Goldman Sachs and it was payout time. The big guy comes out of his office, trundles up to me and hands me a piece of paper and his car keys. He wants me to take his car and go pick up a case of champagne from the liquor store at the address on the paper. Then he wants me to deliver it to Mr. Corzine at Goldman's downtown offices.

>   Me: Do you know Goldman's address?
>
>   The big guy: No.
>
>   Me: Are they expecting me?
>
>   The big guy: Don't worry, when you tell them you have a case of champagne for Corzine, someone will go find him.
>
>   Me: OK, I'm on it.

Let me just be up front. No one has ever accused me of being Magellan. I am extremely geographically impaired, along with all my other afflictions. Uh, oh. Let's recap: I'm 24 years old, driving my boss's new Mercedes from downtown to some liquor store, I've got to pick up a case of champagne without being robbed (this is circa 1989 after all), find my way back downtown to Goldman Sachs, weasel my way in and make the delivery, then drive back to the big guy's garage. All without crashing his car and making an ass out of myself. On a side note, I really need to question the big guy's judgement. I've never been a big champagne guy, but I'm 24 years old and a big drunk and he trusts me to deliver a $1,000 case of champagne? Who could blame me if I ended up taking his black Mercedes and champagne out to my old fraternity house in Bethlehem PA for the party of the century? I'd end up a god-damn legend! Wouldn't that really be his bad, not mine? Think about it.

Before I set out I did make one good decision though. I called Goldman's trading desk and asked them for their address and what floor they were on, and told them to let me up when I called from reception in a few hours. So I was set. As it all worked out, I decided to deliver the booze to the winner rather than become a fugitive and a legend. I got into Goldman's office, tracked down Corzine and made my delivery. I got a grunt and a handshake. Maybe all the big guys are alike at every place. Once again, driving that damn Mercedes around New York City was the most stressful part of the operation.

One of my other responsibilities I had for a short while was being the liaison between the New York trading desk and the London trading desk between 8:30 a.m. and 9 a.m. every day. In those days, the New York cash market did not open until 9 a.m. EST. Before 9 a.m., all trading from our trading desk and NY customers had to be routed to our trading floor in London. This was for turf reasons as well as not having people confused by having multiple trading floors competing with each other. So an arbitrary time to switch from London to NY was 9 a.m. . The reason the action was mostly at 8:30 a.m. was because many important economic releases in the US were at 8:30 a.m. . So the government would release an economic number that changed a trader's or customer's view of where the market should be, and there would be a rush to trade between 8:30 a.m. and 9 a.m. as the market digested the number and settled down. That is where I came in. In order to keep things organized, I'd be on the phone with the London trading desk at 8:30 a.m. when the economic number came out. If any trader in NY or a customer wanted to trade a cash bond, they would yell the order to me and I would relay that order to a person in London who would execute the trades and confirm them back to me. The person doing that job in NY had to have a few firm attributes. They had to listen carefully, be able to prioritize and multi-task, and be able to speak clearly. Yours truly had #1 and #2, but was a huge failure with the whole "be able to speak clearly" thing. I lasted doing that for only about two weeks, as it became apparent my minor speech impediment would not make that job practical. I was just lucky that the traders on both sides of the Atlantic were very thoughtful of my feelings regarding the matter and let me down gently. I'm kidding. "Get the fucking marbles out of your mouth!!" was shouted at me multiple times. From both sides of the Atlantic. Brutal. I think the London desk heard the NY traders screaming that at me and thought it was so funny (and sadly appropriate) that it became their rallying call against me also. FAIL. I was relieved when they found someone else better qualified. It was torture for those two weeks. At some point after that, probably after some major communication screwup that cost the bank a buttload of cash, the handover was done at 8:15 a.m. instead of 9 a.m. , which made much more sense because 8:20 a.m. was the time the Bond futures market opened in Chicago.

 It was about this time (two years into it) that I started

to become a bit more aware of what was happening around me. I started to notice that people my age were being hired directly onto the trading desks as junior traders, or hired onto the sales desk as junior salespeople. I never thought about being a salesperson for a second. Not my thing. Constantly worrying about not offending people, not offending your traders, not offending your clients. Kissing everyone's ass, being dependent on others for getting your business done. No way. That would drive me crazy. As a trader, I figured you live or die by the sword that you wield. You do well, have good ideas and make money, and you will be okay. You suck and lose money, time to find another job. I accept that challenge.

When I looked around and saw what was happening, I realized I'd have to change my plan if I wanted to get on a trading desk as a trader. The new graduates who were being hired directly as Junior traders were from schools like Harvard, University of Chicago, Penn, Cornell, etc. Some had MBA's (graduate degree in business administration) and some were undergrads, but I started to see the writing on the wall. There were two pipelines leading into the bank. One pipeline was the knucklehead pipeline that I was currently crawling through as a clerk. The other pipeline was a more direct line to a trading job and seemed to be separated by education. "Better" schools and higher degrees.

Technically, a person was not allowed to execute any trade until they had their trading license. You had to pass a test called the Series 7, which was a big, long, nasty test. Also a smaller test called the Series 63 test. Those tests consisted of rules, regulations, calculations, etc. All stuff that reminded me of school and made me shudder and cringe. I hated school. Boring and stupid. Period. My bosses at JP Morgan mentioned going back to school at night to get my business degree as a way to move forward. No Fucking Way. First of all, I barely graduated college and there was no way I was going back. Second of all, a man has to have priorities. Do you have any idea how much night school would cut into my happy hour attendance? I needed to find a plan B. And fast.

The new hires as junior traders were immediately able to take the Series 7 and Series 63 test. If they passed, they were on their way. Some failed the first or second time, but most people got through it eventually. Even though most of us clerks had begged to be able to take the test, we were always rebuffed. I definitely understand the reasoning, it did make sense. From the operational management viewpoint, why distract your clerks from their jobs to study and pass a test, a test that, when they passed, they would want to leave operations, thus killing the operations pipeline? From the trading desk, why pay for sending clerks through the testing when they were going to stay in the operations pipeline anyway? I had to find a way to take and pass that test.

In my job as trading assistant to the big guy, I would get to sit next to him on the desk as he was trading and making markets and screaming and yelling back and forth with salespeople. In general, a customer from the outside would go through a salesperson to buy or sell different bonds. In dealing with the customers, a trading desk would often be left with large risk positions that they would have to try to offset. For instance, if the big guy sold $200,000,000 worth of a bond he did not own to an insurance company through our salesforce, he would need to try to find that $200,000,000 somewhere else to offset the risk. There were two ways to do that. If you did not find those exact bonds in the market to deliver to the insurance company, the bank would have to borrow those bonds from someone else until the bonds could be purchased in the market. The process of borrowing bonds was known as a Repurchase Agreement (Repo), and I will go into that in depth next. Many times to find the exact bond and offset your position without borrowing, we would go through a broker.

Every trader had a direct phone line to five or six broker shops. Garvin Guy Butler, Cantor Fitzgerald, RMJ Securities were just a few. The broker shops in bonds were the equivalent of what the Stock Exchange was for equities, but each broker shop was its own exchange. To generalize, at every broker there was a desk with ten brokers. Each broker would cover two primary dealers. All day long the brokers and the bank traders would communicate prices of different bonds, as well as what trades were actually happening between the banks using the broker shops. A system like that was just much more efficient than calling to each bank separately to find a price. Each broker shop spoke to many banks so things moved much quicker. Each broker was basically its own mini exchange.

Now that you get the picture, let's go through a typical trade. A customer wants to sell $100,000,000 of a 30-year bond they had bought a week ago. They call their salesperson at JP Morgan and the jargon starts.

> Customer to salesperson(phone): Bid on 100 million long bonds
>
> Salesperson screams to trading desk: Bid on 100 million long bonds
>
> Trader for 30yr long bonds screams back: One oh two, seven
>
> Salesperson to customer(phone): One oh two, seven
>
> Customer to salesperson: Done! You buy 100 million at One oh two, seven
>
> Salesperson screams to trading desk: Done! You buy 100 million long bonds

The long version of these six lines of dialogue is the following. The customer has agreed to sell $100,000,000 in face amount of the current long bond at a price of 102.21875.

Since bonds trade in 32nds, "seven" equals 7/32's which is where ".21875" comes from. The cash and bonds will exchange the next day (T+1 or regular way) using the Fed wire system. The $100,000,000 of face amount will be sent to JP Morgan and in turn JP Morgan will wire the customer $102,218,750,000 plus accrued interest to pay for the bonds. Since most US bonds pay interest every six months, in between payments is called accrued interest which needs to be added to trades separately. I got a little buzz going right now so that's as far as I go into accrued interest, otherwise we will all be confused!

These types of transactions happen hundreds of times a day. Behind the scenes there are our checkout functions, going over proceeds to the penny, exactly what account at the Federal Reserve the money needs to be deposited in. A lot of moving parts, a lot that can and always did go wrong. That was the challenge. On to the next part of the process.

After the trade with the salesperson, the trading desk has $100,000,000 of a bond that creates risk for the bank. If, after that trade, the bond market goes lower in price, the bank will lose money, and vice versa if the market moves higher. The market moves all the time, every second, especially during regular business hours. For every 32nd this price moves, the bank either profits or loses $3,125. Considering these bonds could move three or four ticks (1 tick = 1/32) in five seconds there was quite a bit of money at risk. That was where the trader skill came in. And sometimes blind luck. The trader had this new risk position and would then have to decide what to do with it to make the most money for the bank. If they felt the market would go higher, they might wait a few minutes or a few hours to sell those bonds. If they thought the market was heading lower, they would get on the horn with the brokers and start dumping those bonds into the market. It was very common to make or lose $20,000 in five minutes as the markets were moving, so decision-making was very important. Traders who froze like a deer in the headlights lasted about as long as a dog that chases cars.

Besides either being right or wrong, it also got dicey when you could not get out of your bonds (risk position) in time. You just bought $100 million in bonds from a client so you go into the broker market and try to sell them because you think the market is going lower. So you really need to sell that $100 million quick. The problem is, the broker markets trade in increments of 1 million most of the time. Uh oh. The market is going down and you are losing money and you do five trades and sell only 5 million of the 100 million you need to sell. In the mean time, you have lost $30,000 of bank money in three minutes. Not a fun situation and I have been there hundreds of times. It can be great when it works out and the market goes higher as you are selling and you make money, or you can be nauseous if you get caught in a losing position. OK, so now the table is set for my first trade, which was not exactly within the rules.

The Big guy is a very busy person. Besides trading, he has meetings all day long with tons of people, so he is in and out all day. It is a very fluid situation so he can be trading one minute and on the way to his office the next. Keep in mind I am 24 years old and probably making $25,000 a year (including overtime) at this point and I do not have my series 7 or series 63 license. Ya know, a knucklehead.

One day I'm sitting at the desk and the big guy is trading as normal. He is not having a good day and is a little agitated. Why? I have no idea, I'm just a knucklehead, remember? Anyway, a salesperson screams over for a price on $100,000,000 in bonds and he buys the bonds. So he decides the market is going lower and he starts trying to sell them in the broker market. He tries for the next ten minutes through three brokers and sells about $12 million of the $100 million he has to sell. He ain't happy. If he ain't happy, I ain't happy, so I ain't happy. He then gets up and looks at me and says, "I have a meeting, get out of these fucking things!" Then he walks to his office. I can feel my sphincter pulsating at 100 miles an hour. What the fuck do I do now? Think Matt, think. I knew that his favorite broker was a middle-aged woman from Cantor Fitzgerald named Susan. She had been in the market forever and was a very calm presence. I had known that because ten or twelve times a day I would have to call her to check trades that the big guy had done with her. In the midst of all the screaming and yelling going on at Cantor, she would calmly check her trades out with me. Yes, call Susan, she will know what to do. There was no way in hell I could reach out to other traders on the desk or my fellow trading assistants. Too embarrassing. The big guy says, "Get out of these fucking things" so I have to "get out of these fucking things." The problem is I don't exactly know how to best "get out of these fucking things." OK, deep breath. I buzz Susan on the Cantor direct line. A direct is a dedicated line that stays open 24 hours a day with no dialing necessary.

>   Me: Susan, it's Matt.

>   Susan: Hi Matt, need to check trades?

>   Me: No, the big guy tasked me to get out of 88 long bonds he just got hit with. He's in a meeting.

>   Susan: What do you want to do?

>   Me: I have no fucking idea, thats why I called you!

>   Susan: If you leave the order with me I will do my best.

>   Me: The order is yours.

I then stayed on the line and listened as she did her magic. I could not have been more impressed. She was screaming at her cohorts, cajoling her cohorts, and pleading with them. What a master. Ten minutes later, "we" are out of the position and I can start breathing again. The best part was we broke even on the whole debacle from start to finish. I will never forget Susan. I doubt the big guy ever knew what happened, but I had caught the trading bug for life. I could not wait to tell the rest of the Edit desk I did my first trade. The problem with opening my big mouth about this trade without thinking was that it was technically a breach of regulations. When my bosses found out what happened, I thought they were going to shit a color TV. It was a big deal and created about a week's worth of problems. Everyone knew it was not my fault so it was not like I was at risk, it just became a firm problem. My bosses saw this problem as a "one off," but little did I know that this bizarre situation would create an opportunity not only for me, but for others going forward.

5

As the furor of my first trade abated, the question at hand was, what could the bosses do going forward so that nothing like that could happen again? The solution was simple and it was a great break for me. As I said, the junior traders were able to take the licensing tests like the Series 7 and Series 63, but the time and money was never going to be wasted on the knuckleheads. Or so it was thought! The only thing everyone could agree to was to start getting licenses for everyone who ever might be in a situation to trade. It made sense in a lot of ways; more education and knowledge of trading regulations would always make the environment safer from a regulation standpoint. I was duly pulled into an office and told that since I was the cause of this, as well as the assistant to the big man, that I would be the first person to take the test. I was also told that since I was the pioneer, I had better pass with a high score on the first try or else no one would be able to take it after me. I was given one try to pass. Oh boy. Now I was under pressure. There were roughly six other people on the desk who had their hearts set on taking that test and becoming traders. What if I fucked it up for all of them? There was pressure but I wanted this so bad, I knew I'd find a way to make it happen even though I hated studying and hated tests. I did have a little advantage that I realized as I started studying for the test. I had a month of studying for the test and even was enrolled in a study class to take the test. It was just in everyone's best interest that the knucklehead pass the test. The advantage I had was that in my first job as a back office clerk, I had gotten extensive knowledge of the futures and options on futures markets. The reports we were reconciling were futures and options on futures so I knew those products inside and out. In those days, at least 30% of the series 7 was centered on options trading. Options are basically Puts and Calls and they are not that tough but certainly there are a few different nuances in them that make it a little challenge to know them well. The questions on the test were tricky also and designed to fluster, so you really had to be on your game. Every test taker had to have a sponsor and the big guy was my sponsor. That meant that my score after I took the test would go directly to him. Oh man. Anyway, the test was on paper and multiple choice and it took about four hours. The score was sent to your sponsor in about a week. After I took the test, I thought I passed but wanted to make sure I got above a 90% to punctuate a win for all knuckleheads. I was not sure I had done that, though. The week I waited between taking the test and getting the results was torturous. A week later the big guy's personal assistant called me over to her desk and gave me a folded piece of paper. I assumed it was the test results and she had a smile on her face so I knew I passed. When I opened the paper and saw 92% I was one happy camper. And one relieved camper. And six hours later you can bet I was one drunk happy camper. For the most part going forward, none of the rest of the desk had any trouble passing the series 7 and they were all glad they had it. The series 63 test was supposed to be a minor, short and easy test. It took about an hour, was done on a computer, and the results were staring you in the face at the end of the test when you pushed the submit button. This test was not trading oriented at all, but all about regulations and not bond trading regulations, but stock trading regulations. I knew virtually nothing about the stock market and didn't care much about it either. The series 63 was a struggle for me and I knew it would be as soon as I started studying for it. I will never forget hitting the 'submit' button on the IBM AT computer. It took about a minute to get to the test results. I felt sick to my stomach. You have to remember how slow and new computers were. Those results would come up in one second nowadays, but back then it sounded like a freaking submarine surfacing right next to me and took forever. Tick tock, tick tock. <u>72%</u>. Holy crap, I had to get a 70%, made it by two points. I remember hoping that my test taking days would be over forever. Tests are for the freaking birds. Nonetheless, I had my required licenses and nothing could stop me now. Except one thing. Finding a trading job. That took another six months of playing my cards right.

After the excitement of the licensing, it was back to the job at hand. Making sure the big guy's account was right every day. While my friends were out getting drunk three times a week, I'd be dragging a five pound calculator back and forth between New York and New Jersey to do all my reconciling by hand at night. That way I'd know it was right at 6 a.m. the next morning without having to wait for the computer printouts to get to the desk. Talk about sacrifice. Me, giving up booze? In reality, I am sure I made up for it on Friday, Saturday and Sunday. I just needed everything to be perfect until I got my opportunity.

The good thing about being on the desk and working for the big guy is that there was plenty of free time. He was probably half on the desk and half in meetings during a typical day. When he was in meetings, I would float around the trading floor sitting with as many traders as I could once all the work was done on the Edit desk. One of the desks I used to frequent was the OTC (Over The Counter) options desk. One of the traders there was a very experienced gentleman who reminded me of a college professor. He never raised his voice, he was always calm. He would have looked right at home in a smoking jacket and a pipe. Calming influence.

TEETH (50) MARKS

Patience of a saint. I was a knucklehead, after all. His desk was situated in the far corner of the trading floor, next to a desk of about twenty people called the REPO (Repurchase Agreement) desk.

I would hang around the OTC desk as much as I could. Some desks you would visit and the traders looked at you like you were a wolf coming to steal their food. They treated the youngsters as competition and would not share a god-damn thing with them. Jeez, you are so god-damn insecure you can't even talk about what you do for fear of being replaced? Or maybe you just had no fucking idea what you were doing in the first place and did not want to be found out. That happened more than you would ever think possible.

The two people now on the OTC desk were pretty friendly so I liked sitting with them. The lady who hit me in the bean bag with her phone when I first started was actually nice, she just had a bad five seconds that probably cost me a few thousand in my sperm count. She had moved on by then so my little Irish raisins were safe. OK, sorry, off on another tangent.

Remember, I had my licenses so I was legal to trade. The college professor and I spent about a month together, and I listened 90% and spoke 10%. Options have three basic parts to them. Time value (time to expiration), intrinsic value (actual worth at that moment), and a little squirmy animal called volatility. The volatility factor in an option is just really a gauge of market participants' sentiment at the moment. If traders are scared, volatility might be high, if they are not scared or the market is quiet, "vol" might be low. To people who know options well this might seem oversimplified, or they might even be offended by my simple views of complex products. Tough shit. I am a simple guy, not terribly smart so I need to make everything simple so *I* can understand it. Capeshe?

Anyway, once I had convinced my new mentor that I was

not as dumb as I looked, we started throwing trade ideas off each other. The difference was, he could put his trades on at will and I was just a knucklehead. At some point I was able to beg and cajole him to execute a very small quantity of my trade in his account and let me manage it. It was a very small trade, maybe with a maximum loss of $2,000 and a maximum gain of $20,000. Small by his standards. The trade was a play on market sentiment by being long volatility. Basically just buying an at-the-money Call and hedging it with a futures contract. The trade made money if the market moved in a big way. I did not care if the market went up...or if it went down. Just as long as it hauled ass one way or the other. If you got lucky and the market moved, you would just fine tune the hedges to lock in your profits. For the month that trade was on, I would painstakingly track its progress, over-analyzing every single second and movement. It turned out to be a pain in the ass. I loved it at the time but it was a massive amount of work just to lock in my $5,000 profit I finally booked in my mentor's account.

It turns out during that time that the professor was almost auditioning me in a quiet sort of way. Let me explain. The desk next to the OTC desk was the REPO desk (more on that product coming) and I was also sitting with them and learning their product. I LOVED sitting with that group. They were my kind of people all around. Rather than being snobby blue-bloods who took themselves WAY too seriously, that desk comprised down-to-earth people who worked their asses off every day to make money as well as service the whole trading floor. They had a sense of family, teamwork and profitability that really just clicked with me.

The odds of me getting on one of the "cream of the crop" desks with my background were slim to none and I was starting to figure that out. At least as my first trading job, it was never going to happen. Between my work on the OTC desk and time spent with the Repo desk and how well we gelled, it became clear I'd be a good fit with that desk. The Repo desk was expanding because the little fledgling JPM Securities subsidiary was expanding as Fixed Income (bond trading) was getting more important as private and public debt issuance started to increase. This was 1989 and interest rates were still pretty high. A mortgage for a house for 30 years was still in the 9% range, still high even though much lower than the 18% seen in the early 1980's. As interest rates came down, the bond market seemed to draw more interest. The Repo desk was expanding because there was a lot more debt to deal with in that arena. I will explain that a bit later. In US government bond trading, there were T-bills, which were short term debt of the government, notes, which were medium term, and bonds, which were long term. One of the most profitable traders at the Repo desk was responsible for the T-bill sector as well as the "specials" (more on that in a bit) sector. He was making so much money in the "specials" sector and it was expanding at a pace where the boss decided they needed a new trader just to handle the T-bill sector. This would allow him more time to concentrate on the more profitable part of his job. The head of the Repo desk checked with my bosses on the Edit desk and when it was approved I was pulled into an office by both of those gents and offered the job trading T-bills on the Repo desk. I think I jumped up and accepted before the first god-damn sentence was out of their mouths. I did not want to give anyone a chance to change their mind.

    Me: I can't wait. Yes! Thank you, thank you.

    It was like I was being proposed to.

    New boss: When can you start?

    Old boss: We need him for another month.

    Me: Can I do both for a month to start learning?

Old boss: Yes.

The deal was done. My first trading job. June of 1989. I was two years in, making $28,000 a year and much further than I ever even expected. I was a happy squealin' little girl.

6

First, a little about the Repo business so you have a flavor for it. The amount of bonds that are traded and positioned on a trading floor is staggering. Billions and billions. In general, trading would mean in and out to offset and close, and positioning would mean parking a bond on the balance sheet to sell at another time, hopefully for a profit.

There is just one little problem with parking $100,000,000 of bonds. You have to pay for them. Virtually no trading firm has that kind of cash to purchase securities. Remember, the bank puts up a starting amount of cash (Capital), then within the subsidiary that small amount of cash needs to be maximized. That is why Repo desks were created. A Repo is a "Repurchase Agreement," basically a collaterized loan which allows a trading floor to function. Think of it this way. A firm starts with only $1,000,000 but wants to buy $100,000,000 in 30-year bonds. The trader buys the $100,000,000 of bonds from a customer or the government. The bonds and the cash will be exchanged tomorrow. It's kinda like a big drug deal. No one trusts the other dude, so the money and the bonds are exchanged at the exact same time the next day. The only thing missing is the guns. That leaves the firm 24 hours to find another $99,000,000 (remember, they start with $1,000,000) to complete the transaction. This is where the Repo desk comes in. They will pay another firm or customer to borrow that $99,000,000 in cash so they can pay for the bonds. Here is the ingenious part. The whole transaction settles simultaneously (remember the drug deal) and the $99,000,000 extra is borrowed by sending the purchased bonds as collateral for the loan. Let me see if I can show this in a simpler way.

> Monday: Trader purchases $100,000,000 in 30-year bonds to clear Tuesday from client A
>
> (Repo desk borrows $99,000,000 vs that same bond to clear Tuesday from client B)
>
> Tuesday: At roughly the same time, like a three-way drug deal, client A hands over its $100,000,000 30-year bonds. The Repo desk takes those bonds and immediately gives them to client B who then hands the Repo desk $99,000,000. The Repo desk takes that $99,000,000 along with the $1,000,000 they already have and hands it to client A.

The only difference in the transactions is that the $99,000,000 with client B is just a loan usually paid back in a day or so. Client B does not mind lending the firm $99,000,000 because if the loan does not get paid back (a default by the firm), Client B just goes into the market and sells the firm's bonds they have as collateral. A very safe investment for Client B.

So the summary of the transactions is that the firm has actually only spent $1,000,000 of its own money, but has control (and the market risk) of $100,000,000 of 30-year bonds. This is how leverage is created. In its most basic form, this would create 100X leverage. Thousands of these transactions are done every day. Leverage is how a securities firm maximizes its profits, finances itself and pays for itself.

The Repo desk greases the skids and allows Wall Street to work.

Doing these collaterized loans to finance the traders that I had been supporting for the last few years was going to be my first job. What I was really excited about was learning the business from the ground up. I knew from my interaction with the traders that the best traders were the ones who knew everything about every business. To be brutal, many of the snobby fucks I had supported previously thought the Repo desk people and function were not as good as they were. They felt it was "below them" to learn any of the nuts and bolts functions of the trading floor. I thought that was just an arrogant and stupid way to do business. The more you know, the better you will do. This would be a common theme for me going forward, watching people snob themselves right out of the business because they refused to roll up their sleeves and get greasy with us knuckleheads. Those same people would squeal like stuck pigs when their ignorance ultimately cost them their jobs. The most successful people I met knew all the nuts and bolts of every part of the business. Common sense, right? Common sense was in short supply on Wall Street during my career, and each year there was less and less of it.

It was late 1989 and I had my first trading job, a job that I had to work like a dog for. It was all great, right? Not quite. The problem was simple. I sucked at that job. I mean I was pretty bad. I loved the desk, loved the people, loved my bosses. But still sucked. Facts are facts. It took me less than a year to come to the conclusion that this job was not right for me. To be successful in that job you needed the instinct and/or the networking skills to identify and exploit weaknesses in the supply of securities. I had neither of those skills. My boss at the time was incredible about it. He sent me on my way to another job on the trading floor and ultimately had a huge role in my future.

It was a dream come true when I started, ya know, before I really figured out how shitty I was at that job. I went to school in Pennsylvania and that is where my wife's family is from. It turns out my new boss's wife hailed from almost the exact same area. He enjoyed going to visit his wife's family near the steel mills and I always loved spending time out there also. It gave us something to talk about and created a bond.

A rite of passage in your first trading job is going out and meeting all of your brokers in a formal, strict, social setting. Boring, right? I'm kidding, I spent a month going out to dinners and basketball games and getting rip-roaring drunk with my brokers. Brokers were the people who sat in circles on their own trading floor and put trades together from two or more firms that had had offsetting views. A broker can find someone in two seconds to execute the trade you need to get done, as opposed to calling around and spending five minutes finding someone yourself. They were a middle man and very efficient part of the process. For the most part they would receive a small commission on every trade they did, based on the size of the trades. The more volume brokers got done, the more money they made. Socializing just greased the skids for both parties, and knowing someone on a social level just made it easier to spend eight hours a day on the phone with that person. Free drinks? Me? Don't mind if I do!

The first day I was on the desk, one of my boss's friends and brokers invited my boss and me to a dinner and a Knicks' game for the next day at Madison Square Garden. Yes, my schedule is clear. The itinerary was set. A few hours of cocktails before the game at a bar near the Garden to get the juices flowing, go see the Knicks, then head to the broker's favorite Italian restaurant in Jersey City. Then a cab home. I was excited and a little nervous, as let's face these important facts:

1) I was a drunken kid

2) I did not know my new boss that well

3) There was gonna be a lotta booze and a free ride home

This could be a dangerous situation for my career.

It turned out fine in that respect, but also a night I would never forget. During the Knick game, the broker turned to me and very seriously said: "I wanted to be your first broker who took you out in your career. You will always remember this night and the guy who took you." I thought it was a bit of a strange thing to say but I also thought it was very nice. After the game we took a cab to his favorite Italian restaurant in Jersey City. The name escapes me... Interesting place. Very Italian, not like the fine dining Italian places in the city. I felt like I was the only Irishman in the joint and was fascinated by the whole thing. Oh yeah, and it was the best Italian food I had ever had.

After I left the Repo desk, I had contact with that broker just a few times over the years, mostly because my boss and he had remained friends. He was right. I never forgot. His name was Ed Mardovich. It was heartbreaking to read his name in a list of the missing in the days after the September 11, 2001 attacks in New York. He was working for Euro brokers in the upper floors of the World Trade Center. Thanks, Ed.

The nights out on that desk were nothing short of spectacular. There were a few young guys like me, and then some withered veterans too. It's funny, the people who I think of as the old timers were probably only three of four years older than I was. A few of the traders on that desk started right out of high school and worked their way up. They may have been only three or four years older, but had seven or eight years more experience than I did.

As the securities part of the bank was expanding, the finance arm (Repo desk) was really ramping up its volume. The brokers were making a ton of money off of our business and for the most part were grizzled veterans of 24-27 years old also. Translation: They wanted mischief just as much as we did. And they were paying. Let me set the scene. Eight guys under thirty years old having cocktails right off of Wall Street. After two hours of drinking, the mood gets very serious as the broker asked the age-old question: Dinner or strip club? It surprises me, in retrospect, that the ratio was usually 50/50. Then again, the times we chose dinner was when the women who worked with us wanted to go out also. If they were headed home after drinks, the broker would call a few cabs for them, then a limo for the knuckleheads to head to midtown to go see the "Ballet." Yes, ballet is what we called the strip club. Remember that the next time you hear some old fart ask his friend if he wants to go to the ballet. Which ballet? Think about it.

The scary thing about the "ballet" was that it was just an atmosphere for shenanigans and it was the first time I saw stuff that I thought could lead to bad things. For instance, the group walks into a club and within two minutes the broker hands $1,000 in funny money to each trader. Funny money is basically strip club dollars. That money could be used for tips and lap dances. I guess the idea behind it is that forcing people to convert cash to funny money will just ensure that more money is spent, since no one will want to leave the premises with funny money on them. Maybe the unattached guys would do that, but even they would be tempted to spend it all.

So you have $6,000 in funny money floating around the group. In that group, there are probably four who just want to have a few drinks and look around, and two who are hard core attendees who think they have found their next wife or girlfriend every time they hit the club. "This one really likes me. I think I can go home with her if I do the work." And my personal favorite: "She says she likes me because I remind her of her first boyfriend." The rest of us just roll our eyes and think to ourselves, *she's got you.* I always had the view that it was 100% fair game for a young lady to separate some dumbass from his money in this way. Just part of the game. Good for her.

After about an hour, the four "watchers" would have a few drinks and get bored. They would still have all their funny money and be calling cabs for the ride home to the suburbs. What to do with that stupid money? Give it to the guys who will use it. So in between lap dances we hand our stash of funny money to the guys who will stay there forever looking for their new love. Let's do the math. Theoretically, you now have two guys with $3,000 in funny money each. That is a lot. Even $1,000 would be tough to spend. So humans being human, we had heard that the people with all the extra funny money would find ways within the club to exchange their ballet currency into cash. They could do this either by finding a new patron looking to exchange and giving them a discount, or even with the dancers or the bouncers. Either way, there were people pocketing cash at the end of those nights out. This was the exception, though, as with the usual ratio of humans, 85% do the right thing, 15% are devious and exploitive. It's always those 15% that end up fucking things up for the rest of us.

After my first few months in this job, which were mediocre at best, it was the time of year for bonuses to be handed out. I knew I might be up for promotion to Associate. Most of the young traders were promoted to Associate pretty quick. A big reason for this is that as an Associate you became a salaried employee with no overtime. That meant they could work you 100 hours a week and pay you the same as if they worked you 40 hours, although they limited our overtime anyway when I was eligible. I would work 80-hour weeks and be limited to putting in for 10 hours of overtime after my 40 hours. The rest was on the house and happily so.

I knew I was up for Associate but had zero expectations for a bonus. Besides show up diligently, I had done nothing to earn my keep. Bonus day was never a great day at JP Morgan Securities. Because it was a bank subsidiary and not an investment bank (like Goldman), the payouts were always smaller. To boot, we were a relatively new little subsidiary with lots of expansion costs, without the revenue to match it. Bonus day was an unhappy day for most people and that is why the "kick the dog" party existed. Relax animal lovers, no actual dogs were harmed at these parties, only brain cells. A few days before bonus day, I was called into my boss's office and told I was being promoted to Associate with a new salary of $50,000 a year with no overtime. I was also now eligible for incentive compensation (ie: bonus). I was thrilled with the promotion as well as the salary. Even with the loss of overtime, it was probably a $15,000 a year kick up. I know what your asking yourself. Did the idiot go out and buy new suits? Not a chance people, at that point I was engaged and saving for a house. I was cheaper than ever, I was eating full time from the JPM cafeteria to save every penny. So once again I was very happy and grateful for where I was.

A few days later was bonus day and the first one I was ever involved with, even if just on the fringes. The boss would do his morning trading duties and then head off to his office once the bonus package was delivered to him. He was still a big volume trader at that time and made a lot of money for the firm. This was a desk where everyone traded and produced, there were no administration people, except one personal assistant who covered the whole desk. So the boss goes back to his office and starts calling people from the desk back one by one. Usually it was title and position on the desk, then going by seniority. For instance, the second in command always got his bonus first, even though he had less time on the desk then some of the traders. Once the desk traders started getting called back, it was usually by seniority. I watched with fascination as people came and went into his office. For the most part, people were poker-faced and just sat back down and went about their work. They knew they could let it loose and kick the dog at the party that night. A few of the traders with spouses came out and immediately called their husbands/wives with their number. For some reason, I got a big chuckle out of that.

After everyone got called in, I was told the boss wanted to see me in his office. Remember, I was expecting zero so did not even expect to get called into his office that day. I will admit that on the walk back to his office I allowed myself the possibility that maybe I would be thrown a few thousand bucks (1-3k) for the hell of it. That would go right into the house down payment account. I got my hopes up on the walk back to his office. SLAP! I sit down, he looks at me and says (not very nicely), "There is zero for you, not even an envelope, what did you expect!?" Holy crap. Where did this anger come from? I very shakily tried to assure him I never expected a penny and was not remotely disappointed. He dismissed me and I scurried back to the desk to lick my wounds. That was so freaking bizarre. But that is what bonus day did to people. It messed with everyone's head, the people giving the bonuses out as well as the people getting them.

He told me a few months later that he had asked his boss for a $2,000 bonus for me to go along with my promotion because he knew I was saving for a house. He said he was so disappointed when my envelope was not in the package that he just took it out on me in the heat of the moment. It was a defense mechanism because he had tried, but failed. I got it. I appreciated the effort but really deserved the goose egg I got.

7

In those days, I would be coming into New York City on the first Path train in the morning. It left Newark, New Jersey, at 6 a.m. and got to the World Trade Center at 6:15 a.m. or so. It was then roughly a ten-minute walk from WTC to the office at 15 Broad, right next to the NY Stock Exchange. At that time of the morning, I was really on autopilot and concentrating on the day ahead as I hustled into the office. I definitely was aware late at night when I was walking around the city to be very smart and conscientious. The city was still a tough place back then. Some sections in Manhattan you just did not want to stray into. For the most part, I would just encounter very aggressive panhandlers on my walk into work and home from work. One beggar became a rock star in our eyes. It was actually funny. A few of us would be walking to the Path train at the WTC and when we passed this guy he'd always yell the same thing. "You got quarta, you got quarta, you got quarta?" Three times, always the same way. But, that's not what made it funny. What happened next is what made it funny. If you bypassed him without giving him change, he would wait until you got two steps by him and SCREAM... "FUCK YOU!!" Hilarious. Day after day, this happened and the hundreds (if not thousands) of commuters all knew the drill so I don't remember him ever getting money from anyone. That was a strange business plan for sure.

One morning I was scooting from the WTC to the office, cutting through the Merrill Lynch park and mindlessly hugging a building to cut the wind before I made a right onto Broadway. Suddenly I am blocked. My head was down like an idiot while I was walking, so I just felt a wall go up. I knew. Uh oh. "Look up and I will blow your fucking head off." Then I felt the gun barrel on my temple. The dude didn't even say good morning. Another rude New Yorker. At that point time stops and you just go into autopilot, like your mind floats out of your body. I didn't even have enough sense to shit my pants. Numb thoughtlessness. "Give me everything you got!" Let me stop here and go over a few problems with this situation. You know how cheap I am, right? Most people I knew walked around the city with hundreds of dollars in their pockets and at least a few pieces of jewelry. Here was my inventory that day:

> 1) Cheap leather wallet with one credit card, one driver's license and one $20 bill. Yes, only 20 bucks.
>
> 2) My new fake gold Timex watch my wife bought me. Functional but a druggie couldn't even get a buzz from the proceeds of selling that thing.
>
> 3) A $15 dollar thin gold wedding ring. I had gotten married a few months earlier and had never worn any jewelry before in my life so I basically had the cheapest ring I could buy.

The dude picked the wrong guy to rob. The question was, how mad was he gonna be when he saw how little he was about to get? I pulled my wallet out of my jacket pocket and he must have been happy. It was a big wallet. Probably six inches long. Almost empty. False advertising for sure. "The watch, too." Bummer, I loved that watch. Here is where it gets dicey to explain the whole thing to my wife. At that point, I took my ring off and handed it to him without him asking for it. By that point I knew he was gonna be pissed and I would have popped a gold filling out to get him the fuck away from me. Autopilot. He takes it all and says, "I'll leave your wallet down the street," as he skulks away. It was then I saw the gun. A 38 caliber revolver. I'd hoped it was a bar of soap carved into the shape of a gun like that old Woody Allen movie but the barrel sure felt like metal against my head.

I sat frozen for a few minutes, then walked down the street following his lead to look for my wallet. Nothing. Interesting. In retrospect I bet he got down the street and checked the wallet and looked at the watch. He was probably sorry he did not shoot me when he realized his haul was probably gonna be $30 total. I'll bet he threw my wallet down the sewer. So not only was he an armed robber, he was a liar too. Prick. Still in a daze, I started back to my office. The first cop I saw was standing just inside of the Stock Exchange. I went in and let him know I'd just been robbed at gun point.

I started to turn around and walk back out, expecting him to follow me back to the scene of the crime. He did not move. Instead he looked at me, rolled his eyes and said, "You want to file a report?" *Of fucking course I do!* Instead I said, "Should I?" and his response was about the last thing I expected. "Nothing will come of it and you will create a lot of work for me. Let me know what you want to do." I folded like the pussy I am and just wandered back to my office.

I immediately called my wife, who was getting ready for work. It was only then that the realization hit me of what had happened. Shaking, tearing etc. I fell apart. After I hung up with my wife someone on the desk had overheard and came over to offer support. People were telling me to go home but I wanted to try and stay. My boss was out that day so I really did not want to leave without permission. I got through about half the day but was a mess so I decided to go home if I could. With my boss out, I decided to let his boss know I was going to leave if it was okay. My boss ran the Repo desk and reported to a guy who was the supervisor of multiple desks. He supervised the Repo desk, Money Market desk, Agency desk and short government bond desk. I did not find him terribly approachable in general so I was a bit nervous finding him and talking to him. When I let him know I had gotten mugged at gun point on my way in to work and was gonna head home to cancel my credit cards and start drinking, you know what that fucker said to me? "That's the price of doing business in the big city." What a douche. For the next three months or so, I would jump three feet in the air if a truck went over a bump, or a dumpster door slammed. My good friend beer and my great wife got me through it.

8

I WENT TO COLLEGE IN BETHLEHEM, Pennsylvania, and my wife's family lives there, so I spent a lot of my weekends there. My boss's wife was also from that area so he had occasion to visit there on weekends too. Both of our fathers-in-law worked at Bethlehem Steel so we had that in common also. Every once in a while, when we were out there we would play golf together. My boss was a good golfer and I was a hacker. We would play a round and then get something to eat and maybe drink also. Haha, no maybe about it, definitely beer was involved. Was there a doubt? Sometimes our foursome would find a local bar, but sometimes we would frequent the Pennsylvania Ballet. It was a place called Erv's BYOB. They charged $10 at the door but you brought your own beer in. It was a fun place where many Bethlehem Steel guys also hung out. It was not a classy upper echelon place like the NY ones but it was fun and the people were friendly. Oh yeah, and totally nude. Some law about not selling liquor allowed them to not wear any clothes at all. Who was I to argue? I love Pennsylvania.

It was during one of these weekends at Erv's with a cooler of beer on our laps (you had to watch your beer closely) that a great idea was hatched. I think the conversation went like this:

Me (slurring): *I love it out here.*

My boss: *Me too.*

Me (slurring more): *I wish the guys in New York could experience it out here. Totally different than any NY experience.*

My boss: *We should bring them all out for a weekend!*

Me (slurrrrrring): *I love you man!*

And that, my friends, is how the GPO was founded. The GPO stood for Greater Pennsylvania Open. The first year was 1989 and it lasted for about twelve years and moved with me as I switched jobs. The first year there were eight people and it got as high as 36 people at its peak. The basic structure of the weekend changed a bit over the years, depending on the interest. In general, a GPO weekend schedule looked like this:

Friday: 7-9 p.m. Dinner at Gregory's Steakhouse

9 p.m.-3 a.m. Bar, club or Erv's

Stay over at a hotel

Saturday: 9 a.m. tee times at local course

2-6 p.m. Erv's

Then home.

I would have everyone tucked back into their beds at home safely Saturday night. Safely tucked in with a nasty hangover. My friend growing up in NJ owned a great steakhouse in the area. They served 40-ounce beers and great steak. No need to eat anywhere else, although the rumor was that the broiled haddock from the strip club kitchen was pretty good. Yes, Erv's had a kitchen and no, we never ordered anything. The hotel on Friday night always caused me a lot of angst. I would book all the rooms under my name and then everyone would pay for their own when they checked in. The problem is that the group was still under my name, which meant that when one of my knuckleheads did something stupid, I would get woken up and told to take charge and fix the situation. Tough to do when your seeing three of everything yourself. Here is just a sample of the issues I dealt with over the years at the hotel and the nightclub attached to it:

> 1) Members of my group actually got into a fight with a bachelorette party. You read that right. *Guys* in my group were beat up and punched out by a rowdy group of ladies celebrating a bride's impending nuptials. Never found out how it started.
>
> 2) One of my brain surgeon knuckleheads decided that after making the sensible decision to get a limo for the night, they would end the night by standing up out of the sun roof of the limo and throwing beer bottles into road signs. I actually will take credit for talking the cops out of an arrest on that one after they woke me up in my room. I had to GUARANTEE them that I would sit on the offending party myself and not let them out of the room.
>
> 3) Someone decided that taking girls from the club on Harley Davidson rides in the hotel parking lot at 2 a.m. after 10 beers was a smashing idea. The problem was that the Harley had no tailpipes and was the loudest machine I ever heard in my life.

Those are just a few examples of the shenanigans that occurred.

The Pennsylvania Ballet was a funny place. You brought your own beer but they sold water and soda and coffee inside. We used to bring in five or six coolers of beer for the bigger GPO events. After you paid your $10 to get in, the bouncers would check the coolers to make sure only beer or hard liquor was in them. A few times a couple of sodas or a water bottle would find its way into the cooler. This infuriated the bouncers:

> Big nasty Bouncer: What the hell is that soda doing in there!!!??? We sell soda inside!! Get that the hell out of there.
>
> Us: Yes, sir.

We always got a kick out of being yelled at for trying to sneak a soda into a strip joint that let you bring in 10 cases of beer.

After the golf was over, everyone went to Erv's for the winners' presentation. Not only was this a "nude" establishment, but you could get a picture taken with a dancer if you chose to. The dancer stood behind a chain and the person paying for the privilege of the picture stood in front of the chain. A separation measure, I guess. Why would you get your picture taken in a place like that? Ordinarily, I would agree with you that it would be insane. However, this was the GPO, after all, so all winning teams, long drive champions, and closest to the pin winners HAD to have their picture taken at Erv's. Sadly, I don't remember anyone arguing with it.

This left me (the GPO chairman) with a yearly file of polaroid pictures of all the winners, past and present. I kept this file at my desk and would show it to any prospective players as a recruiting tool. Since I won a few of the years, I was in some of those pictures too. They just sat right at my desk. Weird nowadays, but back then no one cared. We had women play many of the years too. As an aside, when I switched jobs in 1995 that file had to come home with me for the week I had between jobs. My wife knew all about the pictures and the file (and me being in them), but there was never a need for her to see them. For that week they were at home, I tucked them safely in my office. To be safe, I told my wife they were there just so she could make sure not to stumble over them. Big mistake. She looked and I was in trouble. I could not get that damn file out of there quickly enough. At some point after the dawn of the Internet age that file came home and was safely tucked into my attic. I did not want any of those pics falling into the wrong hands and showing up on the Internet. At some point I grew some additional brains and shredded all the pictures just to be safe. All shredded. I did get a call from someone in one of the pics who wanted to make sure those pics were shredded and gone because he was running for public office. I was glad they were safely gone by then. So was he.

The GPO was also my first real brush with the effects of racism and it really saddened me. One of the traders on the Repo desk was a very nice black man. After the second or third year I asked him why he never came out for the weekend with us. He looked at me and said, "Would you want a black man out there?" I stared at him in shock. "Why the hell would I not want you out there?" I asked him. I was almost offended but then he explained it to me and it really was a sad day for me. He was not accusing me of not wanting him there, he was worried that his presence out in farmland Pennsylvania would create problems for the group. I never would have thought it would have been a problem but I could never convince him to join us. I never blamed him because I guess I could not really answer that question and he did not want to take the chance. Sad.

By the tenth year, we had a trophy, an insignia, and a mascot. The insignia and mascot were created by a great artist who was our computer expert on the Repo desk and an artist, writer, and singer on the side. I still have GPO clothes, shirts, golf balls, and ball markers to this day. The trophy is missing, so if you have it please let me know. The mascot was a cow chewing grass, a little poke on the difference between city and country life. By the third or fourth year it got to the point where instead of putting money into the pot and giving it out to the winner, we'd just turn the whole thing into charity money. It was fun looking around for good causes to support with our GPO money every year. I'm not a fan of charity companies or non profits, but I found some great places where 100% of the money got to the kids or the people that needed it, not just 50% or even less.

Back to work. As I was learning the ins and outs of the Repo market, there was an effort afoot on the desk to add some new products and be a little bit more aggressive in trading. Since I started out in the back office for futures and options on futures, I always had the itch to try to trade them. As it turns out, a few of the traders were also trading small amounts of "Eurodollar" futures which could be a decent way to offset or lower risk by hedging longer term financing trades. I was able to convince my boss to allow me to trade very small amounts to start off. I could trade only a few at a time and I was supposed to lose only a set amount before I had to get out of my risk. I think it was 10 Eurodollar contracts and $1,000 of losses. Even in those days, that was small. I would find a way to screw it up, though.

There were five or six days a month where very important economic numbers would be released by the government. Those releases would change people's outlook on where interest rates were going and the market would move. It was always risky to be holding a market position when these economic numbers were released because the market could "gap." A gapping market moves so abruptly that nothing trades in between prices. If nothing trades, it means you cannot get out of a position that is costing you money. So stupid shit that I am, I decide to have a small position going into a report on inflation for the country. I think I had 30% of my allowable position. When the number came out, it was very different from what I was expecting. By the time I was able to get out of the trade, I had a loss of about $1,200, higher than my $1,000 limit. I had a problem. I was sick to my stomach. If I fucked this up I was afraid not only would it cost me, but that other people would be curtailed also, and the last thing I wanted was for someone else to pay the price. I decided to seek out the advice of one of the grizzled veterans. He had been a mentor to my learning Repo and on the desk for a few years. He was only a few years older than me but he started at the company out of high school, so he had way more experience. I told him what the problem was and he agreed that the boss might clip everyone's wings if the rookie fucked it all up. He did me a huge solid and I never forgot it. We split the trade and he took half the loss and I took half. I still had to explain to my boss why I was so stupid at the end of the day, but at least I was able to stay below my limits. The $600 for the grizzled vet was like nothing, so he was not fazed. I learned a painful lesson and was forever grateful to him. We stayed friends and our lives intertwined for the next twenty years on and off as you will be reading about later.

Meanwhile, my efforts to learn the cash side of this market were not really bearing any profits. I just did not possess the instinct or personality traits needed to be successful in this product. I just sucked. You not only needed to know the interest rate market, which I knew pretty well. You also had to know the supply and demand side of this market in depth to be successful. In the Repo market, there were two types of supply and demand. The first was fundamental, the second was what I called random. Fundamental demand was knowing what bonds your customers owned and which ones they did not own, as well as which bonds other banks owned or which bonds they needed. A bank would need a bond if they sold more bonds than they owned (called being short) and had to borrow that bond until they could find enough bonds to purchase outright. Random demand had to do with another bank's ability to squeeze or corner the market in a particular bond. In those days it was commonplace for a dealer to exploit shortages in the market by buying and buying and buying more. It was called a squeeze and it happened every day. Huge amounts of money were made and lost on squeezing bonds. Here is the basic premise. A dealer who owns these bonds figures out that one or more other dealers have sold many more of these bonds than they own. They then have to borrow them until they can find them in the market. If you remember, a repo is a collaterized loan so if you owned a bond you had to lend it out to borrow the cash and, vice versa, if you needed a specific bond you would have to give someone cash and they would give you the bond you need.

If a dealer owned enough bonds, and enough other dealers needed those bonds, you would often times see the owners buying ALL of them so that there were no bonds left for the dealers that needed them. That would drive the price up. It took instinct, knowledge and an ability to scour your brokers' knowledge and your friends' knowledge to find out this information. You had to know which bonds were needed. If you started buying tons of bonds no dealer needed, it wouldn't make any difference other than make the person doing it look foolish. Since I had no friends and no instincts, I was a failure in this arena and it really did not take me or my boss that long to figure this out. I think for the whole time I was on that desk I pretty much broke even, which really was not good enough. I did get along well with others in general, and I did a good job servicing my traders. So before my boss offloaded me in a new arena I was able to get my first bonus, a hefty $3,000 check. I was extremely happy and there was no kicking the dog for me that night.

9

I REALLY WANTED TO FIND A place within the firm where I could be more valuable. I had loved the cash desk where I used to be an assistant, so my boss spoke to his boss about possible landing spots on one of those desks. You remember his boss, Mr. "that's the price of doing business in the big city" Assclown. Anyway, they needed a junior trader on the Agency desk to help the discount note trader. Let me step back and explain this. Agency debt consisted of discount notes, notes or bonds. Instead of being issued by the US government, they were issued by Sallie Mae (SLMA), Freddie Mac and Federal Home Loan (FHLB). Sallie Mae consisted of student loans, the other two involved mortgages. Notes and bonds are mostly the same from a time-to-maturity perspective, it's just the issuer or how the money is used that is different. Agency Discount notes were the equivalent of US T-bills, usually one year or shorter. Agency Notes will fall in between and bonds always had longer maturities.

My new job was to learn to trade Agency Discount notes. The trader responsible for that sector also was responsible for short Agency notes. As that market was expanding, he was to teach me the Discount notes and then break off and do the short notes while I took over the Discount notes. As far as the trading floor went, it was regarded as a step up from the Repo desk, mostly because the Agency desk was right next to the main US Treasury trading hub on the floor and there was plenty of action.

The whole idea of Discount notes was to use the salesforce to raise money to be used for student loans and mortgages for the country. Discount notes were loans/securities that were one year or less. The agencies (SLMA/FREDDIEMAC/FHLB) would supplement their cash needs by issuing these securities. The key to the job was communication with the salesforce and communication with the issuer. I would spend much of the day trying to find out how much cash the agencies needed to borrow, and for how long. Then I would canvas the salesforce whose accounts had cash to try to line up orders. I was brokering much more than trading, just trying to line up as many orders as I could and making a little commission on each trade. The more volume I executed, the more revenue would come into the firm's coffers.

I now reported to the short Agency trader and he in turn reported jointly to the big guy's deputy as well as my old boss's boss, "big city" assclown, who was in charge of all short end products. Got it? The trader who I now reported to was known as being young, aggressive and very proactive. They had big things in store for him and he was anxious to move up in the world. It took about four months for me to know enough to be able to be let off the leash a bit. For the first four months I was really just a trading assistant who could execute trades for him. He would bark out orders to me all day and I would just run around doing what he told me. We got along well. I thought he was a pretty astute person, and he treated me well and was forthcoming with knowledge. I think he thought I was okay because I would just do what he told me and never complained about making copies or doing little things for him that others would have bitched about.

During a typical day, I would get all the paperwork done from 6-7 a.m. , then start canvassing sales from 7-8:30

a.m. as trading started. The afternoon before, I would have reached out to the Agencies to get a feel for what their needs might be for the next day. Once trading opened up after 8:20 a.m., the race was on between all the Agencies' banks to match up their cash needs to customer orders. That would last for a few hours until all the Agencies' short term cash needs were met. Generally from 11 a.m. to 2 p.m. was when the worry became making sure all the ticket work between the customers and Agencies was correct so that all the trades settled correctly. I was in charge of all that naturally, as that was where I started out. The work from 2 p.m. to 6 p.m. mostly consisted of re-canvassing both sides again for the next day. Rinse and repeat. You get the drill.

The Agencies preferred to have all their cash needs met with pre-packaged orders from our salesforce. However, if they had a cash need to fill that we could not fill at that moment, they would post offerings. We would then dangle these specific offerings in front of our salesforce to try to get a trade done. Every once in a while the main trader would yell over to me to call up the agency and tell them we have sold one of their offerings. The conversation would go like this:

> Trader: I know a customer that will want that posting later. Go tell the Agency we have an order. We will sell it later when our West coast accounts get into the office.
>
> Me: Duh, okay.

Then another day:

> Trader: I like that 2 month offering, call the Agency and tell them we have an order. I'll sell it tomorrow or the next day.
>
> Me: Duh, okay.

As it turned out, there was one little problem with taking their offerings without having an order. It was against the rules! I think I probably had a vague idea only because sometimes our inventory from the Agencies was not advertised transparently, but would be sold to specific clients at specific times.

The whole thing blew up Wall Street wide as the practice became a daily occurrence and the Agencies could not look the other way anymore. The Agencies started a big investigation of the whole practices and procedures and found many dealers (us included) were not following the rules.

It was my first scandal and I was oblivious that it was even going on or being investigated. For about a month I just remember that every order was directly from the Agency to the customer with no time lags anymore. I really did not think anything of it. I was about five months into my new job at this point and absolutely loved it. I loved dealing with the Agencies and also trying to fill their needs with customer orders. I remember thinking I had a long career in the Agency business in front of me. WRONG AGAIN!

As it turned out, a few of our managers had signed agreements that every order was going directly and simultaneously into the customers' hands. Every week those managers signed specific documents to that effect. It was a very big scandal and a black eye when it started to come out. I still had no realization of what was happening. I guess ignorance really is stupidity.

This was the same time that a few primary dealers and especially Solomon Brothers were caught lying to the government about their orders in the auctions and were actually trying to corner certain bond issuances by doing that. The Solomon scandal was a much much bigger deal and took all of the headlines. It very much overshadowed the Agency scandal.

Since it was clear that the rules were not followed at our firm and papers were actually signed weekly by certain managers, it finally became apparent that some drastic changes would have to take place to make the Agencies happy in order for business to go forward again.

One morning out of the blue, I was called into the office by my old boss from the repo desk.

> Him: We have to replace everyone in the Agency short end immediately. You are no longer in that job.
>
> Me (feeling woozy): Am I fired?
>
> Him: Not yet. We have a plan for you but it may take a week or two to sort out. Move your seat back to the Repo desk in the mean time.
>
> Me: Why are *you* talking to me and not my "price of doing business in the big city" boss who ran the whole short end?
>
> Him: He was fired this morning, he is no longer here.

Holy Shit. Holy Shit.

In those days almost no one ever got fired. They would just let you resign quietly and move forward. It was all hush hush stuff. As it turned out they brought a whole new team in the Agency short end and restructured management of the products. My new mentor was quietly shipped off to our Tokyo office and I was sent to the rubber room until they could figure out, "where this moron fits."

10

THIS WAS LATE 1991 AND it was decided that I would join the Money Market desk. I had known the head trader on the desk and we had gotten along very well. Actually, he was one of the nicest people I had ever met on Wall Street. If you could not get along with him, you could not get along with anyone. He must have been feeling charitable because he agreed to take me onto his desk. During my few weeks in limbo, it was bonus season and kick the dog time. They must have felt pity for me being caught in a shitty situation not of my causing because I got a raise to $60,000 a year and a $10,000 bonus. I could not believe I could be getting paid this much to do something I found so fascinating.

The Money Market desk was separated into two smaller desks. The first desk was the Certificate of Deposit (CD) desk and the desk I would be joining was the Commercial Paper (CP) desk. The product was very similar to my beloved Agency Discount Notes. Actually, both CD's and CP are similar in every way to Agency discount notes. CD's were obligations issued by banks to fund their operations. Some banks could issue Commercial Paper also, but for the most part banks issued CD's. Only banks could issue CD's. The Commercial Paper market was dominated by corporations raising money to fund all kinds of various things. Most Commercial Paper was less than nine months in maturity. There were a few different types of Commercial Paper and mostly the different types limited what the money could be used for and how long the maturity could be.

Bank CD's were only registered vaguely with NY and virtually any amounts could be issued to raise money. Most of the time banks would use CD money to buy other securities or make loans for a profit. By comparison, every Commercial Paper program (issuer) had to be registered with a prospectus and a maximum limit. The bulk of Commercial Paper funded payroll and short term cash needs. Here are a few examples:

> CD's - A bank would make a mortgage loan for 10 years to a client that wants to buy a building and charge 6%. The bank would then issue a 1YR CD for 4% and make 2%. When that first CD had to be paid back, they would issue another CD for another year at 4% if they could. At the end of ten years, voila!! The bank makes 2% a year profit for 10 years. Do that enough times and you can actually give out enough bonuses where you don't have to have the kick the dog party!

> 3(a)3 CP – A corporation makes office products. On an ongoing basis, they have to buy paper pulp to make notebooks, various metals to make paper clips, plus pay the payroll. They can issue CP upfront to buy the pulp and metals and then pay back the CP in a month after they make and sell the printer paper and paper clips. It is a very easy and flexible way to raise cash, especially when a corporation's cash needs go up and down constantly.

> 4(2) CP – This was a specially registered program where the money could only be used for a certain specific reason. For instance, a company buys another company for 20 billion dollars. After they

buy the company they might want to sell off parts of the company immediately but they are not sure yet. They issue $20 billion of this Commercial Paper to fund the acquisition short term until they figure out a better, longer term way to fund what they have left.

Not very sexy, I agree with you. Trading Commercial Paper definitely gave me the perfect experience for the things I would be doing down the line. Of course I didn't give a crap about that at the time, I was still just trying to catch on somewhere stable and.... that's right, hit freakin' happy hour!

We had two people trading CD's and four people trading CP. The CP desk was expanding as new issuers were brought on so I was added as the fourth trader. The securities subsidiary of JP Morgan was solidly in middle age at this point; the businesses were started and had expanded fairly rapidly. There was more pressure at this point for the revenue side to catch up to the cost side. Expansion is always an investment that needs to be paid for at some point.

One of the CD traders was some hot shit fella hired right out of Harvard or Yale or Dartmouth. All those blue-blood joints look the same to me. I remember the story being that he graduated number one out of that school. They brought him in to upgrade the business, shake things up, take trading risk and expand the business. What he ended up doing was quite the opposite, but it was funny to watch every day. He was a pretty good guy, just high strung. Yeah, that's it. High strung. He was the future and came with huge expectations so he had a ton of pressure on him. He took tremendous interest rate risks to try to make the money expected of him. I truly believe it started to drive him nuts. Nuts. Speaking of nuts. Towards the end, he would take massive risk positions into big economic numbers. As you may remember, when those numbers were released the markets would gap up or gap down. A trader's risk was 100% at the mercy of the market. You were a goat or a hero immediately, no getting out. You will remember that I was the goat earlier when I lost more than I was allowed. This guy was taking hundreds of times more risk into the economic releases than I had been. Multiple hundreds of times. So in the five minutes before the number was released we noticed he would do the strangest thing. He would take this piece of good luck religious jewelry out of his pocket and rub his balls with it. His BALLS. Thankfully, above his suits pants, but still. Along with the rubbing, we could see his lips move as he was murmuring a little chant:

> Ivy guy (while rubbing his nutsack): "C'mon, be a strong number, be a strong number. C'mon baby, work for me."

He obviously thought he would profit if the economic number printed strong so that is what the good luck charm, and the chant, was trying to make happen. Hope is never a good trading strategy, remember that.

We truly were worried about him and it was decided he needed to move on and try other things. I'm not sure he lost a lot of money, I just don't think he made a lot and we were all worried he was going to kill himself.

In the years after that I would see him on financial news shows quite a bit. I guess he found his sweet spot in the business. Bless him.

Commercial Paper trading was the ultimate rinse and repeat job. It was not glamorous but there were many facets involved that a person had to be good at to be successful. In addition to the four CP traders, we had a wonderful, sweet woman sitting on the desk with us. Her job was to explain all the new programs to our salesforce and our clients and she was the best in the business. We also had a separate group called the Origination group. Origination had four or five people and they would be charged with going out into the world and finding more companies to issue Commercial Paper through us. In those days every program created had a panel of dealers. For instance, if Origination got the bank on a new program, that issuer would decide how many banks they wanted to deal with on a daily basis and formally hire them. If an issuer hired JP Morgan, Lehman and Goldman, those three were the only banks who could sell their paper. This was in opposition to the CD market where a bank could call 100 different banks, dealers or customers direct to raise money.

Each trader had about 20-25 issuers they would be responsible for. The head of the desk would split up the issuers per trader with many things in mind. The head of the desk tried to match up the issuer's personality with the trader's personality. There was a huge amount of time spent on the phone with the issuer so if a trader and issuer did not get along it could be very detrimental to both sides. Our daily contacts on the issuer side were mostly treasurers or assistant treasurers of those companies. They could be tough to handle sometimes. Assignments would also be based on how active the issuer was, as any trader could probably only survive with 10-15 active accounts, the rest would just need money intermittently. Also, some accounts were easy to deal with from a daily transaction standpoint and some were very stressful from a trading perspective. Getting the right mix of issuers per trader was a very tough job for the head trader.

My day would start at 6 a.m. with a few cups of swill. I have always been an old man. It's easy for me to get up at 4 a.m., but difficult for me to stay up past 9 p.m.. I got tons of crap for that in college, let me tell you. But I digress. So I'm at my desk at 6 a.m. with swill in hand, filling out my blank trading blotter for the day. The trading blotter was the bible for a CP trader and a legal document to boot. All blotters had to be stored for five years on the premises. Every trader created a blotter template that fit how they wanted to view the day's work. Each blotter was probably the size of four 8"x11" pieces of paper put together. Hundreds of pieces of info would be written in pencil every day on that blotter. Some blotters would have names. My colleague created a blotter and had it professionally printed out for him. Two hundred copies. He called it the "battleship." A lot of his information was pre-printed on the blotter so that he would not have to set it up each day. When he first showed me the "battleship," I was in awe. It was a piece of artistry and would save him a half hour a day. OK, I'll admit it. We were totally fucking immature over these blotters and would try to outdo each other. I'm not proud of it but two weeks later I showed up at work with a monstrosity that barely fit on my desk. I called it the "aircraft carrier." The shame. As it turns out, the joke was on us. One day my colleague walked up and threw a whole case of white-out on my desk. White-out being the paint you use on paper to fix your little fuck-ups. I said to him "What's up with this, kimosabee?" He laughed and pined to me that we just hired another trader for the desk and all of the hundred issuer accounts were going to have to be re-assigned. All that freakin' work and all those copies we had to fix and move. Didn't save us squat time-wise in the end. Just going to prove, once a knucklehead, always a knucklehead.

Moving on. Get in at 6ish, finish getting the aircraft carrier prepared for the day. Information that would reside on the aircraft carrier at the end of the day would be items such as each issuer's name, how much money they needed to raise; the rates in each maturity that you suggested they could raise money at, along with the rates you had agreed to for that day. Economic releases, time stamps as well as every single trade that was executed with an issuer or a customer. Let's do some simple math (simple math is all I'm capable of). Twenty issuers, ten time frames per issuer of rates, five trades per day with the issuer, which creates a hundred trades with customers. Add in five different economic reports plus time stamps for each trade. Can't you see why we needed the aircraft carrier? That is at least 400 penciled items per day on a legal document. I write left-handed too so it's all freakin' smeared on the page, thanks to my hand being backwards. Let's just add that I write like a Parkinson's patient also. I'm tired just thinking about what the god-damn thing looked like at the end of the day.

OK Matt, start again. Aircraft carrier starting to take shape. Start calling European clients at 6:30 a.m. (11:30 a.m. Europe time). You always wanted to get European clients on the horn before noon their time. Many times they leave for lunch at noon and you find out they gave all their orders to the person in NY who was the early bird. That's why I wanted to be the early bird. Missing their orders before they left for lunch became even more frustrating when you talked to one of your issuers and realized they had two bottles of wine with their lunch. So not only did you lose their business, but when they get back from lunch two hours later you are being berated by someone who's half in the bag from a long lunch. Not my idea of fun.

Get your Europe orders squared away, then finish putting in your guesstimated rates for each issuer on the aircraft carrier. By that time it's after 7:30 a.m. and your day is starting to take shape. From 7:30 to 8:30 you are back and forth between calling your issuers on the phone and canvassing your salesforce so they can show their customers the most attractive deals. At 8 a.m. you start putting what orders for cash you have from your issuers up on the screen. By that time, computers are a bit better and networks have been created. We had a rudimentary computer network where we could post our offerings and inventory to our salesforce. The salesforce had customers who had the cash to invest.

Our offerings start to go up on the screen and the frenzy starts. We would have forty salespeople crawling over our postings and showing them to their clients. It was a madhouse. We used to have these little intercoms, like walkie-talkies, on our desk. The salespeople in our general area would scream at us to execute a trade but other salespeople 100 feet away would use the little intercoms. Each trader had a three-digit number corresponding to their desk intercom. A salesperson would punch in your code and scream their order at you. The intercom had a waiting or busy function too. If you punched up an intercom that was in use, you could sit and be next up. Sometimes this whole process fell apart when two or more salespeople would want to buy the same piece of CP for their customer. Supply was limited folks, that is why it was a feeding frenzy. It was strictly on a first-come, first-served basis. That gave the screamers the advantage over the intercommers. Is that even a word? It is now. Anyway, the salespeople who missed the piece of CP they wanted would have to report back to their customer that the trade was not done. Letting a customer know they missed a trade was not pleasant for a salesperson. Since us traders were immature, sometimes we would chuckle to ourselves when a salesperson we did not like missed a trade. Human nature, right? Don't judge me. Customers were many times like spoiled little brats. If they decided to do a trade with your firm, many expected that it was such a privilege that they should be treated like the King of England. To call them and tell them "nothing done" elicited screaming, yelling and belittling, as well as threats of cutting off. As we all know, shit flows downhill but sometimes shit flows downhill in slow motion. Let me explain.

    I explained about the feeding frenzy. From 8 a.m. to 11:30 a.m. it was 100 miles an hour. No stop for anyone, sales or trading. There was too much stuff for us to get done during the morning to lose focus. When you cut out a salesperson on a trade there was no choice for both of us but to move on to the next trade. The salesperson would have to fend off the screams from their customer and keep selling. Sometimes the customer would boycott them as the morning went on. This created a lot of seething anger in the salesperson that could not be released during the frenzy. At the same time, traders would get frustrated if our salesforce could not sell something during the morning and that inventory was pulled away from us and sent to Goldman Sachs to be sold by their salesforce. Can you see where this is going? We have seething salespeople and resentful traders, but we are both too busy to vent. Guess what happens at 11:30 when things slow down? You guessed it. Fights. Sometimes nasty scream-a-thons. Everyone tried to discuss the morning's events in a civilized way so that things would be smoother going forward. Of course, I'm kidding. We were all like a bunch of three-year-olds that got a smaller piece of cake than the kid next to us. I remember when a very intense saleswoman got so mad at me for a missed trade that she kicked the back of my chair with her high heel. Then she pushed forward on the top of my chair to try to topple me over. Why do all these chicks want to hurt me? Who says trading is not a contact sport? The worst screaming match I have ever seen on a trading floor happened right smack dab in the middle of the frenzy. Keep in mind that these were two people who did not get along to begin with. Personally, I always though there might be a little sexual tension going on between these two. To be fair though, I'm immature enough to always think that. Here is the recap then we move on:

> Saleswoman (screaming to desk): I WILL TAKE 100 MILLION OF THE PEPSI PAPER!
>
> Trader (screaming back): NOTHING DONE, IT ALREADY SOLD
>
> Saleswoman (screaming): THAT'S NOT FAIR!

The trader stands up and looks over at her. I'm thinking he is going to say something conciliatory since she lost out.

Instead he pauses, sticks his chin out and YELLS: "You would not know fair if it fucked you up the ass!"

I can't even bring myself to capitalize that quote. To this day I cringe. We spent a lot of time in the office trying to figure out how to fix that one. I'm not even sure he would have gotten fired. To the saleswoman's credit, she took it much better than anyone expected. She was willing to move on. As it turned out the trader had just gotten another job so he was leaving anyway. This was just his parting shot at the salesforce. All's well that ends well?

So we are at midday now. All the "airing of grievances" is finished after the morning feeding frenzy. The battleship now has maybe 50 to 100 different trades on it that need to be verified and put into some system so the cash can change hands. Did I mention that 90% of these trades were settled the same day and were worth multiple billions of dollars? That means that before 4 p.m. that day the morning frenzy had to be sorted out and battened down. We did it all ourselves. Traders checked trades with their issuers, salespeople with their customers, and then traders with the salespeople.

By 1:30 or so our trades are all checked and entered in the system. At some point we would have stolen away to the cafeteria and grabbed a quick lunch to eat at our desks while we did our paperwork. I was a peanut butter & jelly guy, along with graham crackers. That and the stress explains my 6' 0", 230-pound body that had me going through clothes faster than I could take them on and off. 34" waist, 36" waist, 38" waist, 40" waist. I was expanding faster than the universe.

Finally at 1:30 or so we slow down and then start thinking about tomorrow's trading. We look to see what trades are maturing tomorrow from previous days and do some pre-work with our issuers and salesforce to line up as much as we could for the next day. Rinse and repeat.

From 3 p.m. to 4 p.m. we would have to monitor all the trades and wires going in and out to make sure all the money changed hands and the customers and issuers were happy. Then from 4 p.m. to 5 p.m. we would circle back with our issuers to finalize any information about their cash needs for the next day so that we could start updating our "aircraft carriers" for the next day to start.

Let's talk about how we dealt with our issuers on the trading side. As I said, most of our daily contacts on the issuance side were treasurers and assistant treasurers. They were well educated, most had high fallutin MBA's from places that would have laughed at me if I had even mentioned their name in high school. They were mostly type A personalities who were under a lot of pressure also. For the most part they were very professional and very fair people but like everything else…always exceptions.

Let me finish setting the stage for you. Some fucking moron at JP Morgan decided a great marketing strategy for our business would be that, "We have never been fired from a Commercial Paper program." That marketing strategy might have been okay at the beginning of the business in the late 80's, but by the early to mid 90's it was ridiculous to continue with. First of all we HAD gotten fired. Management would just call it something else or ignore all together that it happened. One issuer we even claimed *we* had fired. I used to say that, "Yes, we fired them…right after they fired us!"

Let me revisit my 85%/15% rule of humanity. 85% of everyone, race, age, gender, nationality, religion, are good, normal people who treat people right. EVERY sector of people included. It's the 15% that are the problem. Craziness, irrationality, lying, exploiting, manipulating. All the bad stuff. Here are just a few examples of what the 15% of the issuers used to do to us.

As a general rule, every market participant knew that every price was "subject" right as an economic number was announced. For instance, let's say a market maker makes a price on Apple stock so that they will sell it to a customer at $99 a share one minute before Apple's earnings come out. If the earnings come out much stronger, it would be unfair and unethical to force that market maker to sell to the customer at $99, when it is trading at $105 one minute after the earnings. We actually had issuers who would make us quote a price to them one minute before an economic number was released, then force us to transact at an instant loss (and instant gain for them) after the number was released. If we refused, as was general practice in the market, they would threaten to fire us as their dealer. Guess what? Since we were not *allowed* to be fired and would be scared of being fired ourselves if we were kicked off the program, we allowed ourselves to be dumped on time and time again. The 15% scumbag factor was killing us.

We also had issuers who would put prices in front of us that they knew we would lose money on after selling to our customers. They would lie to us and threaten us that if we did not take the loss our dealership would be in jeopardy. Those issuers would do that constantly and line their own pockets and their companies' pockets at our expense. Talk about frustrating. All because we were scared to stick up for ourselves because our marketing was that we had never gotten fired. Cost us millions of dollars over the years.

Remember, that was just the 15% that were killing us. The other 85% were professionals doing their good business by cutting hard nosed deals with us....and we respected that. There were plenty of absolutely incredible people I will never forget as our issuers. Marsha from Bausch & Laumb, Tim from Merck Pharma, Ginny from Mallinkrodt. Just great people to do business with and great human beings. There were plenty more good ones too. It's always the 15% that screw up life for people.

11

From 1991 to 1994 there were many changes to our company, some good and some bad. We moved to our new headquarters at 60 Wall Street, I was on the third floor and it was a beautiful change from the rat trap that was 15 Broad Street. The Securities subsidiary was fully expanded into all the products. That meant instead of investing in the businesses, the bank was expecting more profits to justify the outlays. Those revenues were never forthcoming in the subsidiary as a whole, or even in the Commercial Paper business specifically. This put a whole new set of pressures on every person on the trading floor.

The Commercial Paper business had a lot of overhead costs associated with it. Traders, investor relations, the origination department, legal costs, and other capital costs. We were a loss leader business that hopefully led to other business in the firm, but we were never going to make lots of money for the bank. Throw in the fact that we were not allowed to get fired, and it was just a frustratingly bad business model that management would not let us change.

Personally, I was happier than a pig in shit. I loved my job, and had even been promoted to Vice President and head trader of the desk. A head trader in general is in charge of day to day trading but does not have management responsibilities or the ability to raise or lower bonuses.

Think of a head trader as a manager of a baseball team, with executives and supervisors being more like the general manager of the baseball team. I had no say in my personnel or how much they got paid; I was charged only with taking care of the daily trading problems. Perfect for me. My salary through those years rose steadily and I think it was 90k a year after I was promoted to VP. My bonus climbed from 15k to 65k from 1991 to 1994. While being frustrated with the business model, I had found a job I was truly good at and thought I'd hit my peak and would be doing that until I retired.

Close to the time we made our move from ratty 15 Broad to 60 Wall Street, the first bombing of the twin towers occurred in 1993. We were a good quarter-mile away, but it was a deeply disturbing event. Many people we knew had to be evacuated from their office, and many did not return to work for some time. Only my commute was affected, as I was still taking the Path train from Newark to the World Trade Center at 6 a.m. every day. There were structural concerns with the buildings after the bombing, so the Path trains were idle until the buildings could take the rumble and vibration of the train. I made damn sure I was on the first train back into the World Trade Center that next Monday. It was a patriotic thing. My small contribution. I was scared but wanted that god-damn train to be full to show them we were not scared. My wife says I would tell her several times after… "They are not finished, some day they will try to finish the job."

As far as JP Morgan, in 1994 and 1995 the pressure was on to start turning profits for every group. Some businesses did well, others did not, but all were under pressure and at risk. Our trading floor was just starting to get more heavily involved in mortgage-backed trading. Banks used to make the bulk of their profits by lending to individuals to buy homes or to businesses to buy buildings. It was a simple and profitable business. The advent of GSE changed that dramatically. A GSE is a Government Sponsored Enterprise.

TEETH (94) MARKS

They are companies that are not fully guaranteed by the government, but have the implicit guarantee of the government. FHLMC and GNMA were two big ones that were ramping up operations to make it easier for the general public to get mortgages to purchase homes. Since these enterprises have the implicit backing of the government, they could borrow money cheaper than a bank could. That meant, in turn, that they could lend money to homeowners cheaper than banks could. Sounds great, right? Who does not want to make it easier for people to buy homes? The problem is that it cut the banks out of the generic mortgage business. Who would borrow from a bank at 7% when they could go another route for 6%, right? To offset this business loss, the GSE created ways for banks to sell their mortgages into securitized products. In addition, bankers tried to create more complex ways to lend people money. One of the offshoots of this change was a huge increase in the trading of mortgage-backed securities on Wall Street and the warehousing of these products on bank books. Banks were trying to replace the lost revenue from GSE competition.

Economics 101 lesson. Since a mortgage on a home can be paid back at any time for any reason, the securities themselves carry tremendous risk. Say I decide to lend $20,000 to someone to buy a house at 6% for 30 years. I could have bought a 30-year bond at 5% interest, but 6% is better than 5%, right? If two years later, a person can get a 4% 30-year mortgage, they can just get a 4% mortgage and use the proceeds to pre-pay the loan they took from me. At the same time, that 5% 30-year bond is now 3%. Uh oh. So instead of getting 5% interest assured for 30 years, I get 6% for two years and settle for 3% for the next 28 years. I am not a happy camper. I was depending on 6%, now I am getting 3%. In addition, if you lend someone a mortgage for 30 years, they can just sell their house and pay you back and you have to go invest your money again. No reason at all, other than the fact that someone wants to move. Prepayment risk and default risk will always make mortgage-backed securities extremely risky to trade. Period.

In 1994-1995 our firm started taking huge risk in mortgage-backed securities. Not my desk, but another bunch of traders with degrees a knucklehead like me could only dream of. It was borne out of pressure to succeed and turn a profit. As the risk on the floor was ramping up, my desk was having a pretty good year in 1995 so I was hoping for a decent bonus. As the fourth quarter began, I was told I'd be getting a 75k bonus for the year. Happy days. It was all gravy to me. I had paid off my 26k in student loans in 1992 after my bonus crept past 20k. My bonus was just going to go to paying off my mortgage because my wife and I always lived on our salaries and saved whatever bonus I was lucky enough to get. At that time, the first boss I had as a trader had worked his way up to be in charge of the whole short end. Not just Repo any more, but Commercial Paper and Certificates of Deposit as well. He was now my boss's boss. The general rule of thumb was to give people a vague view of their bonus a few months beforehand, because we all know how people hate to be blindsided in money matters. He had let me know I was pretty much a shoe-in for a 75k bonus. In the month after that discussion I had made a lot more money trading than expected. Still, I was happy with the 75k I figured I had coming. All gravy, I'm just happy to be here.

Disaster. Financial disaster. Some bozo in the mortgage-backed department had suddenly lost hundreds of millions of dollars out of the blue. There were rumors around the trading floor but no one knew the details. Apparently this loss was the last straw for the securities subsidiary and the patience with our fledgling little company had finally run out. How were we told? Matt, the boss wants to see you in his office. Uh-oh.

Boss's boss: Bad news, since Joe Blow (he used

the person's real name) lost 164 million dollars, every bonus has been cut 18% across the board.

Me: Everyone?

Boss's boss: Everyone. We were actually told to use the trader's name who caused it. This place is ridiculous.

Me: Agreed.

Talk about kick the dog? I was not happy with the dude who lost 164 million bucks, but man it was harsh for him that they singled him out. If I did a few bad trades, would they then turn around and tell everyone they were cutting all bonuses by .0000005% because Matt lost $10,000 because one of his issuers stuffed him with a loss? The place I loved was going to the dogs. That is when I first became disenchanted. It was a month before bonus time and the whole floor was freaking out.

It did not take long after that for the wheels to come off. A week later, we got corralled into a conference room where the new top guy of the floor addressed us. The original big guy had moved onto greener pastures and his old deputy was now the top guy. You remember, the guy who absolved me after the auction where I put a line through the three zeros. The dude scared everyone. No one wanted to mess with him or get on his bad side. When we got into the room (about twenty of us) he announced that my boss's boss, my Repo desk first trading boss, fellow GPO founder, had resigned that morning. He was taking a job at Deutsche Bank, along with two or three others from JPM. WOW! The guy moves fast when he's pissed off.

It was clear that things were changing at JPM Securities, and not for the better. The new group of executives and supervisors who moved in were either people I was not thrilled with, or very technical people who I knew (as a knucklehead) I would clash with. I started to think about looking around for another bank job, or leaving the industry totally. I really wanted to move back to Pennsylvania and coach baseball, which I had played through my college years. Time to check how much "fuck you" money I have.

Let's talk about what I like to call "fuck you" money. Wall Street and banking is all about ego, control of people, and empire-building. Ego and controlling people are two things I hate and empire building is something I have never been comfortable with. On Wall Street, empire building means that no matter what happens, you keep expanding and trying to get as many people under your crown as you can. I have seen people losing money hand over fist and they keep adding and adding and lying and lying. You know who pays in the end? The worker bees pay. They are the ones who end up getting fired when the whole thing blows up. By the time they realize the emperor has no clothes, the emperor is suntanning on his yacht while we end up holding the bag. Take my word for it.

To counter these things, I made sure I always had "fuck you" money. Fuck you money was six months of living money in the bank so that I could quit on the dime and then start looking for a job. I did not want to be controlled or manipulated. If a person was living day to day on Wall Street, or was too frightened to pull the plug, they were ripe to be controlled and taken advantage of. I saw it many times and swore it would never happen to me. I saw many good people who went into management and demanded more money. Demanded. Many times those squeaky wheels were able to get more money via the "lockup." When a manager "locks up" an employee, they guarantee a salary and bonus in total during a certain time period. The standard was two years. The employee usually gets a big bump in pay regardless of whether they do a good job or not. When they "locked up" a trader, even if that trader lost a ton of money for the bank, the trader still took his big check home. I have a problem with the bad incentives that creates. Bad business. On the other side, management keeps "control" of that employee. Control in this instance means two things. First, keeping that employee means the boss does not have to look bad when that person leaves. I never quite understood why the control was so important to management. I guess it's the type A personality thing. Second, locking someone up meant you could work them to death and beat the living crap out of them, figuratively.

A mediocre worker comes in and demands to be locked up. The ego in the manager agrees to the lockup selfishly (so they don't look bad), but they know the worker is not worth it. So what do you think the manager does? They give that employee every crappy job, they berate and take out their frustrations on that person. It is just human nature. Most people I knew who demanded a lockup were happy for about a week and then 100% miserable for the next 1 year and 51 weeks. Most of them left after their contract was up. The pursuit of money can make you miserable.

I had my "fuck you" money and had decided to look around after my bonus. Then I got a call at home from my fellow GPO founder who had resigned to take a job with Deutsche Bank.

> Old Repo desk boss: How would you like to move the GPO to a German bank?
>
> Him again (more seriously): I am starting a whole unit in the short end and am looking for someone to start a Commercial Paper desk from scratch. You interested?
>
> Me: Maybe. I really was thinking about doing something else. I'm not sure I can start over again, I'm not sure I have the energy.

At this point, I am 30 years old and that is getting old for Wall Street. I truly felt like time was running out on my shelf life.

Old Repo desk boss: Come talk to us and then decide. I have a feeling you will like what we have to say.

Me: Okay. *What do I have to lose? I'll probably get some beers afterwards from my old boss.*

I then set up an afternoon to take a subway up to midtown and meet a few people at my old boss's new place. Deutsche Bank. Everyone had heard the name and knew they were huge in Germany but I did not even know they had an operation in the states. The office was on the corner of 52nd Street and 6th Avenue. I got buzzed in and took the elevator up and went through the big wooden doors to the trading floor. *Jeez, what a dump this place is.*

While I was waiting for my old boss I looked around the floor. Something struck me when I looked at this big, almost empty floor. *A blank canvas.* A trading floor big enough for 400 people with only 60 people in it. Yes, it was a dump. But building could be fun. I was immediately in a more receptive frame of mind. I wonder if he made me wait on purpose. Clever bastard. We entered his office and he started to tell me what the bank wanted from him. He said they had hired some hot-shit investment banker from Merrill Lynch to take Deutsche bank from zero to top 5 in the United States. That banker had hired him and now he was coming for me and another guy in our group. Starting from scratch sounded good and I really liked the other trader who my old boss was trying to reel in. This may work out. My old boss said if I was interested, he wanted to have us both back the next day to meet his boss from Germany who was flying in. I said I'd be happy to, so we made an appointment for the next day at 1 p.m. back in midtown.

I went to work the next morning and started slopping Commercial Paper around as usual to my salesforce. Just a normal day. Late morning, I get called back to my boss's office. She sits me down and tells me I was seen going into

Deutsche Bank's office the day before. *Are they fucking spying on me?* Outrageous. Why would she even tell me that? I'm sure it's just a coincidence that someone saw me and ratted me out. Weasels. She then proceeds to tell me that the new big guy told her, "Matt is one of my guys, he won't leave." *They already had a meeting about me?* I'm just a nobody, this makes no sense. For once in my life, I shut my big fucking mouth but I was pissed that someone would just assume they had control over me. Control. It's all about control.

Later that day, my cohort and I went up to midtown to meet with the guy from Germany. We met with him and my old boss for about an hour and talked about the whole business and new management's five-year plan in New York. He was a German who spoke English well and we hit it off immediately. I thought the guy was great. Dry sense of humor, extremely knowledgeable of how the business worked. He just seemed like my type of guy.

At one point that day it was me, my old boss, and the guy from Germany in the office, just shootin' the shit about German versus American beer. Then the guy from Germany says out of the blue: Your old boss says there is no one better and we only want to best. What would it take for you to sign on right now?

> Me: I don't think that's possible. Maybe we can talk next month after I get my bonus.

Never in a million years did I think anyone on this earth would pay a knucklehead like me up front to do anything so the next words out of his mouth blew my mind.

> German guy: We don't pay bonuses for another two months but if you come over now we will guarantee you a 75k bonus and a title of Vice President and salary of 100k a year.

I was very flustered and did a quick pro/con conversation in my mind. It went something like this:

> Me (to myself): *Are these people stupid? They want to pay me 75k just to show up? I'll get 13k more in my bonus, 10k more in salary...and I can start a business however I want? Where do I sign??!!*
>
> Me to German guy and my old boss: I'm happy to be aboard.

We shook hands and that was that. The deal was done and there was no turning back. By the next day they had sent the paperwork to me by overnight courier. *These people don't fuck around.* I have a habit of being way too trusting, so I did not have anyone look at the papers, I just signed them and sent them back. Once they got the papers, I could go in and resign from JP Morgan, wait a week or two, and then start my new life at Deutsche Bank.

It all happened so fast. I barely even had time to run it all by my wife. It really made her uncomfortable because she had never heard of Deutsche Bank and knew I was fairly entrenched at JP Morgan. She did not give a rat's ass about the money either, it was just the stability she questioned. She trusted me and took my word on the whole thing.

When you resign from a trading floor job, it's a bit different than most resignations. It's a little bit of a dance. You go in and give your two-week notice like a normal human being would... Then they usually kick your ass out of the office within 15 minutes. No two weeks in the office. You resign, you go to Human Resources, and within a ½ hour you are heading home. They clean out whatever is left of your desk and send it to you. They even pay you for the two weeks' notice you gave them. If it's done right, it's like a little vacation before you start your next job. My problem was everything had happened so fast and I was expected to resign within a day or two, so I had not had time to start taking my belongings home. My desk was still full of my stuff. Luckily, I was able to smuggle my pictures and notebooks and GPO file out of the office the next night, before I had resigned. The last thing I needed was for some woman tasked with going through my desk to find the GPO file with the polaroids from the strip club. I also had 100 pages of the dirtiest, nastiest jokes ever told on the face of the earth. Ask me what a "Tony Danza" is, if you are daring enough.

Grant you, this all happened within a week. So fast my head was still spinning. It was October 30, 1995, and I was supposed to resign the next day. My last day was going to be Halloween of 1995. Frightening.

The day I resigned is a blur and so strange it's a little hazy. I'll do the best I can. It was considered bad etiquette to resign at the end of the day. It was always courtesy to resign first thing in the morning. I guess in a trading job they were worried that you would sabotage something on your last day. Kind of a stupid thought process to me. Why would you purposely screw something up and take a chance on your way out? How about the day before? You know you're leaving the day before, right? I'll never be able to figure out why people think the way they do.

I get into the office and am looking for my boss, so I can resign. As it turns out, she is out of the office that day. It was Halloween, after all. Oh no, not good. Do you know why it's not good? Because that means I have to resign to her boss, the guy in charge of the trading floor who I wanted no part of. He was also the guy who said I would never leave. I'll be honest, I was looking forward to resigning to my boss and being back home by 10 a.m. . My boss was a nice lady who just didn't really give all that much of a shit. Now my plans were a mess.

I find him in his office and tell him. He freaks out.

Him: Deutsche Bank? Why would you go to

> Deutsche Bank? There is nothing there. How much are they paying you?
>
> Me: A 10k salary hike and a 75k bonus in two months.
>
> Him: What? That's it? What about next year? Don't tell me you didn't even get a two-year contract?
>
> Me: No, those are the terms.
>
> Him: How much will it take to get you to stay? Name your price and we will try.
>
> Me: I'm leaving, there is no negotiating. I already shook their hands.

We went back and forth a little bit. I have never seen him so mad. In retrospect, I think the way I left made him look bad in some way. Because it's not like I got some great deal with millions guaranteed. I think the fact that I left for just a little bit more pay to a place that had nothing really bothered him. I think it really offended his ego when I would not give him a chance to outbid Deutsche Bank. If anything, every minute and every word out of his mouth fucking infuriated me. So they would pay me whatever amount more money if they could control me? But they would not pay me unless I threatened to leave? I was insulted and just wanted to get the fuck out of there. He would not let me leave. He would not release me until he ran people in and out to convince me to stay. Three hours later, I was still in his office. Then who walks in? The President of JP Morgan Securities. Higher than the guy that runs the trading floor. I had never seen him before. He was not happy to get dragged into the office to convince some peon not to leave. He could not even hide it. He was condescending and was actually bitching at me because he was having this conversation. I did not ask for this conversation. I just wanted to resign. All I saw was arrogance because their egos had been bruised. I barely said a word to him and just said the decision was irreversible. He huffed out like a pissed off 14-year-old teen-age girl. Get a grip, dude.

The other guy came back, it was probably 2 p.m. by now. Jeez, I just want to get home and drag a wagon of beer around with my neighbors while my one-year-old trick or treats for the first time.

> Him: I do not accept your resignation. You think about it and talk it over with your wife. I will call you at 10 a.m. tomorrow morning. If you still feel this way, I will let you go. Have a good night.

Finally! Holy crap, I was gonna need a beer IV drip for this night.

There was no conversation at home because there didn't need to be. The decision was made, I was sure it was the right decision, and I did not renege on my deals. I had nothing to lose. I did not have a contract other than the 75k bonus they agreed they would pay me in two months. I was missing my 62k bonus from JPM, and Deutsche Bank was happy to get the word out that they were seriously recruiting people. That is the real reason they did not wait two months. That 75k they spent on me was basically public relations money. I would have gotten my bonus at JPM then left for nothing. I did not want a contract and I did not want extra money. If I did not like how Deutsche Bank worked out, I wanted to be able to just walk away after a year and not feel like I ripped them off. Nothing to lose.

I was in the line at the grocery store the next morning when my Nokia cell phone buzzed. I knew it was him.

> Me: Hello.
>
> Him: What's your decision?
>
> Me: Thank you for everything but I'm leaving.

Him (after a pause): Very well. I know those people in charge over there so good luck with that!

Click.

What the fuck was that supposed to mean?

Time for my two-week vacation before reporting to Deutsche Bank.

PART II
DEUTSCHE BANK

12

The move to Deutsche Bank was happening fast, so fast that I was looking forward to my two-week "garden leave" to take a deep breath and restart my engines. Garden leave is what they call the forced vacation people need to take while switching firms. Usually it's anywhere from two weeks to three months. I never worked in my fucking garden during those weeks, that I can tell you.

Much of those two weeks I spent fending off beatings from my wife after she stumbled across the GPO file and the yearly polaroids of winners posing with strippers. During quieter moments, we both did a lot of thinking about the decision I made and our future. We had a one-year-old kid and a mortgage and here I am galavanting off to a place that really had no footprint in the United States, after spending the previous nine years at one of the most prestigious banks in the US. Am I nuts?

So while soul-searching and convincing myself I did the right thing, my wife and I discussed what planning we might do just in case things went sour at Deutsche Bank. We probably spent five straight days pining over the whole thing. After all that talk of plans, security, moving, career, future, do you know what our fucking solution was to figure it all out? Go see a psychic, of course! Perfectly logical. Time to back up again.

The previous year we had our first child. I knew he was mine because he was born with a huge head, and a forehead a 747 could land on. So no paternity test needed. Anyway, the poor little guy was born a few months early and weighed a smidgeon over 3 pounds. In the next week he dropped to 2 ½ pounds and we were worried. In the hospital he would stop breathing and turn purple. The alarms would go off and the nurses would have to resuscitate him, many times in front of us. They ended up putting an apnea mattress under him that would pop him up in the air when his heart stopped to get it going again. Scariest time of my life. Here is where the psychic comes in.

My wife worked with a wonderful lady who was a psychic on the side. People would go to her to ask about their future. My wife and she were very close so when my wife and I were scared shitless, she asked to come and visit the little guy in the NICU. I don't know what NICU means, but that is where all the babies in intensive care were situated. She pops in one day and the little squirt has a lot going on. He's got an apnea mattress bouncing him up in the air to keep his heart going. An intravenous line is running into his head because they had already tapped all of his veins. And the little guy is 2 ½ lbs. Yes, I was feeling sorry for myself. Maybe I had caused this by drinking too much beer all those years?..... Nah, can't be.

So our friend rolls in and hugs my wife and me. She walks over to the lad and reaches in and touches his leg and looks at him for about a minute. Then she smiles and withdraws her hand from the plastic incubator type thing. She looks at us and says, "This boy is going to thrive. I see a healthy blue aura all around him. You should not worry." She was 100% confident, not a doubt in her. He came home three months later from the hospital and was just fine. She was right all around and it was just what we needed to hear at that time.

TEETH (110) MARKS

We decide that since the psychic was a help with our son that maybe she could make us feel more confident about my future at work. I made an appointment and insisted on paying her fee this time. I don't remember a god-damn thing about that hour. She recorded the whole thing on an audio cassette that I'm sure is still up in my attic. My wife and I listened to it a few times and when it came to my job move, she was nothing but hopeful. She said in the tape that when she looked at me (probably my forehead) and thought of my new place she actually could see me climbing up a rope ladder with a smile on my face. She took that as a sign my move would be happy and prosperous. That helped settle us down a bit. Sometimes it's just good to hear what you want to hear, right? Hey, maybe she was right again.

All I remember about my first day at Deutsche Bank (DB) was the first meeting with my boss and how absolutely empty the trading floor was. I think I farted and could hear it echo.

After my cohort and I got our ID badges, we sat down with our boss. I was in charge of starting a Commercial Paper (CP) desk and my cohort was starting a Certificate of Deposit (CD) desk. We would back each other up also. The boss was in charge of CP, CD's, Repo and also the Asset & Liability desk (bank funding desk). Since JP Morgan was a US institution under the Glass-Steagall Act, what I call Core banking activities and Investment banking activities were separated by what was called a Chinese wall. The Chinese wall was basically when two parts of the bank were forbidden to even talk to each other. During my years at JP Morgan, their Asset & Liability (funding) desk was on a different floor from the Securities subsidiary and we were not even allowed contact with them. The Asset & Liability desk at JP Morgan saw fifty times the business the Securities division did, so being separated from that flow of information was always a lament of ours from 1987 to 1995 when I left.

Glass-Steagall was the law passed during the Depression in 1933 that separated Core banking from Investment banking. Core banking consisting of checking and savings accounts and actual banking payment activity including deposits and loans. Investment banking would include Securities trading for other clients and advising clients on mergers & acquisitions, as well as other customer related activity. The spirit behind the law was that by separating the more risky Investment banking from the stodgier Core banking, the Core banking would stay safer and the country better off as a result.

For some reason, in the US office of foreign banks Glass-Steagall was not a barrier so all these desks could sit together and exchange information. This was a huge advantage to foreign banks in the US vs their domestic counterparts. I knew absolutely nothing about Core banking at the time but market information was market information, and the more the better.

After my boss finished explaining what he was in charge of, he gave us our task as laid out to him by Edson Mitchell and his boss from Germany. Edson was brought over from Merrill Lynch with the goal of turning DB into a bulge bracket (top 5) firm in the United States. That was a huge aspiration because we had diddly squat in the US at the time. In order to formulate goals that can be attained, the resources to reach that goal need to be available. It's just common sense. At JP Morgan, they wanted top 5 rankings but they really fucked up the resources expended. For instance, they spent millions and millions for fancy computer systems but then had no capital left for the firm to support its operations with a balance sheet. 'Supporting operations with a balance sheet' is just a fancy term for being able to warehouse securities on your own books until you could sell them for a bigger profit.

The instructions we got from my boss were simple.

Make money and expand your market presence as fast as possible. He said we would get any resource we needed to get that job done. He told us we would be in charge of our own systems, our own people, our own operations group and almost everything else. It also meant we could trade just about any product associated with fixed income (aka bonds) and have unlimited balance sheet. He told us that we had no more excuses, if we failed it was 100% on us because we were 100% in charge. He let us know that these people were very serious and if they did not see results in a year we would be out on our asses. He was blunt and I was happy. Challenge accepted. I would work my ass off and if it worked out that would be great, and if I got shitcanned I could go out to Pennsylvania and coach baseball.

He escorted us out to our desk. His empire was two little trading areas next to each other. Before my cohort and I walked in that morning he had about ten employees. Each little trading area had ten desks and chairs pushed together. One area was the Repo desk and one area was for the new "Money Market" group which consisted of the Asset & Liability desk, CP desk, CD desk and the salesforce. The Money Market desk was occupied by two bank funding traders on the Asset & Liability desk and two salespeople. My cohort and I were the new additions, which made six in that group. On the Repo side there were six people who financed the government bond trading operation a few desks away. After quick introductions I got right down to brass tacks. "Where can I get a coffee and how are the bars around here?" I was never much for trying to impress people.

The first weeks were extremely busy trying to get set up to do our first trades. We literally had a desk and a blank computer that just had an email address attached to it. We could not even see our markets until we went around the trading floor to the various desks and saw what market data they had and decided what we liked and how much it cost. Each different desk we looked at had different systems in place for the products they traded. In most banks, management made those "big picture" decisions and tried to centralize the cost to save money. At Deutsche Bank we found out fast it was a series of fiefdoms and it was every man for himself.

We even had our pick of back office groups. We went downstairs and visited the four or five operations groups. They all had different systems, and different managers, and were also little fiefdoms. We were courted by each of the different managers of the operations groups. What was happening is that as DB was adding groups and products to the trading floor, they were each bringing over their own operations people. Since our group was starting at zero and very small, we decided we would just pick from an existing group to support our trading. All the managers wanted us to pick them because they figured the more traders and businesses they supported, the safer their jobs were. It took us about a month to sort all that stuff out and after we did we were ready to do our first trades at the new place.

Neither I nor my CD cohort had any official clients to do trades with in our respective products. It was a bit easier for my cohort because CD's are a bank product and as such they did not generally hire other banks to support their CD programs. Translation: Banks are whores and will deal with anyone who can give them the best price. In the Commercial Paper market, dealerships were more exclusive and 95% of corporations or banks would not deal with you unless you were able to get yourself hired on the program. We did not even have a marketing group to get hired on any programs yet, so it would be a slower start for me. My cohort started banging around CD's in good size and was doing pretty well for himself. I was able to beg a few CP brokers to throw me some paper to trade and a couple of DB customers sold me some of the paper they had already bought, so I was able to scrape together a little bit. We were getting there, albeit slowly.

TEETH (114) MARKS

My boss was in charge of hiring a person to start the origination group at DB. As you remember, the origination group contacts existing bank customers and tries to woo them to hire us officially on to their programs. It was a much more political process than in the CD market, where you could just call a bank and trade if they liked your price. After a month we hired a guy from Merrill Lynch to be our originator. Merrill had a fantastic CP business and Edson (the new big guy) was from Merrill so it made sense he would help us poach.

Deutsche Bank would become known as the biggest, nastiest poacher of talent in the market. Fortunately our poaching of talent was basically just 1995 and 1996 as we were starting our business. Poaching is a nasty, greedy business. You negotiate in good faith and shake hands on a deal to bring someone aboard, then they turn around and get themselves locked up in their existing shop. Ends up the whole thing was just a ploy by them to get a big contract where they already worked. I was also handcuffed by the fact that I would only bring people in on one-year contracts. I knew too many people would take the money and just sit on their ass collecting their guarantee and then walk after the contract was over. I learned a lot in that first two years about how people would lie, cheat and steal to get more money one way or the other. Either by going back to their old firms or by overestimating their value to their new place. I was generally not a good judge of value from interviews and got burned a few times. I can be a naive sucker.

At JP Morgan, the salesforce just showed up and I had no say in who was hired or what they were paid. At DB, a few of us were in charge of who we wanted to hire and then my boss would negotiate the deals. It took about a year to bring in a sales manager to help us build our salesforce. Even after we brought in the manager, we still made some bad decisions but he was much better at deciphering who were the true talents and who were the pretenders.

I was absolutely terrible hiring people from interviews, especially salespeople. Salespeople are slick marketers, and most of them are in the business of marketing themselves. A sucker like me who would sit through an interview believing every word out of a person's mouth is just fodder for being taken advantage of. Luckily we had a few good, down to earth, aggressive salespeople when we started because I was zero for fucking four hiring salespeople and some of them were given two-year contracts by my boss. For a few of them, we figured out after about two weeks they had lied through their teeth about the business they could generate and their relationships with their clients. It was frustrating to know you were used by someone with no pride or principles and then have to stare at them day after day as they laughed at how stupid you were for hiring them. But as we all know, what does not kill you makes you stronger and I learned so much about people during that first year... both good and bad.

From the outset, we were under intense pressure to become profitable. Profitable in the sense that every single expense was tracked and recorded in the way only Germans can do it. We would get a sheet of paper every day with our revenue vs our expenses and every item was listed on the expense line. We were extremely restricted in the products we were allowed to trade at JP Morgan, but DB basically let us trade anything we could make a reasonable case was relevant to our business. One product that we wanted to trade was Interest Rate Swaps. Let me explain what a swap or derivative is. It's really not as complex as the egos on Wall Street want people to believe. The more these assclowns can convince people they are so smart and no one can understand it like they can, the more they can get paid and the more they become irreplaceable. That is total rubbish. A swap is simply a bet. The difference is the bet pays not a set price, but the amount you are right or wrong. Here is an example. Let's say two neighbors are sitting on their deck having a few drinks. One neighbor looks across the yard at the house next door and says, "I heard your neighbor is putting a huge deck and hot tub on his house. I bet the value of the house goes way up afterwards." The other neighbor had heard the contractor doing the work does shoddy work and that the deck will be a monstrosity. The 2nd neighbor says, "Zillow says the house is worth $300,000 now, let's bet on where the value is a year from now and the difference from $300,000 is the payout." Okay, you have a bet! If the deck sinks into the backyard and the value of the house drops to $280,000 on Zillow a year forward, neighbor 1 has to pay neighbor 2 $20,000, the difference between the initial price and the final price. If the deck is spectacular and the house goes to $320,000, neighbor 2 pays neighbor 1 $20,000. A swap is simply a bet on the value of "something" going forward. Yes, you can layer a million things on it and make it as complex as you want, but that is really what it comes down to in its basic form. Many different types of swaps are created to tie multiple different futures contracts together in order to have one simpler index to track.

My cohort and I decide to do our first swap as a bet that interest rates would go lower over the next year. It was a learning experience that did not kill me. I guess that shows you how it went. Not well. We got our asses kicked on that trade because interest rates started to creep up. The swap we put on was a trade that "swapped" a one-year fixed rate for a series of twelve one-month floating rates. If the one year fixed rate was 3%, and the average of all of the one-month rates was 3%, we would break even. If lower than 3%, we make money and happy days! If the average of the one-month rates is higher than 3%, we lose money. We lost. Not hugely but enough to make my sphincter tighten for a few months until we made up for it.

13

About a year into my new endeavor, we got our feet below us and started to pick up ground. My cohort on the CD side was hitting the ball out of the park and I had gotten hired on five or so good CP programs that were starting to give DB a footprint in the business. Finally I was able to see my revenue outpace my expenses, not by much but my boss was thrilled because they had planned on it taking three years to break even and we were "flat" after a year. Our strategy was to try to get hired on as many German Commercial Paper programs as possible. Henkel, Bayer, Siemens, Daimler Benz. Good German companies that may have a soft spot for the new German kid on the block. Since Commercial Paper marketing is also subject to some "massaging of the numbers," we counted Deutsche Bank's own Commercial Paper amounts in our numbers also.

Trying to make yourself look as big as possible was always part of the equation. When you talked about a bulge bracket (top 5ish) firm, it was always revenue AND volume. When you shop for a surgeon about a knee replacement, you want the dude who has done the most knee replacements, right? You can't really look at his tax return but you can see how many operations he has performed and say, "He must be good if everyone hires him." It was the same way in investment banking. High volumes many times led to higher revenues. On Wall Street they called it "League Table."

Sometimes League Table business was break even and sometimes it was loss leader business. Loss leader business is business where you lose at first but once you get your foot in the door you can raise prices and make some money. When I worked at JP Morgan we were more about the League Table and less about the revenue. In banking, at some point the revenue needs to catch up to the investment or the business fails. At Deutsche Bank it was much, much more about the revenue and less about the League Table.

As we were trying to ramp up the Commercial Paper business in 1995 and 1996, I was scraping for ways to make money. Our volumes in CP were growing slowly but still very low and I was struggling for ways to pay for myself and the overhead of my business until it became self sustaining. Deutsche Bank was like the wild west. If someone put a proposal in front of management that could add to the business and the revenue, it was always easy to get approval. I was able to add about five new products to trade to try to make money at Deutsche Bank. Swaps/derivatives were one and cash Treasury Bills were another. I still had the itch to trade US Government Securities because that is where I cut my teeth. I got my approvals early at DB to trade some of these products while I waited to grow my business to a point where I could concentrate on CP.

A few months after I started, many new people started showing up on the trading floor. Most of the early hires by Edson Mitchell were Merrill Lynch people he poached, with just a sprinkling of people from other banks. I guess at some point it was decided that too many people were coming from Merrill so they started poaching from others. The US Treasury trading desk had three or four people trading all the products and was in need of expansion after the increase in salespeople on the trading floor.

One day, a guy started walking around the trading floor. He was getting a tour and was walking around like he owned the place. He was wearing cowboy boots. Interesting. We knew looking at him that he was a newly poached employee coming to claim his piece of the fiefdom. We found out from our boss that he was hired from Goldman Sachs to expand the US Treasury desk and also start a mortgage-backed securities trading operation. He was also bringing forty people with him. Forty people? Holy crap, this place is serious. The Cowboy was also hired to be unofficial head of the whole floor. When the dust settled I reported to my regular boss who brought me from JP Morgan but also unofficially to the Cowboy, as everyone now did on the trading floor. My boss reported to the guy in Germany and the Cowboy reported to Edson. Now my two bosses were in totally different management chains that no one could figure out. And the in-fighting had not even started yet!

I thought the Cowboy was great and just what the trading floor needed. He was a leadership figure and skilled in tying together about ten different fiefdoms into a cohesive group. He brought in traders, a new set of operations people, technical analysts, as well as research people. This guy did not fuck around. He also instituted casual Fridays which I was a big fan of.

With the addition of the Cowboy and all his indians, the US Treasury desk was booming. My boss had the Repo desk and the Repo desk financed and supported the US Treasury desk. The expansion under the Cowboy made it necessary for the Repo desk to have to expand greatly also. This allowed my boss to ramp up the Repo desk and he was happy about that so he and the Cowboy got along just fine. We were told to expect more hires in our group as the Repo desk expanded. When I started we had to order computers and other supplies for each desk individually after the fact, but my boss was starting to get more efficient. We always knew when a new set of people were showing up in our little fiefdom because computer support people would be scurrying around setting up a computer the day before the new person arrived.

One afternoon, we saw a new computer going in so we knew to expect a new arrival on the Repo desk the next day. Don't you know the next morning around 9:30 a.m. a guy in a black overcoat wanders over towards us and looks lost. He asks my cohort and me where the Repo desk is and we introduce ourselves and tell him where we think his computer has been set up. He thanks us and walks over to his computer and looks around his desk. Then he takes about 30 seconds to figure out his phone and all the buttons on his phone bank. Each desk had a phone bank with a handset and about 50 preset buttons. Ten of those buttons were dial tone outside lines and the rest were dedicated direct lines. A direct line went to a specific place and there was no dial tone. Generally any direct line was picked up within five seconds as it was a general rule anywhere that a call on a direct line meant something important. Like a hotline. Almost all of our brokers had a dedicated hotline and that is what he was looking for. The broker lines.

He finds the line he wants and picks it up and asks for a market in one year General Collateral. He then proceeds to sell 1 billion dollars worth of one-year collateral in the broker market. That was a huge trade. The guy was standing up, still in his god-damn black overcoat, and was trading massive amounts. He did his first trade within five minutes of walking in the door. Insane. This guy was serious and we knew we were amateurs in comparison. He continued to trade sitting at his desk and by the end of the day had built up a risk position five times higher than my cohort or me. Incredible.

He was a big help to my cohort and me. He brought in computer models and different ways for us to look at the markets. He allowed us to expand our knowledge of the markets with the information he brought in and maybe we helped him a little. Wishful thinking!

As the Repo desk added three or four new traders to better service the Treasury desk, it was also time for my cohort and me to add someone to help with our growing volumes. I was adamant that we would bring up a person from inside Deutsche Bank and not go poach someone. I came up from the bush leagues as a clerk when I started, so it was important to me that those people get a fair shake at a trading job. In addition, I had showed myself to be a total sucker and a terrible initial judge of talent during the interview process. We had a kid working for us downstairs settling our trades who was talented, aggressive and very good at supporting us. We decided he would make a perfect third wheel to our little group. We would teach him the business from the ground up and he already knew the nuts and bolts on how to settle securities as well as the associated paperwork. I also liked the fact that he did not have some fancy pants education.

We spoke to his boss downstairs, whose fiefdom had expanded since we chose his group to support us. He owed us but was not thrilled to lose one of his best guys. My boss stepped in and overruled his initial rejection of our effort to steal one of his guys. The kid was happy and was ours from the next day forward.

I'll be honest, I was in year six of kissing client ass and Treasurers' ass to get business and I was sick and tired of it. The CP business seemed on firm footing at Deutsche Bank by that time and I had had enough snooty Treasurers of corporations to last me a lifetime. So when we hired this kid I laid out his job description very clearly to him:

> Me: Learn the business, settle the trades and most importantly you have to go out and drink whenever a client asks, or I or my cohort asks. No

saying no. Your job is to deal with our clients so I don't have to.

Him: Do I get an expense account?

Me: Yes, almost unlimited.

He was a happy guy, I think. A young, hungry kid who just got a career break and his bosses wanted him to go out all the time and booze it up? He could not sign on fast enough. To his credit he was a war horse in the going out department. We made him go out with our clients, we made him go out with us. Sometimes with no notice at all. He never missed a call and always showed up raring to go the next day. My type of guy.

At the same time, the Repo desk doubled in just those few weeks. The older crew that had been on the Repo desk when we all came in was having a tougher adjustment. Not surprisingly, they felt threatened with all the changes and were worried about their jobs. A few did a good job sucking it up and learning to live within the new regime. One or two, however, decided to make life miserable in turn for the new Repo desk hires and this created many days of fighting, nasty comments and backstabbing, for about a year. Ya know, all the fun stuff. It was like a reality show and over at our desk we were happy it was not us. At some point during that year, my boss hired a new manager for the Repo desk. My boss was building his empire, as was the Wall Street norm. The new Repo desk manager was not going to allow this infighting to continue and decided to fire a few people to bring harmony to the desk. It was a tough call on his part as the desk was making a ton of money at this point and the trader causing the most problems was a very big producer. They dumped him like a sack of potatoes. It was pretty bad but I don't think they had a choice. He went on to a long and profitable career at another bank. He was a funny guy, no bullshit about him. I rather enjoyed him but we could all see the writing on the wall.

It was both fun and stressful building the business during those years. The stress and chaos is what made it fun. Oh, don't get me wrong, I was a whining, complaining little bitch at times. It's healthier to let it all out. I was not one to keep my feelings inside. If I was in a bad trade and getting my ass kicked, there was no way I could hide it. Most people were pretty good at that, not me. Some of my bosses would view that as a major weakness on my part. Fuck them. Hey, at least people always knew where I stood. I hated the "Slick Willy" mentality of many of the people on Wall Street, trying to hide the fact that they were human. They could pretend all they wanted, but we are all human and there is no changing that. A few of the salespeople and traders who would never "show weakness" at work were on wife #3 or wife #4, and miserable. They could try all they wanted to hide it. People figure it out anyway.

After the Cowboy came, the US Treasury desk went from four traders to twenty. Just like our Repo desk, there were the four originals and then all new people who came in. I'm sure those four were enduring the same growing pains and insecurities that the originals at the Repo desk were going through.

So as the expansion effort created tension within each desk, it also created tension between desks as they traded and interacted together. The culture was a mishmash of five other cultures on Wall Street and it was tough to navigate. The Merrill people thought things should work one way, the Goldman people all thought it should work another way. The small number of JP Morgan people thought their way and then you throw in people from First Boston, Natwest, Morgan Grenfell, as well as the originals. Oh yeah, did I tell you that most of these people were type A egos as well? Talk about an accident waiting to happen. The fights and screaming matches between desks were monumental. Our Money Market/Repo group traded many Treasury bonds so our fights with the Treasury desk were the highlight of many a people's day on the trading floor. I'm sure the other groups wanted to break out a bowl of popcorn and a soda to watch some of our fights between desks. Growing pains.

I was progressing along in building my business when my old Repo boss who ran the group suggested I spend a week in London to see how they were doing things. At the time there was a move afoot for more communication globally and more sharing of knowledge. Our relationship with our desk in London was a bit shaky. As we were getting bigger in New York we were running into our London office in the markets more, and they were somewhat protective of their turf as anyone would be. Human nature, no problem. So I scheduled a week to fly over during December of 1996.

14

Spending a week in London was a great experience for me and a huge eye opener. The operation was huge compared to ours, and so much more sophisticated. My colleagues were wonderful. Even though I was a total stranger to them, they were very forthcoming about how they ran their business as I rotated through various desks that week.

I brought a thick, hard-covered blue notebook and spent the week furiously scribbling my notes about all these new things. I wanted to make sure when I got back to New York I could remember as much as possible so I could help our business expand into other avenues. The main area I was supposed to visit was the Euro Commercial Paper desk but I wanted to see it all. I really wanted to learn about the Asset & Liability side because I had no experience in that arena. I was interested in the hedging of the Asset & Liability book with interest rate swaps, also using currency arbitrage to take an asset or liability in one currency and swap it into the same asset or liability in a whole other currency. That was before the advent of the Euro, so on a daily basis the group had a trader whose sole job was arbitraging between 25 different currencies to manage their liquidity risk and their interest rate risk. I sat with the cash traders, the foreign exchange swap traders, the Libor traders and just about anyone else I could fit in.

And the pubs were out of heaven. I had heard the beer would be warm but I managed to find pint after pint after pint of cold brew that was very tasty. Every single night the guys and gals would hit the Brass Monkey or one of the other pubs right down the block from our office. So many pubs, so little time. They were a very close knit group and spent a lot of time after work with each other, as well as with their counterparts from other banks.

Enough about the beer, let's talk food. I'm a picky eater, so the first day or two I stuck to deli food and I even tried a Burger King next door. I was not a happy camper. It was pretty nasty. Who puts beans on toast? What a dumbass American I was. On the second day I met up with our Commercial Paper Originator from NY, who was also in the office that week, and I bitched about the food. He told me I was doing it all wrong and that London had the best restaurants in the world. He invited me for dinner the third night. I told him I'd go but it would have to be after I visited the Brass Monkey for a pint or two. I was starting to fit right in.

He takes me to a famous old steak house called Simpsons on the Strand. Sounds great, right? When we got out of the cab, I looked at him like he had three heads. "Dude, I'm not eating here." Let's back up a bit. At that point in 1996, London was in the midst of the mad cow scare. It was a big thing and I was not eating beef in the UK. No way. But he explained it this way. "Matt, use your brain. The crisis is almost over, I guarantee you that you will never have a safer piece of beef in your life. Can you imagine how many tests are being done on all this beef to make sure it's safe?" Ah, reverse logic. I was starting to understand his thinking. He said it's almost impossible to get reservations here normally so we should be happy and jump in with both feet. This was from a guy who ate monkey brains and snake in China and survived so I figured he knew what he was talking about. He was so right. First of all, the restaurant was deserted. Maybe one other full table besides us. The waiters and waitresses and management were so happy we were there and they treated us like kings and not the knuckleheads we were. One of the best steaks I ever had. I also ordered bubble and squeak and of course being the child I am, I had to order "spotted dick" when I saw it on the menu. I learned a valuable lesson that night. Don't listen to the hoopla or other people's fears, use your own brain to make your own decisions.

My only knocking heads that week with the London desk was when they tried to get me to buy a pink shirt. Pink shirt, me? Not happening. On the Friday of every month when the US employment numbers were released, the desk in London all wore pink shirts. They had a name for it, which escapes me. They kept telling me the whole week I HAD to wear a pink shirt that Friday when the employment report came out. Or don't come in the office. It was a haze-the-new-guy type of thing but there was no fucking way cheapo pants Matt is going out to buy a $100 pink shirt he will never wear again. So we had a standoff. My solution after being harassed was to go to the cafeteria and get 10 pink napkins and stuff them in my shirt collar and pockets and wrap them around my arm. Fuck you guys! They laughed and let me off the hook.

Now all you pink people who are offended by my refusal to wear pink, just settle down. Don't get your panties in a bunch. I don't do color coordination. Have no clue what matches with what and never have. That is why my shirts were white, my shoes were black and my suits were gray, blue and black only. My ties were only colors that went with all of that. It was an idiot-proof plan for the idiot. I never had to decide, I could wear everything I had and my wife and daughter would not have to be embarrassed by my "unfortunate" fashion sense.

In 1996 my business made a little money, and overall my effort was considered to be a pretty decent success. My bonus went from $75,000 to $90,000 that year. I was still a

Vice President and my salary got bumped to $100,000. How happy was I? Very. More money than I could ever hope for and having the freedom to build a business.

I was trading a lot of US Treasury Bills. Sometimes I would buy them through DB's Treasury desk, and sometimes I would trade them directly with other banks where I had contacts. The trader who traded bills at DB's desk was not happy about me not dealing exclusively with him. Sorry bro, this is wild west Deutsche Bank and I can do whatever the fuck I want. I never trusted the fellow so wanted to keep him on his toes by making sure he was in competition.

We had an internal broadcasting system that had been hastily put together in the last year as the trading floor was getting bigger. It was basically a chat room for the whole trading floor but was not heavily used. A few traders would broadcast their trading interests to the salesforce. The whole salesforce was forced to be on this system so they did not miss anything. Since I had a lot of points of contact with my salesforce for my Commercial Paper effort, I would always have this system up to see what people were up to.

One day I gave an order on Bills to the trader on the Treasury desk to get me out of a particular position of a T-Bill I owned. There were two ways of executing trades. You could ask for a live price and do the trade immediately, or you could get the trader to work an order for you. Executing trades off a live price was less risky because you were out of your risk immediately. Working an order consisted of telling the trader the price you were hoping for, and then they would try to get that price for you. If that market never gets to your price and starts going the other way, you are dead. That's the risk.

I give the trader my order to work for the rest of the day with his brokers and customers. I go back to slinging around Commercial Paper at my desk. About an hour later I pop up the internal group messaging system to see what the salesforce is up to. I see a message from the bill trader to the salesforce regarding the exact T-bill I have on order with him. My initial thought, being the patsy I am, is, *Wow, this guy is really working hard for me. Cool.* I had just assumed he was working my order with the salesforce to help me execute my trade. Then I look closer. It seems he is working the opposite order I gave him. Hmmmm. Of course I just assume I fucked up and relayed my order in the wrong way so I call him on the intercom to confirm my order. Yes, he has my order the right way around. That is strange, maybe it's a coincidence that he is actively doing something that will hurt me. Maybe he has an opposite order with another customer. So no trade gets done that day with him but at happy hour that night my mind is racing, thinking that this guy is actually working against me. My solution? A test for him.

The next day I take a similar position I have in T-bills and give him another order. I confirm the order with him and go take a quick leak and then head back to my desk. I had started drinking a lot of coffee by then. A lot. Let's just say I wore the carpet out walking back and forth to the bathroom. OK Matt, soldier on with the story.

I get back to my desk and bring up the messaging system and lo and freakin' behold...the same thing. I see his message, trying to get his customers to move that particular bill's price against me. So not only do I not get out of my risk, but the price moves against me and I lose money. I'm steaming now. Steaming. There have probably been five times in my life when I have gotten so angry that my vision starts to close in on me and I feel like I am going to black out. This was one of those times.

I stalk over to him and ask him how he can be working an order from me and at the same time trying to get his clients to push the price against me? TWICE in two days. He looks at me and says, "I think that T-bill is too expensive too and want our customers to sell it." That explains nothing. I withdraw my order and stomp over to my desk like the little bitch I am. I then go into paranoid Matt mode.

I go back into the messaging system and print out all his messages for the past five days. There are three of them and two are the messages that are designed to screw me. I then print out a copy of the bill positions that I have from my system and march right into my boss's office to vent. I tell him the story and I see smoke coming from his ears, he is so mad. It's tough enough to be successful in this business without someone in your own bank working to screw you. I was surprised when my boss got up and said we were going to the Cowboy's office to sort this out.

It was a two-minute conversation with the Cowboy. He was just as pissed as we were. He took my printouts and said, "Leave this with me." I'm leaving that office thinking that the trader is gonna get a beatdown and from now on he will do the right thing by me. Not quite.

The next day my boss calls me into his office. On my way back I am thinking of what I have done wrong to get this call, just like a little kid getting the call into his parents' room before the spanking. I sit down and here it goes:

> My boss: Cowboy fired the Bill trader this morning.
>
> Me: Wow, I was not expecting that. I just wanted him to stop doin' it.
>
> My boss: The Cowboy and I want you to take his place. He thinks you moving over to his desk will quell some of the bad blood between the two desks.
>
> You could have knocked me over with a feather, I was so surprised.
>
> Me: Are you sure? When?

My boss: Two weeks.

He then told me that one of our salespeople who used to be a commercial paper trader at another firm was interested in getting back into trading. We would spend two weeks transitioning him and then I was packing my bags and moving forty feet to a different world.

Just like that. Another move so fast I could not even process it. I was pretty happy with this development, as I was getting sick of the old job. It was pretty much built out, the CP business at DB was entering middle age, and so I was good to move on. I was going back to the desk where I originally started on the trading floor as a clerk at JP Morgan, and was always eager to see if I'd be good at it. After all, I had made some money trading T-bills and other US bonds over the years while also trading commercial paper.

15

Two weeks later I moved into my new desk and was excited for another brand new start. It was late 1997. I was thirty-two years old and had plenty of "fuck you" money in the bank, so I was okay starting again with no net under me. My family always lived on my salary, and any bonus I had left after taxes was used to pay off student loans or the mortgage, or put right into savings for when my lucky streak ended.

My new desk consisted of about 20 or 25 people involved in trading US government bonds. The US had a few years of budget surpluses under Bill Clinton, so that meant the government needed less money to operate and was issuing fewer securities. Some "experts" in the market were talking about how in a few years the US would have no debt and there would be no bonds left. Experts, my ass. How wrong were those over-educated experts? Maybe they were the knuckleheads and I was the sane one? Nah... I'm the king of the knuckleheads.

For as wrong as the long term predictions were in the US debt department, these short term surpluses reduced the amount of bills/notes/bonds that were issued. That created scarcity value and scarcity value in T-bills was accentuated, because while demand was rising due to trade imbalances, the Treasury department was cutting the sizes of T-bill issuances because they did not need the cash.

As far as trade imbalances go, it was pretty simple. Other countries sell their products into the United States and get our dollars for their products. For example, China sells apparel into the US, Japan sells us electronics and Saudi Arabia sells us oil. Those countries generally wanted most of that money sitting in dollars for use later, so they buy US Government securities through the Federal Reserve Bank. The money just sits in that country's account at the Federal Reserve earning interest, until they need it.

Trading bills is somewhat like CP except you have only one issuer, the US government. Every Monday the government would auction a 3-month bill and a 6-month bill. Once a month they would auction off a 1-year bill. It was my job as a bill trader to participate in these auctions and help the government get the money they need to run, then to get these bills into the final investors' hands. As an example, I might buy 2 billion dollars worth of bills at the Monday auction and by Friday sell them all to forty accounts that will sit with those bills in their accounts until the securities mature, then buy them again. Rinse and repeat, right?

I had all the pre-requisites to be a good bill trader. Knowledge of securities distribution, check. Knowledge of the auction process, check. Ability to trade bills and make money, check. Solid contacts in the bill trading market, check. On paper, I was the perfect candidate. I could not miss, right? Only one little problem. I sucked at it. Terrible. After three months, I decided if I kept doing this, at some point I would get a tap on the shoulder with the Cowboy pointing his thumb towards the door with the words, "You, get the fuck out!"

Let's go through the checklist after three months. I had lost about $100,000 trading. I was supposed to have bought my share of 5% of all the auctions from the government but instead I had 1% and had the government bitching at me as well as my head trader. Because I never bought enough bills I never had enough inventory when the customers came in to buy them so my customer numbers were bad.

My new bosses kept telling me they were not that upset with my numbers overall but that I really needed to pull my auction numbers up. At that time the auctions were getting so small that to buy anything direct from the government a dealer had to pay "through the market" and lose money. I hated doing that. To keep their numbers up, other dealers would use bills as a loss leader and bid though the market in the auction, then dump them either in the broker market or to customers directly at a loss. I was struggling to keep my head above water on a daily basis so I was oblivious to what was going on around me.

The Cowboy's group had about 25 people. There were nine of us who were on the "Flow" desk. That meant each trader had a specific sector of the market and would "flow" securities from the auctions into the customers' accounts while trying to make markets and make money. Making markets generally just meant always providing liquidity, or a price to buy or sell to anyone who asked. There was a head trader who oversaw the flow traders and also traded whatever he wanted on a day to day basis. Behind me sat the proprietary desk. "Prop" desks were a fairly new phenomenon on Wall Street. These people generally had no customer contact and would simply try to find anomalies to arbitrage or just plain guess which way the market was going. Arbitrage is just a fancy way of describing someone who buys a T-shirt at a garage sale for a buck and goes on eBay and finds someone to pay 10 bucks for it. That's all.

Anyway, the three behind me on the prop desk were a close-knit group that had worked together for a while, and I'll bet Deutsche poached them from Goldman also. The only real contact I had with them was in the first few weeks. The elder statesman of the group was appalled by my ratty suits. Appalled. Some things never change. Why would I ever spend more than $400 on a suit or $20 on a tie? Anyway, this gentleman looks me over, shakes his head and says this:

"A young guy like you can't dress like you're living in a dumpster. Take this business card. These two ladies will come up to the office and fit you for some suits. They will cost $3,000 each but you will be happy you did it."

So let me get this straight. I'm gonna let two chicks fit me for a suit, they are going to go out and buy those suits for $1,500, then sell them to me for $3,000? Sounds like arbitrage to me.

Not happenin', my friend.

The desk also had two economists who tried to make sense of all the economic data and what that data meant for interest rates and what direction the Fed would push interest rates. We also employed two technical analysts. They would use charts or tea leaves or any other ideas to get a sense of how interest rates would be moving. Technical analysts had a reputation for being a little quirky. As opposed to fundamental analysts who tried to predict the markets' direction using known facts or "fundamentals," a technical analyst would try to predict market direction from the shapes of a trading chart or regression analysis or something more forward-looking.

The desk also had two trading clerks and two system clerks. The trading clerks were basically junior traders and would move around where needed, while the system clerks would be in charge of the computers and making sure trading tickets were correctly input into all the systems.

Out of the 20 people, 15 were probably poached from Goldman or Merrill Lynch and maybe four or five were traders who had been there for a while. The original Deutsche people on that desk were an island unto ourselves (I included myself), while it seemed the 15 poached people were in a little clique with the Cowboy. That being said, the overall morale of the desk was high and everyone was pretty nice to each other. My only real problem was that I sucked at my job. Other than that, life was good.

As I said, the group of three behind me were proprietary traders. One desk to my right sat an Asian fellow who I really enjoyed. He was a computer programmer, helping the group build out all their trading models. As I was in my first few months, he was transitioning from a programmer to a trader. His name was Tony. What I thought hilarious at the time was that he would be heavily involved in other very risky trades and not blink an eye, but being long or short just a few futures contracts outright would drive him crazy. He would fidget in his seat when he had any naked risk. His main programming focus was either basis risk or curve risk. An example of basis risk might be buying a five-year bond in Europe versus selling a five-year bond in the US market. An example of curve risk might be buying two-year bonds in the US versus selling ten year bonds in the US. In that instance, a trader thinks the two-year bonds will outperform the ten-year bonds. Basis trades and curve trades are very risky and a person can make or lose millions of dollars in each. Being long or short "outright" just means it's a standalone simple trade. A trader wants the market to go up if they are long, and down if they are short. Simple. Being long or short a few contracts vs the basis and curve risk his group was responsible for is like a person who smokes a single cigarette being as worried about cancer as someone who has smoked for thirty years.

Two seats to my right was the main driver of most of the computer-driven trading strategies in the whole group. He was just a kid. I was 32 years old at the time and he was about 25 and looked 16. He was considered the genius of the whole department and was treated as such. When he was poached from Goldman Sachs early in his time there (he was 24 years old for Christ sakes!!), it was considered a huge win for Deutsche Bank. He graduated from MIT a few years earlier and brought over a few of his MIT cronies as well. He always had a cooler full of cold Mountain Dew soda under his desk that they would all draw off of during the day. I'll stick to my coffee, thank you very much.

The kid and I were about as far away in mental attributes as two people could be on this earth. I was a knucklehead who hated math and just struggled my way through this whole Wall Street thing. He had it all planned out, was a mathematical genius who came from Goldman to Deutsche with a big check and a promise he could build whatever he wanted and hire whoever he wanted. I made sure I chiseled in on any little meetings those guys had on the desk. I wanted to learn as much as I could about what the hell they were doing in that little computer group. In addition to being responsible for the computer trading, the kid oversaw all flow trading in a big sector of the US Treasury market for our desk. It was a combination of flow trading with customers and computer generated strategy. Cutting edge stuff and I wanted to learn it if I could. The way I figured it, I sucked so much trading bills the way I was doing it, I might as well learn something new and try to change my luck in this job.

When I did weasel into their little MIT powwows, I might as well have been attending a meeting in another country with a different language. I'm not a big math guy so as they were talking NASA math and computer code I must have looked like a US tourist asking for directions in the streets of Japan. I knew I was dumb, but now I have to be slapped in the face with how much of a dope I am every day? Anyway, they were a pretty fun group and I did manage to learn quite a bit. We had even heard the rumor that the whole group of them were banned from Atlantic City for counting cards. I'm not sure if that was a myth or not.

One day the kid called me over to his desk about fifteen minutes before a big economic number was being released by the government. The market moved big on these days and people were a little nervous before the release because it usually meant a busy day with a ton of money made.... or lost. I'm sure I was going over my positions to try to see what I could do not to get my ass kicked by the market. Tough times, zero confidence in myself. When I get over to his desk, I am thinking that I am going to get some piece of wisdom to help me make some money or some strategy pep talk for the day. On his desk he had four fixed computer monitors, but he kept all his important stuff on his laptop that went everywhere he went. He reaches for his laptop and opens it up and I'm thinking, *Holy crap, he is actually going to show me the big secret trading model.* Alas, not today. He says, "I really want you to see this" and I look at the screen and guess what pops up? Nope, not porn but that was a good guess on your part. It was that video on the web where the circus clown runs down the little red and white ramp towards the back end of a horse. Then the clown ducks down and his whole head disappears into the horse's ass. He laughs as he slams the laptop shut, looks at me and says very quietly, "Now go make some money." I was laughing so hard. There was no way I would have expected that in a million years. Classic.

One of the original non-poached traders on the desk was in charge of keeping the head trader abreast of the P&L (profit & loss) estimates at the end of the day. During the day each trader would informally let the head trader know how the day was shaping up. At the end of the day there was a formal process where every trader on the desk would compute the day's P&L and give it to that trader. He would then tally up the day's gains or losses for the whole desk and report the estimate to the head trader, who would then report that number to the Cowboy. It was just an estimate, but if your number came out way differently the next day when the real number was printed, you had some explaining to do. Not only did they not want people fudging on the estimate to make themselves look better, but getting the estimate right was a sign you knew your market and your positions. When the trader filled in the estimate numbers he would write gains on the day as regular numbers and losses on the day would have brackets around them. Then he would just add and subtract to arrive at the day's estimate for the desk. He was a good guy with a great sense of humor. My luck was so bad after the first few months that he used to make sure when he asked me my estimate that I could see his sheet. The fucker had already put the brackets in my spot where he reported the number. A set of loss brackets next to my name, just so he could fill in my loss. Then he would laugh his ass off. Even I had to laugh.

One Monday I came into the office and sat down at my desk. I was usually one of the first ones in so the floor was always empty. Something was not right. I went through my whole desk and everything was in order. My computer. My notebooks. My blotter. My scrap paper. The amount of wasted paper on a trading floor used to crush me. There was not much recycling going on so it went right in the garbage. I hated that. So I used to rip big stacks of paper into four sections and pile them up on my desk. Two or three feet high. I'd use them like my own little note pads. It made me feel better about the waste. My desk drawers were all there also and populated but something was not right. Then it hit me. It was not my desk that was not right. The desk to my right, where Tony sat, was gone. Well, the desk was there but literally every single thing at his workspace was gone, including his chair. No computer. No papers. No desk drawers. No name plate. Nothing. My first thought was that it could not have been due to losing money because I would have been out on my ass before he was. Something big must have happened. The people who obviously knew would not speak about it and the rest of us were clueless.

At some point later, we found out or read in the papers that the bank and the FBI had been investigating him for some type of computer sabotage. Apparently he was on his way to another firm and decided to wreak havoc on his Deutsche Bank cohorts by leaving a little time bomb in the computer systems. He got caught because the wiz kid had a program running to log everyone who made changes to the system so that he could track and confirm them. You can read about it in the papers, like I did.

Speaking of all this computer stuff and automated trading and computer models...I might as well give you my feelings on that. You will not be surprised that I think 95% of it is all a bunch of hoo-ha and a scam. Regression analysis is the key to the bulk of this stuff and it's not that complex. The basic premise of regression analysis is that more relationships will revert to their average relationship over time. If a person can put enough plots on a chart and determine which plots are out of sync with their historical averages, you can then decide to put a trade on to profit when those relationships go back to their historic averages. I don't do math that well but even I know what an average is. In the bond market it might go like this. If you plot three specific bond yields and how they differ from each other right now, then put into a basic computer model where that statistical average has been over the last ten or twenty years, then it's not that difficult to determine if that relationship is near its historical average or has popped away from it. If it's far enough away from the average, a trade can be executed that will profit when those three bonds inevitably revert to their average. It's just a matter of waiting through the short-term noise until you get what you want. The scam part occurs when people mask the simplicity of their model by heaping on globs of useless variables over the top of the simple model and then decry how complex and proprietary it is.

That being said, if that trade gets put on and the market continues to stay away from its historical average or goes farther awry, it can make for some heavy losses and put people out of business. The market saying for that is, "The market can stay irrational longer than you can stay solvent." A trading desk with a huge amount of capital to take the initial losses can reap massive benefits when the market trades back to its historical norm. Even I get it.

What has taken over the markets over the past 20 years is that these models have been taken to such an extreme level that NO ONE can figure them out. I have seen many computer model traders take basic regression analysis and layer fifty other variables onto the analysis and then claim they have the newest answer to trading the markets. Sometimes those people make money and sometimes they don't, but it always made me laugh when someone could talk a bank or a hedge fund into some mammoth guaranteed personal contract to move their "model" from one firm to another. And then it all blows up. The firm takes the losses and the shareholders lose but the trader walks away with millions and millions of dollars in his pocket. It was scary to see the hot shot executives who were supposed to be the adults in the room fall for this obvious ploy. Just in the name of stealing someone away and saying they had the newest, brightest, coolest toy on the block. OK, enough of that.

My addition to the government bond desk at Deutsche Bank was a rocky road for me personally. I was definitely struggling to stay alive each day. It seemed to me that the desk in general was doing just fine. As a desk we had made inroads into new customers and had increasing volume numbers. As far as revenue, none of the line traders (dopes like me) could see the overall numbers but what we could see looked pretty healthy. I was hoping I could find my way to right my personal ship. Trading T-bills sucked but when some of the other traders were on vacation, I would jump in and trade their sectors of the market and I did a much better job there than in my own sector. Maybe someone will leave and I can get bumped up into a sector I like better? Keep plugging, Matt.

At some point in that first six months I could sense a little change in the group. More subtle tension. It was tough to put my finger on but the Cowboy was not the same, and the three proprietary traders behind me and he were always cooped up in his office discussing who knows what. Something was off. All we knew was the numbers were good so it should all be okay. Our new mortgage backed area under the Cowboy was doing well also. Remember, this is Deutsche Bank after all and the place was a roller coaster of change and empire building even in 1997 so we took nothing for granted.

Then the shoe dropped. I walk in the door one morning, holding my two 20-ounce coffees that I got from the little cart outside, and my group's area is inhabited by beings from outer space. Or so it seemed. There were ten people I did not recognize sitting in people's chairs going through all the computer reports and computers. I had seen a lot of strange things up to that point but this was taking it to a new level. Jeezus, how much did I have to drink last night? Am I still drunk?

At some point that morning the line traders (those like me who traded the different sectors) were pulled into an office and told that because of a massive loss in our group the Cowboy, his head trader and a few others, including the three proprietary traders (who sat behind me) were no longer at the firm. We were told that the aliens inhabiting our desk that morning were people from London and our mortgage trading desk in NY. They would be there to help until the new structure got sorted. *This place is a fucking madhouse.* And to think I thought the Cowboy would help bring stability to the organization.

We got through our daily duties and then headed to the bar to try to sort out what had happened and what it meant to our future. For three nights we met and started to piece the story together. The first thing we had to figure out is how these big losses occurred. The line trader who was in charge of the daily estimate said he had seen nothing bad at all in his daily estimates. His words: "Matt, we all had made plenty of money to make up for you." True, but still harsh. He said it with a smile, he was one of the best guys I ever worked with and had a very sarcastic sense of humor.

From what we pieced together, certain members of the desk had put on a huge trade together with another bank. It was some kind of bet that two-year yields would not rise as fast as ten or thirty-year yields. That was called a curve trade because it's a bet on the shape of the yield curve. So this bet was put on with the other bank and it was executed using the other bank's books and records and then at the end of the trade they would split off the profit or the loss. As with the best laid plans of mice and men, they expected to put half of a profit on our books but instead they slapped a big ass loss right out of the blue onto Deutsche Bank's books. Sorry folks, but if that ain't grounds for getting fired, I don't know what is. We never found out if the super higher-ups ever knew about the trade or whether it was dumped on them at the last minute also.

This whole thing was really bizarre in every way. First off, how do you not reflect your full risk on your own books and records? Crazy. Secondly, how do you put a trade on with another bank and not let your line traders for that sector know you are doing it? Let me explain that. One of our line traders was responsible for the two-year sector of the curve. He made every price to clients at Deutsche Bank and was responsible for knowing what was going on in his sector. He had noticed very strange and bizarre trade movements in his sector for the past month but could not explain them. Can you imagine his feeling of betrayal when he finds out his own coworkers and bosses are doing massive trades with another firm and not even bothering to tell him?

TEETH (144) MARKS

16

The good news, at least for the bank, was that the mortgage-backed trading area was still doing well. Since Deutsche Bank was a "to the victor goes the spoils" type of place, management decided that the guy they had poached from Goldman a few years ago to run our mortgage business would be the perfect guy to run our desk too. All the line traders were given an address of some bar uptown and told to report there at 6 p.m. on the night we got our new boss, the guy who ran the mortgage department at Deutsche. We all take the subway up to this place and it's some big weird Miami type of bar and we are ushered into the back room which is quiet and small. *Hey, where the fuck is my drink?* We didn't even get a drink. Bullshit, man. The guy comes in with a small entourage of people we did not know. He looks at us and says, "Nice to meet you, any questions?" *Any questions? Yeah, like a hundred of them.* But instead I kept my mouth shut because it's better to be quiet and thought a knucklehead than to open my mouth and remove all doubts. Besides, I knew these guys I worked with would not take any shit. I was right. They asked about ten questions of him and he did not answer a single one. Weirdest meeting of my life.

> Line trader: Do you want us to change the way we do business or keep doing it as usual?
>
> Mortgage guy: What does that question mean?

Line trader: Ya know, since you are in charge should we do things different or the same?

Mortgage guy: I don't understand the question.

I swear it went on that way for ten questions until people just were too fed up to ask any more. It was absolutely bizarre. We were then dismissed. *Let's blow this clambake and go find a real bar.*

We decided over drinks that for us things would not change. We would keep doing business as a group the way we always had. We did not need anyone else. The new guy left us alone and life went on for the next few weeks pretty much as normal.

A month later, word started to get out that they had uncovered some very large losses in the mortgage department also. Just when you thought it was safe to go back in the water. For us, not a big deal because the mortgage guy was never around and we did everything the same way we did two months earlier. I still could not make any money trading my own product but we were a little shorthanded and I was really enjoying trading the longer duration sectors when people were on vacation. I even made a little money doing it.

Then we heard that Mr. Mortgage guy had up and disappeared. They were calling him and looking for him so they could fire him due to all the losses, but he had vanished like a fart in the wind. How bizarre. So mortgage guy is now out of the picture and we hear that they are bringing in three people from the bond trading department in our London office to take over our desk permanently. We also hear that everyone is going to get fired and they are going to start over again with their own people. Not a good week.

The guys from London show up and I catch a break. The new boss of the desk is a guy who came over from JP Morgan around the time my Repo boss and I did. I used to support him when I was a clerk and he was a line trader at JP Morgan. I knew he was a solid guy and would make rational decisions. He was an Irishman who reminded me of James Bond. The Pierce Brosnan Bond.

Since he knew me from our previous lives and obviously lacked good judgement, he asked me to help him understand what had been going on in NY the last six months. They were going to clean house and people had a week or two to audition for their jobs while 007 (that's what we called him) decided the new structure of the desk. After a few days, he sat me down for a heart to heart.

> 007: Matt, you're the first one to go because you're new and you haven't made any money. I'd like to give you a chance to save your job if we can get your numbers up.

> Me: Thanks. I appreciate that but I might be an anchor around your neck because I struggle in this job and I refuse to lose money on purpose to keep my numbers up.

> 007: I appreciate your honesty, what do you think of the other line traders?

> Me: I think you'd be crazy not to give them a chance because they all have good revenue numbers, good market penetration numbers and the salesforce likes them.

> 007: I'll keep that in mind. Over the next month, do me a favor and start looking for your replacement to trade bills. Just get someone good, I don't care where they come from.

> Me: Got it.

What a strange feeling coming out of that meeting. I had no idea where I stood job-wise and I was tasked at finding my own replacement in a job I totally sucked at. To boot, I'd be bringing someone in to a shit job in a shit situation. The desk was a mess and middle management of the trading floor was in disarray because of all the firings. I decided that I could not live with myself if I brought in a trader who had a good job at another bank and sat him down in the middle of this disaster. I decided I would recruit my replacement from out-of-work bill traders. The volumes were getting much smaller because of the government's budget surplus, so banks were laying off bill traders.

In the middle of all this chaos, it was getting close to bonus time for 1997. I was told by 007 that he was more concerned with trying to save my job than getting me a bonus. I should not expect a bonus at all, but he would do the best he could. I appreciated his honesty. I'll take brutal honesty over stupid lies any day. I was fine with no bonus. I hadn't done shit to deserve one. My plan was to do a solid job for my old JP Morgan bro 007 by hiring someone good, then getting fired and going to the next stage of my life. I fully expected the knucklehead fairytale to end right there.

I started talking to other bill traders and the brokers to decide who I should bring in to interview for my job. After a few days of nosing around to get other people's opinions, I started to zero in on one trader who had lost his job a few months back. You will remember how much I suck at interviewing people and how I had made hiring mistakes in the past. I wanted to make sure I did it differently this time. I wanted other people who had worked closely with this person to make my decision for me. I was too much of a sucker in an interview to be trusted.

Anyway, this guy was given high marks from other traders and salespeople all around. He was also out of a job so I would not have to feel bad bringing him into this debacle. It was a win-win for everyone involved. I guess maybe not for me since I was on the outs, but I was ready to roll at that point with two years of "fuck you" money in the bank. The guy came in and interviewed and was a hit with everyone and we hired him immediately. I don't even think we gave him anything guaranteed, but I'm not 100% sure. He ended up being my best hire and stayed forever and was great at his job. How funny is it that my best outside hire to that point was the guy I hired to replace me? I love the irony of life.

It was a week before bonus time and I'm taking a few things home from my desk every day. That way, when I get escorted out after my firing, there will not be much they have to ship to me. You never knew if you would be allowed back to your desk or not. Sometimes people were allowed fifteen minutes to clean their desk and say goodbye and sometimes you were just escorted from the Human Resources office out to the sidewalk. I get called into 007's office.

> 007: Sit. I have good news. Not only was I able to get you a small bonus but I found you a job. Your old Repo boss didn't think firing you was fair since he put you over there in the first place and it was not your fault it all blew up. I'm sorry I could not get you a bigger bonus. I thought you did an okay job all things considered and only lost a small amount of money in a tough job.

> Me: Thanks, but I can't go back to trading CP. I just can't do it.

> 007: It's not CP, he is revamping the Asset & Liability desk and thinks you would be a great fit.

> Me: That's great! Thank you so much.

So my bonus was $60,000, a 1/3 cut from the previous year but more than I deserved. After a week of getting the new bill trader settled in, I said my goodbyes and moved all my shit back to my new desk in my old Money Markets Department.

17

It was early 1998 and I was slinking back to my old stomping grounds to learn a new business. I am a curious person who loves new things so I was genuinely excited to get started and learn a part of the business in which I had no experience. I was grateful to my old Repo boss for saving my ass from oblivion. Since I had left Money Markets the previous year it had been restructured and the name of the group was Money Market Finance. Fancy schmancy. The group still consisted of the CP, CD, Repo and Asset & Liability desks, and a short-term swap desk was now under our group's umbrella. The sales group that used to report to the head of our group now reported centrally up the chain into a global sales group headed by someone brought in from Merrill Lynch by Edson Mitchell. The overall management structure of the bank was changed subtly to have a more global focus as opposed to a local focus. Instead of just worrying about what NY was doing, management wanted traders and salespeople to know what was happening in London, Frankfurt and Asia also.

As part of the changes that occurred in the previous year on the trading floor, my cohort trader who came with me from JP Morgan to Deutsche Bank was put in charge of the Asset & Liability desk in New York. I was now reporting to him and there were three others for a total of five. At that point it was also called the Money Market Funding desk and was not investment banking related, but closer to the core bank.

Up until now all my experience had been in investment banking. Dealing with clients as issuers, trading securities and moving assets on and off the balance sheet. Core banking was more the loans and deposits associated with funding the bank. Loans and deposits are not securities so they just keep piling up on the balance sheet until they mature. For example, if you buy and sell $100,000,000 of Commercial Paper with a one-year maturity the only thing left is the profit or loss you made, otherwise the security does not show up on the balance sheet. In core banking, if you make a one-year loan and then take a one-year deposit, your risk is matched off but both the loan and deposit sit on the balance sheet until they mature. It's a different world.

Our main responsibility was raising cash to fund the bank's US Dollar operations. Our desk would deal with brokers and our salesforce to issue Deutsche Bank Commercial Paper, Deutsche Bank CD's and Deutsche Bank Time Deposits, then funnel that money through our Treasury Group to the business units within Deutsche Bank. For instance, our equity group would buy a bunch of stock from a company to sell over the next few weeks. We would raise the cash for Treasury in the market, then they would fund the equity group's purchase of that stock.

Our desk was the face to the market and the Treasury group was the face to the business units within Deutsche Bank. The Treasury group was in charge of coming up with limits and enforcing them. They were also charged with settling the bank's accounts with the Federal Reserve at the end of the night, using the fedwire. At that time our job was pretty simple. Just raise cash from the markets and get it to our Treasury department. Our liabilities would be the CP, CD's and deposits we took in the bank's name from customers, and our assets would be the loans we made to Treasury to fund the bank's balance sheet. That was why we were called the Asset & Liability desk, or funding desk.

I knew the basics of the products, but how they all went together, I had no clue at all. My boss was fantastic and just told me to spend the next four months learning the business and trading as much as I wanted. I was anxious to lick my trading wounds and start to get the feeling back of making a little money again and not dreading the beginning of my day, knowing the odds were that I was gonna get my assed kicked.

Besides jumping in to learn all this new stuff, I was happy just trading for the bank's account. Trading interest rate futures to make money for my boss's desk and the bank. I was taking more risk and starting to understand the ins and outs of interest rate trading. As always, there were ups and downs. Some of our futures brokers we had on the "hoot & holler." That was a direct line that could be set up on speaker so that you could talk back and forth. Generally you would take a broker who did not annoy the shit out of you and throw him on the hoot so he could give you second-by-second updates and color of what was happening in the market. Certain brokers were so annoying to listen to that they could never go on the hoot. You'd rather chew foil than listen to them all day. My guy on the hoot was a real hoot. It was like a comedy show all day. The guy was nuts. One day he and I were discussing a trade that he had recommended. I thought it fit with my view of the market so I put on a big chunk of the trade. Not three hours later the Federal Reserve entered the market and did something totally unexpected. The markets starting moving far and fast and the trade I just put on was a calendar spread, or a forward curve trade. Not complex at all (remember, I'm a knucklehead), but when the markets are screaming sometimes it's not clear what range the price of those trades will settle into. So while I was trying to figure out whether this trade was going to make me a hero or a goat after what the Fed just did, my broker cleared that up in a minute with what he SCREAMED over the hoot. "Matt, this trade is going to make your ass look like the Lincoln tunnel!" Well, that clears that up. I guess I'm gonna be the goat today. The best part about it was that everyone within thirty feet could hear it and that phrase became an instant classic and was trotted out whenever a trade was going against the desk.

News update: Mr. Mortgage, who was my boss for a few months, was found during this time and promptly fired. After all the chaos he created and the losses he had under his lead, he actually had the balls to get Jesse Jackson to march into Deutsche Bank's lobby and demand millions of dollars in severance. And they were dumb enough to pay. This business is nuts.

A few years later, Mr. Mortgage was arrested for laundering money for terrorists which involved missiles that could be used to shoot down airliners. You can read about it in the papers, like I did. You can't make this shit up.

Also during this time the politically correct police started to finally show up at Deutsche Bank. When I worked at JP Morgan it was an absolute no-no to drink during working hours or drink at lunch, especially after the bar in the basement at 15 Broad was closed down as I came aboard. Yes, I can't let it go, I am still pissed I missed that experience. Deutsche Bank was the exact opposite when I started, so I made up for it a bit.

In the first few weeks, I would always notice empty Beck's beer bottles in the conference rooms. I kinda thought on the weekends the people putting in long hours would grab a couple of cold ones at night. No harm done, right? I always wondered why the beer was always Beck's and only Beck's. I found out from a salesperson that Beck's was Deutsche Bank's "official" beer and that if you were having a meeting or a conference during the day, instead of ordering coffee and soda you could order Beck's beer. Can you believe it? Sitting at meetings during the day, with or without clients, and having a few cold ones. Too good to be true.

Luckily for me it was still drilled into my psyche from my previous job to stay away from booze during the day (at least at work). I only drank twice that I remember in the office. Once was a floor-wide cocktail hour to celebrate a record-breaking month of revenue for the trading floor and the other time I will get into later. Not drinking in the office is nothing to be proud of, Rusty. The Beck's gravy train was eventually cancelled as the American party poopers started to be more prominent in New York.

There were now five people on the Asset & Liability desk and the responsibilities were starting to flesh themselves out. We had my old cohort who ran the desk, did most of the risk taking, and was in charge of guiding the ship (our desk risk) in the right direction. We also had a guy who knew all the nuts and bolts of our desk and the Treasury desk. He mostly traded the more complex swaps in his trading book, along with being a liaison with the Treasury group and helping the bank raise long term money. At that time our group was responsible for raising money inside of two years of maturity and the Treasury group was the "face to the market" for two years out to thirty years. Then there were two guys who did the day-to-day funding and admin, sprinkled in with some trading. My responsibilities were flowing to the side of being the troubleshooter for the desk and also setting up risk management systems so my boss could track his risk more closely so that he could safely take even more risk.

During this time, as I was jumping into the Asset & Liability desk I always had my nose in my blue notebook where I had taken all those notes the week I was in London a few years prior. I was not able to use anything I learned in

London after I moved to trade T-bills, but I was going to put all that information to work now.

My cohort boss who did most of the trading had been "lighting up" the short term swap desk with volume the last few years. As he expanded the Asset & Liability desk he had to do much more hedging, and he was using our own swap desk to hedge the interest rate risk of the portfolio. If the desk made a one-year loan and could not take one-year cash at that moment to offset it perfectly, a swap would be done to "swap" the one-year risk into a more manageable, even shorter-term risk. These swaps were used to turn longer maturity interest rate risk into either one-month Libor risk or three-month Libor risk. Libor is an index based on an average of where a panel of banks estimate they can raise cash in certain time periods. A one-week estimate, a one-month estimate, a three-month estimate, all the way out to one year. Once the risk was converted into one or three month Libor risk, it could be managed with cash, which is much more available within three months than outside of three months. The more the Asset & Liability desk ramped up its volume, the more it had to hedge and it used Libor to hedge most of the risk. The traders on that desk, especially the Libor guys, were making tons of money from the flow from the Asset & Liability desk.

The desk had also ramped up using foreign exchange forwards to convert loans and deposits in one currency into US dollars to help fund the portfolio. I had brought back a computer model that London was good enough to give me on my trip there and my desk was putting it to good use. Foreign Exchange Forwards (F/X forwards) are basically a simultaneous loan in one currency versus a deposit in another for a certain period of time. The difference between an F/X spot trade between currencies and a forward is that a spot trade converts between currency forever, while an F/X forward does it for a specific amount of time and then converts back at the end of the contract. Here is a basic example of how our desk would use the F/X forward market. As our desk in New York was making loans and taking deposits, so were all the other branches of Deutsche Bank around the world. At that time the only real retail branches of Deutsche Bank that had savings and checking account deposits was in Germany and maybe a few other European currencies. In the example, Deutsche Bank in Germany had many more deposits of Deutschmarks (the currency before the Euro) than it needed. New York had zero retail deposits and a growing US Dollar balance sheet to fund. Our German branch had a choice to make. Either lend out their Deutschmarks to other banks in Germany and take the risk of not being paid back, or use F/X Forwards to convert Deutschmarks to US Dollars and lend to DB New York. Since an F/X forward is an internal transaction, it is much cleaner on the books than lending to another German bank. Germany or New York could also reverse the transaction internally and not "gross up" the balance sheet. Since internal Deutsche Bank trades would net out to zero, they looked much better on the balance sheet than twenty loans and deposits to other German banks that always sat layered on the balance sheet until they matured, therefore "grossing it up." It was mentally tiring just thinking about explaining that. Time for a refill.

The year 1998 was fun. I was learning a brand new product in a brand new world with a great group of people. The balance sheet at Deutsche Bank in New York was expanding dramatically with the addition of all the new businesses and it was our job to find the cash to lend to those businesses within Deutsche Bank. All this business created a ton of interest rate and liquidity risk that we had to find a way to manage. Truth be told, we were getting so much flow business that you could sit a monkey down at our desk and that monkey would be able to make money. The real trick of that job was managing the risk of the flow and then creating alpha from the flow. Alpha is basically the extra revenue you can make by leveraging your built-in "monkey money" from the flow, and adding on to it by making correct hedging or interest rate risk decisions.

I was becoming the desk expert on using our existing systems and building new systems to track and manage the risk. I'm gonna let you in on a little secret that you should know by now. I'm not that smart. Pretty simple, as a matter of fact. For that reason I need to break things down to basics so I can understand them. If I can get the basic concept, I can build something that makes it even easier to track and monitor. It's the only way I can survive. When I say "build," don't let me fool you. I could never build shit myself in the systems or model world. I was pretty good, however, at hooking on to brilliant people and having them build or rebuild things to my startlingly simplistic specifications.

In November of 1998, a few senior people in our Money Market Finance group were brought into an office, where my old Repo boss who ran the group and an executive from London were waiting to talk to us. The executive from London announced that Deutsche Bank was buying Bankers Trust, a New York bank. The reason was to both boost the investment banking operation in the US, but also to get our hands on an extra ten or fifteen billion dollars of stable US unsecured funding. We could use that funding to relieve our current funding stresses as the balance sheet expanded. He said it was a straight purchase and that Deutsche Bank people would be in charge and we would have nothing to worry about. He thought the merger would close sometime around the middle of 1999. Looking back, we did not really think much of it. Things changed fast at Deutsche Bank and you never knew what was going to happen next. No big deal, especially since it would be six months until we would have to start working on it for real. A lot of these mergers were announced over the years and then fell apart, so we were not fazed at all. The merger was announced in the press the following day. I wondered if Bankers Trust allowed Beck's beer in their meetings? Doubtful.

My old Repo boss who was in charge of the Money Market Finance group was making a name for himself and took over the whole business globally. It was a big move considering the business in New York was only a few years old and Deutsche Bank was a European bank. He was becoming more powerful globally, and, in turn, helped those who worked under him in NY gain more stature and more recognition. In the previous year, one of the New York Asset & Liability traders was sent off to Singapore for two years to help bring the North American and Asian businesses closer together. He was alone and had a big job and some of our projects with trading systems overlapped. So it was decided I'd spend a week in Singapore with him to see if any of my system enhancements could be folded into his business. So the knucklehead was heading to Singapore for a week in December of 1998.

18

I WAS NOT THRILLED ABOUT MAKING this trip, for many reasons. I did not like being away from my family when I had two little ones at home. I was not looking forward to 19 hours on a plane each way. I had never been to Asia. What kind of food was I going to throw down my piehole? I heard they only had one type of beer. Tiger beer. What if I didn't like it? Do I sound like a whiny little bitch or what?

At that time in 1998 Bill Clinton was having a little showdown with Saddam Hussein over Iraq's unwillingness to be transparent with the UN inspectors, a condition agreed to after the first Iraq war. There were rumors the US was going to invade again or at least do a bunch of bombing runs. I had no interest being anywhere near the area at that time, but I was ordered to go so over I went.

Singapore. The cleanest place on earth. When I was waiting outside the airport for my cab, I saw one lonely Coke can strewn under a bush. The whole week I was there, that was the only litter I saw. Period. I did not even see one splotch of chewing gum flattened on the ground. Pretty amazing.

As far as business went, it was a great week. We got tons accomplished, I learned a boatload about the Asia operation, and I was able to help out my comrade by upgrading all his risk management systems and models to what we were using in NY. Just a few other subjects worth talking about.

Taking a crap. OK, bear with me on this. Let's be honest, everyone has to go. It's just a fact of life. It can be a traumatic experience too, right? You have to feel safe in your "environment" or it can really muck with your system and make you feel lousy. You still with me?

It's my second day in the Singapore office and my comrade knows how the human body works and he knows I have had about four cups of coffee, so he gives me a little piece of friendly advice. "Don't use the first two stalls because they are unhealthy. They are not cleaned correctly and people have had to go to the hospital after using them. Only use stall #3, that's the one all of us use." When the mood hits I mosey along back to the "little generals" room and bypass runway #1 and runway #2 as instructed. I pop open the door to runway #3 and stop dead in my tracks. Panic immediately sets in. It's a freakin' pit in the floor. A pit. To use it you have to squat over the pit. To add insult to injury, it's out of toilet paper. That is not happening. No way. Think fast, Matt. You got to figure a plan B. The train has left the station and the turtle's head is popping out. The lightbulb in my head pops on. I got it!

I waddle out to the desk and urgently demand from my comrade: "Give me the keys to your apartment, I'm calling a cab. Now!" To which he replies, "My keys are in my jacket in the first floor closet of this office." He could barely keep a straight face and I was figuring it out. It turns out he had played an elaborate prank on me. Runway #1 and runway #2 are normal toilets and #3 is where you can squat over a pit if you want to do #2. He enjoyed that thoroughly.

I had a very difficult time with the food. The second day for lunch I tried their version of fast food and had to chuck it before my first bite when I saw some type of vein in my pressed meat burger. Nope. That night they decide we should go to the quay (I'm not sure what that is, but that's the word they used) and get a fancy seafood dinner. Okay, I'm good with that. Besides shrimp cocktail and scallops I'm not big on seafood, but hopefully I will like Tiger beer.

The quay (maybe it means pier?) and restaurant was out on the water and a beautiful setting. We had dropped in to a bar for a few drinks before dinner, and guess what? Tiger beer was awesome! Things were looking up. Five of us from the office went to dinner. One of the guys was an Australian who had lived in Singapore for a few years and knew all the ropes. During that week he insisted on accompanying me when I shopped for electronics and jewelry for my kids and my wife. I was so happy he was with me because he screamed and yelled and negotiated with the vendors and saved me a ton of money.

After a few more Tigers at the table we decide on our seafood. Basically you just order big buckets of seafood and pass it around the table. The Australian guy who knows all the ropes is going to take care of the ordering. The waiter comes over and they start talking about the order and then they start screaming at each other. As they are going back and forth, the Australian guy stands up and puffs his chest out. I'm thinking punches are flying next and I'm wondering if I can fit under the table. More screaming. Then it suddenly settles down and the waiter writes on his pad and scurries away. "What was that about?" I asked. He explained how that was just normal negotiations in Singapore and that the waiter was trying to overcharge us so he negotiated the price down. *There is no fucking way I am eating anything that waiter brings to us.* C'mon man, your telling me that the waiter is not in back hocking big loogies and spitting into our food? Looks like I am going hungry again. They ate like the ship was going down while I drank Tiger beer and ate nothing. I made my comrade cook spaghetti and tomato sauce for me when we got back to his apartment. He had sucked down a bunch of vodkas that night so he was not happy to be cooking. It was his penance for almost making me shit in my pants in runway #3.

It was Vietnamese food the next night. Not a fancy place but an authentic place in the middle of the city that was very rundown. They called it a "noodle" place so I thought I'd be fine. Tough to fuck up a bowl of noodles, right? The group ordered all kinds of food for themselves and were very excited about it. I have no idea what it was, but since I love cats and dogs as pets, I figured I would pass on the meat. I ordered a big bowl of plain noodles with butter. My bowl came and at first glance it looked edible. Just a bowl of noodles with chopsticks. I can handle this. I start mixing the noodles and I realize there is more butter or broth or whatever the hell it is than there are noodles. Swimming in butter. *OK, as long as that is butter I can deal with this.* Butter is good. I swirl and grab a gnarly sized portion of noodles and as it's making its way up to my big piehole I notice something disturbing. Not in the noodles, but on my chopsticks. *Are those teeth marks on my chopsticks?* Confirmed. There were someone else's teethmarks on my chopsticks. Matt's going hungry again. "I'll have another Tiger, please."

There was a little Iraq flavor to my trip as well. Flying from Frankfurt to Singapore during this time, the rumors of a bombing of Iraq made Lufthansa change their route. Normally the route would have gone close or over Iraq, but someone smart figured it would be better not to be a big fat 747 target over Iraq when the shooting starts. Bravo. So the route was changed and it added another hour to the flight each way. I also ate at an Iraqi restaurant, against my will.

I was a little nervous about the whole Iraqi thing going on, being an American in that part of the world. It was a mistake for me to let my comrade and his Australian counterpart know that. They decided it would be funny to take me out to dinner at an Iraqi restaurant before they dropped me off at the airport for my trip home. Only they did not share that with me. They said they felt bad about my food issues and there was a "perfect restaurant you will love" on the way to the airport. It was uncomfortable, to say the least. The people at the restaurant were absolutely fine; the awkwardness was all on me. I did not say a word the entire meal because I did not want to be identified as an American. I have always been paranoid. I could not understand anything on the menu but finally decided the only thing I had a shot of getting down was some type of lamb ball. So I pointed at the dish I wanted (still mute) and hoped for the best. When my dish arrived, the waiter was carrying it with what looked to be a dirty towel. The plate must have been hot. It was only a baseball-sized ball of chopped meat. As he was putting it down, the baseball started to roll off the plate and unfortunately the waiter was able to save it. He saved it by flopping the dirty towel up and using it to roll the baseball back up as he lowered my plate. Appetizing. But the worst was yet to come. You could see the finger marks of the person who molded my lamb ball into its baseball shape. They weren't the dainty fingers of some beautiful dark and exotic lady of my fantasies, either. They were big-ass man fingers that molded my dinner and I was going hungry again into my flight home. There was always good food on the flights so I ended up doing just fine.

Bonuses for the year 1998 were to be announced in early 1999. It was a very good year profit wise for our whole area, and with my old Repo boss now taking over global responsibility, he was able to have a much bigger say in bonuses and promotions. If I'm not mistaken, that was the year three people in the Money Markets group in New York made Managing Director (MD). Being an MD was the most sought after promotion at the bank. It was akin to being made a partner at a law firm. Once you got that promotion, you were in the rarified atmosphere of power and money. My cohort boss, with whom I came over from JP Morgan, made MD that year. I was still a VP but my bonus that year shot up to $225,000. Hog heaven, baby. Never in my wildest dreams.

More importantly, I LOVED the job and could have done it for the rest of my life. Building risk and trading systems, being able to trade all I wanted. And most important, not having to hobnob and kiss anyone's ass. I had zero ambition of being in charge of anything or managing people.

19

When my old Repo boss had his duties expanded globally, he inherited all the offices around the world. He spent about half a year putting a structure in place where more junior MD's were in charge of the offices and he only had regional MD's reporting to him. I'll clue you in to a little-known tactic of the big-shot executives. Have as many minions working for you as you can so your empire is as big and as powerful as possible. At the same time, have as few people reporting directly to you as you can. That way you can reap all the rewards while minimizing the management of people. You know I'm right. It's just human nature. I just like to cut through the bullshit.

After all that restructuring was done, my boss could not figure out where our Toronto office fit in the puzzle. The Toronto office was struggling mightily and the Money Market side was not doing well either. A few years before, some brain surgeon in Canada had opened a twenty-year unbreakable lease on large office spaces in Montreal and Toronto. That overhead was killing their numbers, along with not being able to compete on even terms with the domestic Canadian banks.

It was not a good situation and no one wanted to touch it from a US management perspective. Since my cohort boss was a newly minted MD, my Repo boss dumped it on him.

Since it was a hot potato he did not want, he dumped it on me. See how that works? To be fair, my cohort boss had a lot on his plate at the time. Adding products to the trading mix, switching over from accrual accounting to mark-to-market accounting, dealing with increased funding pressures and getting himself more involved with London, Frankfurt and Asia. He had a lot going on.

My instructions from my old Repo boss were clear. Go up to Toronto and fire the guy running Money Markets and then evaluate whether we should hire someone to try to save it, or just pull the plug on the whole operation. He did not like the guy he had up there and wanted him gone. My thoughts were a bit different. I had never managed anyone before and never wanted to. Direct order or not, I was not firing anyone unless I thought it was the right thing to do for the business. The consequences of firing someone are too important to take someone else's word for. I was going up there with an open mind. After a few phone conversations, I made plans to spend a week up in Toronto to meet the people and immerse myself in the operation. I had heard Canadian beer is thirst-quenching.

Our relationship did not start out well. In the few weeks between me being announced as the new sucker in charge of Toronto and when I planned my visit, a global Money Markets Finance conference was held in Europe and thank goodness I was not invited. Not my idea of a good time. Listening to bloated egos pounding their chests, telling everyone how great they are, there is not enough beer in the world to make up for that annoyance. The Toronto guy was not invited either, but insisted on putting a short presentation in front of the conference. I did not blame him for that, as he was just trying to save his job and prove the Toronto office was worth saving. But get this, the prick refused to show me his presentation. *Dude, I'm your freaking boss.* Nope, he would not budge. He faxed the presentation over to the hotel in Europe and got someone at the conference to hand it out. I had someone from the conference fax it to me. Dysfunction. I thrive on it.

A week later, I took the one-hour flight from New York into Toronto and then popped in a cab for the twenty-minute ride into the office. Very easy commute from New York. What a beautiful city Toronto is. I had a good feeling on the cab ride in. That good feeling lasted about two minutes into my first appearance on our Toronto office's trading floor. The guy I was supposed to fire pulled me into a conference room before I could even hang up my overcoat. It was all hush hush.

He was a wee little neurotic fella. He spent two hours going through every detail of the politics of the office. Nothing regarding business was discussed that first day. I met next with the guy in charge of Repo, and then the guy doing sales and a few other chores for us. What an absolutely fucked up place. Twenty people on the whole floor with room for two hundred and there was enough paranoia, hate and dysfunction to fill a trading floor of five hundred. *How do I even begin to sort this place out?* I was not sure how to answer that question but I know where I do my best thinking. No, not the bathroom. But good guess. At a bar with a beer in my hand.

So, reluctantly, the four of us went to happy hour. The three were so paranoid they didn't even really want to be around each other. It was strange. My first Labatt's Blue beer. Honey, where have you been my whole life? Great beer. Not much was accomplished that first night except for the fact that the three of them bonded enough to make a complete ass out of me. Let me explain. I love beer. Surprised? As I found out the hard way that night, the alcohol content in Canadian beers was higher than in the US, but Matt's drinking speed was not adjusted for Canadian beer content. Do you know what that equals? Me being much more drunk after two hours than I was used to. Thank goodness I did not puke. The funny thing is I was not the first person to fall for this. They had a good laugh throughout the night as I made my way to a hot sloppy mess. They rolled me to my hotel and poured me into my room. Bastards.

We had a good laugh the next day when I got into the office. It was a soft laugh, though, because my hangover could not tolerate loud laughs. It broke the ice a little but I still was wondering if I was over my head here. Nothing of note was accomplished that week except me trying to figure out where the pieces all fit in the puzzle.

When I got back to New York I started to formulate a rough plan. Actually two plans. A short term plan and a long term plan. The short term plan had be be triage. Just stop the bleeding and give me a few months of room to sort out the long term plan. I went to my old Repo boss in New York, the guy who wanted the wee little man in Toronto out. I said that since our merger with Bankers Trust seemed like it might move along within the next few months, wouldn't it be prudent to see if we picked up any Toronto people currently working for Bankers Trust and then move the pieces around after the close as needed? He agreed, with one stipulation. "I don't want to hear from that guy in the mean time. Not a peep." OK I told him, I will take care of it. Triage.

I get on the phone with the guy in Toronto and tell him that under no circumstances is he to contact my boss or my old Repo boss. If he had any problems or issues, the "three amigos" in Toronto should come straight to me and only me. I would then work on the problem. I further clarified to him that the old Repo boss is too damn busy to insert himself into your desk squabbles and turf wars. Stay away from him for your own good. He got it after that. OK, so I stopped the bleeding and gave myself a few months of breathing room to get moving on a longer term plan.

Over the next few weeks, I went over the notes of my trip and talked to them every day. The plan we decided on was basically three parts. The first part was to stop all the infighting within the desk up there and start working together as one group, not three different armies. I had them all cross train in each other's jobs and back each other up. Secondly, the Global Markets group in Toronto consisted of four of five different groups, of which the three amigos were one. Each of these little groups sat away from the other groups, so no wonder they could not get along. It was like five little fiefdoms with no cohesion. They ended up moving all the groups together and acting like a trading floor instead of battling each other. The last part was that we had to keep our group 100% Canadian and all three were Canadian. Canada at the time was the opposite of the US in that domestic banks had all the edges in the market and foreign banks had much more regulations and rules. It was almost impossible to break into the top, being a foreign bank. Your only real chance was stocking up on Canadians with good contacts. Trying to bring in non-Canadians was never going to work. They would be shunned and isolated. The wee little man was highly educated and had many contacts so it made sense to give him another chance. So we got to work.

I was going up to Toronto monthly or bi-monthly. One thing I can tell you about the boys up there is they like their strip clubs. I must admit I frequented the ballet with them a few times myself. Nothing to be proud of, Rusty. What I did find out on these trips is that no matter what country you go to, men are all the same. It always made me chuckle. "I think she likes me, maybe I can get her number." I heard that multiple times after watching a guy spend 200 Canadian dollars on lap dances. Then he gets shut down, always good for a laugh. Speaking of lap dances, with the conversion rate of the currency, a lap dance was only $14 in Canada vs $20 in the United States. I'm just sayin'.

One last story before we move along. After one of these trips to Toronto, I came home late Friday night and threw all my laundry in the hamper. The next morning I was sitting at my son's basketball game when my wife arrived. She walked over and flipped a plastic card at me and said, "Next time, check your pockets before you throw your laundry in the hamper!" Then she walks away and watches the game away from me. Uh-Oh. *What did I do now?* I pick the card up and turn it over and it says, 'Admit one to Brass Rail VIP lounge,' with a drawing of an obvious non-ballet dancer on it. It may have even had a little glitter on it. Holy crap. Thank goodness I was not sitting with anyone. It took me a while to get back in good graces. When you make a mistake, fess up and make amends. That's what I did.

One more laundry story before we move on. Back in New York around this time, I am running a meeting with fifteen or so systems people, IT people, accountants and the Operations department. Guys and gals. I'm sitting in my white shirt and yipping and yapping about who knows what when I feel a lump in my arm below my shirt. Without thinking, I reach into my shirt and before I know it I'm holding up....voila!!, a pair of my wife's freshly laundered white panties that must have gotten caught in my sleeve. The place broke up in laughter. I was tempted to try that trick at other meetings when I was falling on my face with the crowd!

20

This brings us to the few months before the Bankers Trust merger. There were all kinds of rules regarding how much information two companies could share before a merger closed. For that reason, we got very little information on the structure of the bank we were merging with or the personnel involved. I was excited to get a huge block of stable US dollar deposits to alleviate some of the funding pressures we were starting to face in the market. Since our desk was mainly unsecured funding, it was limited or a scarce resource (like a credit card limit). In general, collateralized funding (such as Repo) has less of a limit since the creditor has both the collateral and your credit quality to fall back on. I knew the merger would be a pain in the butt but the diversity of the funding would make it worth it.

Toronto had settled down a bit and the three amigos up there were hard at work. That made the sucker (me) free to be the person from Money Markets picked to manage the group level integration between the two banks. At Deutsche Bank we had two separate groups doing the total funding operation, Money Markets and Treasury. Bankers Trust had one group combining it all. That set up a turf war within Deutsche Bank for how the Bankers Trust group would be split when they came over. Nothin' is easy, right? It's okay, as long as that slug of deposit money folds into Deutsche, life will be just grand and it will be worth it.

The only real information I get in the month leading up to the close is about ten pages of notes on how their group is structured and which of their personnel resides in what group. Otherwise, no more information can be passed around. What's the big fucking secret?

My old Repo boss who has charged me with this has very clear instructions to me. Make no mistake, we are buying Bankers Trust, he said. This is not a merger. On day one every single thing in that building, including the people, are ours to do as we please with. Your job is to make sure the day of the close goes well and then decide the structure of the combined groups going forward. Businesses and systems, as well as the people. As long as my bosses don't have political problems with what you decide, I will go with whatever you say. Whoa. Whoa. Whoa. This is way too much responsibility for a knucklehead. Well, as long as we get those damn deposits we need, I will find a way.

Update: A week later, we get the word. Disaster. Because of "emerging legal" issues between the entities of the merger, certain businesses at Bankers Trust will not be able to be folded into Deutsche Bank. Maybe never. "Are my deposits still coming over?" No, they were not. *Can't we pull the plug on this disaster then?* Too late. We are going through with it.

It turns out the "emerging legal" issues are a well known regulation called 23A from the Federal Reserve Act. I want to know what fucking moron was in charge of vetting this merger and missing that one? I'm sure he got promoted. This was the biggest fuckup I had ever seen on Wall Street.

A week before the merger close in June of 1999, I was allowed to go down to the Bankers Trust building at 130 Liberty Street and try to figure out what I could do on my own before the close went through. I think there were three or four others from other businesses at Deutsche that joined me. One of the first things I was to do was to re-interview everyone for their jobs and to get as much information from those interviews as I could. I was told the people at Bankers knew about the re-interviewing.

At that time Deutsche Bank's offices were still at 31 West 52nd street in mid-town. The trading floor was way over-capacity and it was the most disgusting dump of a place I ever worked in. We probably had twice the number of people that Drexel Burnham Lambert envisioned when the floor was built. When you have lines in front of the crapper stalls after the morning coffee rush and the afternoon coffee rush, you know it's time to lease a bigger space. FYI...I never waited in line. I had found a secret set of bathrooms in the basement with two stalls. Shhh, don't tell anyone. The floor had these huge air conditioner units we had to walk around and turn up on days it was warm or when we had bad hangovers.

My first trip up into 130 Liberty that first morning was amazing. The trading floor was up high and the views of the lower Manhattan waterways and bridges were incredible. At west 52nd our only view was a wall of bricks from the buildings next door. Looking back, about the only redeeming quality of the 31 West 52nd office was when the guys in accounting used to tell us they could see the Rockettes sunbathing topless on the roof of Radio City music hall. I may have to call bullshit on that one. One of these days, I will have to do a satellite search of that area of New York to see if the logistics make that possible. Back to my new temporary digs at 130 Liberty.

Not only were the views amazing at 130 Liberty, but the trading floor was spectacular. Wood paneled walls, new technology. It smelled of old money all right. I was walking around like I was in fantasy land and was lulled into a false sense of peace. Little did I know I was walking into a war zone and should have asked for battle pay. I had no idea of the emotions that were going on in that building at the time.

During that week before the close, I encountered three types of people. Hostile, helpful and "I don't give a shit." Within the category of hostile was also a subcategory of being hostile to me but helpful to the merger. Let me explain that subcategory first. Deutsche Bank bought Bankers Trust for cash and not stock. The premium DB offered over the market was somewhere near 30%. That meant that highly compensated Bankers Trust people who owned stock were going to be "cashed out" at $93 a share from Deutsche Bank, rather than where the market had been before the merger talks, which was anywhere from $50 or $60 a share. So for them this merger HAD to go through for them to reap this massive reward. At the same time most of them had been at Bankers Trust for long enough to have a real bond to the bank and the people. So while they were openly nasty and hostile to me, they were also running around like chickens making sure everything was done by the book so the merger could go through. That was helpful to me because they were helping me do the job I was supposed to do.

I had plenty of desks to park my Irish ass in because about forty percent of the staff just didn't show up the last few weeks, or had already agreed to terms of departure and had left. My main concern was making sure that on the day of the close I knew all the market risks that were left in the groups we were taking over. That, as well as figuring out the personnel stuff.

That first day I mapped out who did what and what systems they traded on. Just the basics. I kept to myself and tried to stay off the radar. People were walking around spouting really irrational shit about DB and its people. I was surprised at the anger, but looking back, I guess I get it. On one hand DB was the sugar daddy, but on the other, it was the monster in the closet.

Once I had the basics, on the second day I started re-interviewing people. My first interview shocked and pissed me off at the same time:

> Me: Hi, nice to meet you. I'm not really good at interviews so I hope you bear with me.
>
> Cocky guy (indignant): This is not an interview!
>
> Me (to myself): *Well what the fuck is it then?*
>
> Me: It's not?
>
> Cocky guy: No, this is an exchange of ideas between equals!
>
> Me (to myself): *Your gonna be the first one I fire. Thanks for making it easy.*
>
> Me: OK, so tell me what you do?

It was a short "exchange of ideas," but I got the basics, which is all I needed. He was the first one out but maybe that's exactly what he wanted. Good times.

By the second day, I was calling my old Repo boss in charge of everything and begging him to get them to move our offices from midtown down to 130 Liberty. What a place, built to be a real trading floor, not like our floor, which seemed like it was built to be a fucking paint ball field. The boss told me that since all the DB hotshots lived in Connecticut and did not want the extra commute, that plan was shot down. Figures those pussies would not take one for the team. The reality is that the building and trading floor were not big enough for the future. I still marveled at the food and coffee cart that served the whole floor all day. In between dodging staplers that the restless natives were aiming my way, I didn't even have to leave my seat to get coffee! Oh, and no wait at all if you had to go see a man about a horse. Just like everything in life, good as well as bad.

I met some very professional people that week who were

a huge help and kept me from getting beat up. I was warned who the angry ones were, so I tried to navigate around them. Can't we all just get along?

At DB we always struggled with our systems coordination, due to how we were built. Deutsche Bank New York was built by having nine different little empires come in with their own systems, operations, and reporting. It was always an obstacle to our growth and our stability. During the first weeks down at 130 Liberty, I kept hearing about this magician who ran the systems at Bankers Trust. His name kept popping up in all my conversations with the people who would actually speak to me. I needed to meet this guy and make sure that he was happy and protected at all costs. I needed him to help move our combined group forward for the next five years after we merged. I was not the only one who felt that way about him, so it was a concerted effort to make sure he was happy to stay. He was a huge help during that period, to say the least.

The morning before the close was interesting. The IT people left at Bankers Trust decided they would start selling everything they could get their hands on to people in the building. I have no idea where that money went. I was told not to interfere by my DB masters. They were selling computers, printers, TV's. Who knows what else. All morning long, the staff were carrying booty out to their cars. You can't make this shit up. That night all the groups have their final meetings together to give it the go signal and report back to their masters in midtown. We are a go. It's June 3, 1999, and the close is set for tomorrow. If it's a clusterfuck for our group, it's going to be a clusterfuck for Matt, so I felt I had a lot at stake. Just make it through the first day.

The day of the close was a bit anti-climatic. The morning was the worst. People crying, drinking at their desks, and generally emotional. And that was just me! Kidding. Most of those people had cleared out with their booty by noon and then it was time to start getting more involved and tracking everything. For the most part, everything ended up working that day, so it was generally considered a success.

I met some great people from Bankers Trust in those weeks and the weeks after the close. Not just those who ended up in my world, but others who I ended up working closely with over the years. As with everything in life, the merger was both good and bad for Deutsche Bank overall. We benefitted from the experience and the outlook and professionalism of those we kept for many years.

I continued down at 130 Liberty for the next few months until we could start moving pieces and people up to midtown. Once the Bankers Trust operation was relatively stable, then it was time to start making sure that Y2K systems and risk management would not be an obstacle for our business and our bank. The calendar flipping from 1999 to 2000 was causing all kinds of craziness in the world. There was widespread fear that at the stroke of midnight at the end of 1999, that instead of turning over to 1/1/2000, that all electronics would cease to work. Bank stocks, bank bonds, and bank funding would be affected. Hoopla and panic in the markets.

21

In the months after the close of the Bankers Trust merger, I had met a few times with the systems magician we inherited and he impressed me more and more. By the second or third meeting I was begging him to jump in to all of our current Deutsche Bank systems and our Y2K risks. On a scale of 1-10, my confidence in our current DB systems people was a 1. Half the time there was no one to call and no one took responsibility for any problems. The bulk of our systems were either outsourced to other companies or managed from Frankfurt or London. When the knucklehead from New York with the big forehead (me) called to complain or ask for an enhancement, I could feel their eyes rolling at me five thousand miles away. It drove me nuts. I was looking to change it and I saw a glimpse of hope in the magician.

To his credit, he jumped right in and muscled his way into all of our systems bureaucracies to check the computer code for Y2K risks. People in the markets were freaking out about it, along with everyone else in the world. People were actually talking about planes falling from the sky. The story going around was that China was so worried about Y2K bugs making planes fall out of the sky that they decreed that the CEOs of all their airlines had to be in the air on commercial flights when the clock struck midnight. Now if that ain't good incentive to get something fixed, I don't know what is.

By early August, the magician made his report on the Y2K readiness of our systems. I had not gotten any word from any people from DB, except to know that they were running around like chickens with their heads cut off trying to get their code for the year 2000 up to date.

Magician: You should have absolutely zero Y2K problems on your systems. Y2K concern is totally overblown everywhere, it's not going to be a big deal. The only glitch I found was in one of our own Bankers Trust systems. I will have that fixed by September 1. The status in general of your Deutsche Bank systems is borderline critical. Someone needs to start paying attention to the links between your systems and the CHIPS and Fed payment systems. They are all teetering and the back-up systems are virtually non-existent.

Uh, oh. That was not good news but not surprising, either. My conversation with him was so important because I already trusted him 100%. If he told me that Y2K was going to be fine then I was going to stop worrying about it and start focusing on other problems. He also alerted me to a bigger problem with the system links that was going to take years to rebuild correctly. His information allowed me to bring details to my management and allow my old Repo boss to start to muscle into Frankfurt and London to get the magician in on those conversations. The magician was indispensable for years. He was considered a "support" person, but he was more than that. It would have been impossible for us to expand and survive if he was not with us. That is the truth. Y2K came and went like he said. Nothing.

Wouldn't you know it, it's bonus time for 1999. The group and the desk had another good year and we had survived the merger and Y2K. Toronto was stabilized. My cohort boss was now an MD who was global co-head of all the Asset & Liability desks along with a guy they had brought in from Deutsche Bank Australia to take over Frankfurt and London. It was already almost impossible to figure out who reported to who. Global focus, regional focus, dotted lines. We never had any idea, we just assumed we reported to everyone somewhere. The German guy who originally hired me ended up around this time moving up to Global Treasurer of Deutsche Bank, which was a huge job. Our little starter group from 1995 was starting to move up the chain and get some respect. The desk that year was the beneficiary of trickle-down economics. As our bosses were getting global recognition, they were able to take care of those below them. Accordingly, three or four people in the group were promoted from VP to Director. I was one of them. I was also given a stunning bonus of $350,000 and with my promotion came a salary of $125,000. Pinch me. What could possibly stop our business now?

Let's just say that the year 2000 would make my decision to deposit my bonus directly into the "Fuck you" fund a wise decision.

A few months into 2000 my old Repo boss calls my cohort boss and me into his office. He tells us that they had done an analysis on our books in London and that when we make the switch-over to our new accounting methodology the desk will have to take a 15 million-dollar hit on day one. This was shocking news. We were never even told the analysis was happening (typical DB London) or when the change-over would be made. That sum was probably half of what we made the whole last year. This was really my expertise, so I took over with the indignant questions to the big boss:

> Me: There is no way that's right. No way. I can see a few million but 15 is ludicrous. Let's see the analysis.
>
> Old Repo boss: No.
>
> Me: What do you mean, NO?
>
> Old Repo boss: I just got the number, no backing details.

Me: Do you know the methodology?

Old Repo boss: No.

Me: Don't you think it would be prudent to rip into this ourselves to see if we agree with this? It's not like any of us trust the London stuff, their business is totally different than ours.

Old Repo boss: I'll try.

My cohort boss (I thought his head was about to explode): Don't throw these numbers at us again until we know exactly what they represent and what the methodology is!

We both got up and stomped out like angry four-year-olds. We were furious and felt betrayed. As we left the office he told me to start our own analyses to come up with a better representation of reality. We had always loosely kept track of the other methodology. There were so many different ways to do it, so we had to wait until we saw the exact method London was employing before we could compare the numbers.

I will try to explain the difference between the two methodologies. While investment banking is done on a mark-to-market basis, core banking had been on accrual accounting for the most part. The theory on mark-to-market is that if you liquidate that portfolio on any given day, the gain or loss will not be outsized because the portfolio value moves daily with the market. Accrual accounting ignores the day-to-day movement of the market and focuses on the difference between the rates at which your assets accrue interest versus the interest you pay for your liabilities.

Here is a basic example, but in a stock world. Say someone would lend you money forever at 1% and you took that cash and bought a stock at $50 whose dividend would be the cash equivalent of 4% forever. Every day you would accrue 4% on your stock (asset) but only pay 1% on the money you borrowed (liability), so you would accrue a profit of 3%

daily and 3% yearly. Whether the stock price went to $70 or whether it went to $30, as long as your dividend stayed the same it would not matter since it was forever.

Mark-to-market would add or subtract to the accrual number the liquidation value daily of the difference between the cost ($50) and the current market. So in this example if the stock went to $40 your profit/loss statement would be a combination of the daily net interest (we called it carry) minus the $10 loss on the stock. It's the same number at the end of the trade no matter what happens. Accrual accounting just assumes your trades will all stay on either forever or until they are contracted to end. The problem with accrual accounting is that it can be very deceiving as far as hiding numbers. No bank wants to make thirty-year, open-ended commitments, and accrual accounting could force a bank into that. If a portfolio is structured by lending out money (assets) for thirty years and funding that asset with 15 two-year bonds (liabilities), an accrual accounting statement might show a small gain in net interest every day while in reality there could be a huge loss in the last twenty-eight years of the trade that will go un-noticed. This would happen if the two-year rate for the tail of the trade (twenty-eight years) rises above the thirty-year loan rate. So mark-to-market is the way to go for safety's sake. The mark-to-market methodology can be a touchy little beast with many different nuances for a multi-product portfolio, so it was important we knew how the London people were arriving at this number they jammed down our throats.

While that issue started to create angst with everyone on the desk, we were starting to come off our merger honeymoon with Bankers Trust. During the merger people are running around trying to move parts around and wondering where they fit in the process. It's so busy there is not a lot of time to think. Once the merger goes through everyone shares some relief that it is over and life goes on. That's when the problem starts. People are not dumb and are capable of doing the math themselves. Anyone can look around our Asset & Liability desk and Corporate Treasury and see the combined group has way too many bodies. Corporate Treasury was the group that housed the Treasurer of NY and Group Treasury was the global Treasury in Frankfurt. While we were the face to the market, they were in charge of the payment systems, policy, long term funding and negotiating and enforcing funding limits. My old Repo boss could see the writing on the wall and he could also tell his strength in the bank was waning as the power base was shifting to London. At that time he started shifting pieces of the chess board around so he would have to fire the fewest number of people possible and also keep the ones he wanted. He transferred a trader on our desk who had about the same seniority as me and sent him to our group in Tokyo. Like magic, he was gone. He had been in charge of the swaption book, one of our trading products that was part of the accrual to mark-to-market conversion. A swaption is a combination of an interest rate swap and an option wrapped in the same package. In our case the desk would purchase a swap with positive daily carry (net interest) but that swap could be called back before it matured and then it would have to be replaced. My head hurts just thinking about those things. Another trader found a good job with another German bank because he did not want to sit through the uncertainty of a big turnover.

As a group and as a desk, we had full plates. We knew we were overstaffed, we were fighting with London about accounting methodology that might show a loss that would get us fired, plus we were trying to trade and make money. At least Toronto was fairly stable. The last thing we needed was for more extraneous events to occur. So guess what? Boom, it hits the papers. "Deutsche Bank and Dresdner Bank to merge." Are you fucking kidding me? I bet the same idiot that fucked up the Bankers Trust merger was trying to cover it up by doing this one. It really was chaos after that one. A few days after the announcement, a CD-Rom is delivered to my old Repo boss. After he inserts the CD-Rom into his computer it graphically shows him how the new combined bank will be structured. None of us ever saw it because he refused to show it to us. He did tell us he had the CD and had watched it. His comments to us after he watched it? "You guys better hope this merger does not go through." That ain't good, right? I guess that meant the Dresdner crew would be taking over the short end after the merge.

I was less worried about my job than I was about all the stupid shit going on that was not ALLOWING me to do my job. The bullshit was just tiring. Considering the fact that I was knee-deep in every issue going on within the group ('cause I'm a sucker), it probably helped my chances I might survive at least initially. It was a frenetic time and I know my cohort boss was out of his mind with stress. Worse for him than me, no doubt.

Thankfully, about a month later word came down that the merger was cancelled because the little girls couldn't agree on the final details. We were all thankful it failed. It made no sense and was pursued only for ego reasons and to cover up failures in other areas. Many of these mergers are done out of ego and these type A personalities who are just obsessed with the notion that, "My dick is bigger than yours." Sad but true. Most mergers make no real business sense when you break them down. But society celebrates them like they are a good thing. Weird.

OK, so where were we? Yes, disaster averted on the Dresdner merger. It's mid 2000 and we are trying to sort through tons of issues plus trade and make money. I'm ripping apart our whole portfolio and trying to do a mark-to-market myself, so when those dopes from London finally share some information with us, I can refute them intelligently. Doing things intelligently is always a struggle for me, that we all know.

22

Around that time, I flew to Toronto to spend a week with the three amigos, something I tried to do every month or so. A few days into my visit, I get a call on the desk from my old Repo boss.

> Him: Get a flight home tonight and be sitting at your desk in NY at 6 a.m. tomorrow.
>
> Me: Why, what's going on?
>
> Him: You will have to wait until tomorrow.
>
> Click.

I sat there in shock for about ten minutes, then called the airline to switch my flights. On the flight home that night I was running through every scenario possible. Every scenario led to me being fired the next morning. I wonder what I did or who I pissed off this time?

The next morning I drove directly into work and parked by the building. Multiple reasons. First off, he told me 6 a.m. and the first train got me to my desk at 6:15 a.m. and I did not want to be late for my own demise. More importantly, I had a lot of crap at my desk that I would have to carry home afterwards so I figured that would make life easier. I had the usual pictures of the family, GPO stuff (the trophy, etc) and my Cover Your Ass files. I had about a foot-tall file of papers, printed emails, and all my blue notebooks that I would have to get home. I was an obsessive note-taker and documenter. I have always been paranoid and working at Deutsche Bank with all its craziness had brought those feelings front and center in my psyche.

At 6:30 a.m. my old Repo boss called me into his office. Here we go! The end of the knucklehead fairytale.

> Him (talking about my cohort current boss): He is no longer working at Deutsche Bank. He had it all and lost it when he betrayed me. We made him resign yesterday.
>
> Me: Am I fired too?
>
> (I still did not realize what was going on or why.)
>
> Him: You're fine. I listened to every phone call of yours and read every email for the last two months to make sure you were not part of it. You came out clean.
>
> Me: Part of what?
>
> Him: You don't need to know. Go out and tell the desk the news and calm them down.
>
> Then he names one of our specific brokers.
>
> Him: He is never allowed to pick up a Deutsche broker line again. Make sure he never does.
>
> *What the fuck is this all about? This is insane.*
>
> Him: We are bringing over the guy who used to run London's book to replace him.
>
> (He was talking about the guy who tried to make me buy a pink shirt in 1996.)
>
> Him (again): One more piece of advice. You need to pay more attention to the inappropriate things

you say on the phone and write in your emails. I don't need to be sitting in a room with two DB lawyers listening to one of your brokers telling you he is so bored he is, "Sitting with his dick in his hand."

Wait a second. How the fuck is that my fault?

Truth be told, I was the most inappropriate person on the phone and email. That's just the truth and I was too fucking old at that point to change. I wasn't going to tell him that. He looked like he wanted to rip my eyeballs out.

Me: Okay, sorry.

Meeting adjourned.

As the day went on, I started thinking about things more. I had the conversation with the desk and told them that we were getting a new boss from London. Apparently the guy from London was in limbo because the big Australian guy who was the co-head with my boss had come to London and taken over.

Over the next few days, I thought long and hard about the possibilities of how this would or would not work out. The more I thought about it, the more I was hurt that I wasn't considered for the job. Too late now. Unbeknownst to me at the time, the trader who was on his way out to another German bank had met with my old Repo boss and told him that it made no sense to bring the guy from London over when I was the best person for the job. He had once worked in London, so he knew all the parties involved.

In the mean time, I had decided that I was going to resign. There was no way I could work for the London guy. He wasn't a bad guy and I respected him, but we clashed. One of us would kill the other and he was bigger than me. I needed a boss who would allow me to speak my mind and he was forever lecturing me on "getting on my soapbox" at meetings or on conference calls. Not gonna work. After getting my wife's approval, I called a meeting with my Old Repo boss.

> Me: I can't tell you how to run your business and I accept your decision but I needed to tell you that the day the guy from London walks in the office, I am going to resign. I just thought you should know so it does not come back to hurt you in some way. I want you to be prepared.
>
> Him: I never thought of you as a replacement to take over. You do a great job but you show no ambition to move up in the world.

True. But still an ouch!

> Me: I understand and you are probably right. It's up to you. I'll take over if that's an option you are offering.
>
> Him: You can have the job and I will stop the transfer but since you are not a Managing Director you will have to report directly to the big Australian who will be the sole global head now.
>
> Me: I accept. Thank you.

So that is how I got my first real management job. I had managed the guys in Toronto, but that was more of a hobby than a job since my performance up there was not really linked to anything. I never had any ambition to manage people. But this seemed like it was a no-win situation if I did not take it.

In the next few weeks the big Australian guy and I tried to get to know each other. It did not work out too well at first. I was really fed up and tired and was being a dick to everyone. I was especially a dick to him. Did I tell you I'm really not that smart? He did absolutely nothing wrong and I was being a little bitch. He asked me a few things about our business in New York and my response was that, "I don't like to be managed." I could tell he wanted to reach through the phone line and smash my head on the desk. I was terrible. The guy had the patience of a saint and I have no idea why he did not fire me. He probably knew that my old Repo boss, who was his boss, and I went back a long way so he gave me an extra long leash. Hopefully his patience was rewarded.

In the mean time, I was ripping apart the portfolio both to analyze the mark-to-market adjustment and also to figure out what my cohort boss had left me. I needed to have my numbers up to date and solid by November of 2000 when discussions on bonuses were started and then locked in by December. In the process of reviewing the portfolio, one of the products I zeroed in on was Libor. My cohort boss used Libor products extensively to hedge our cash exposures. I was not so sure it made sense. In my trading in 1999 and 2000, I saw some Libor swings within a week or two of the actual settings that made no sense. Libor and cash were supposed to correlate pretty much 100%, but there were strange moves happening that I could not figure out. As I isolated the products, I also tracked the moves between cash and Libor and did a more thorough analysis.

I came to three possible conclusions. One, Libor was being manipulated by collusion caused by the London banks. Two, I was missing something and just did not understand the product from a New York perspective. Three, Libor and specifically the spot settings of Libor were not the best way for a New York branch to hedge its exposures. From that time forward, the Asset & Liability desk would stop using Libor, except the forward market for hedging. This would ratchet down Libor-setting risk. We used a number of products instead, one of them being the fledgling OIS product. OIS swaps are Overnight Index Swaps and are derived by averaging the bulk of overnight trades that occurred in the US during the day. It was calculated by the Federal Reserve by taking actual trades from the various brokers and doing a weighted average. It was a real market rate calculated in New York and therefore a much more robust rate.

By the time November came, I had my analysis done for mark-to-market for the whole portfolio. While I had calculated a loss in the swaptions book and a loss in the cash book, my analysis showed the cutover number when we made the switch would be closer to three million dollars, not the fifteen that London accountants had arrived at. After I made my presentation to my old Repo boss, he let me know that London had made some "refinements" to the methodology and the fifteen-million dollar loss was now closer to ten million. That was still a huge gap and I asked again to get more information on how London was calculating the number. It was not forthcoming. I was incredibly frustrated and my old Repo boss told me to be patient. He said we would have time to compare our numbers and methodology. I sensed a slaughter coming.

I was right, in multiple ways. During bonus discussions in December, I was told that the bonuses for our desk would all be frozen until the mark-to-market issue was sorted out. Here's how it went down:

My old Repo boss: You took over the desk and did a great job and your accrual profit was up. The problem is we don't know whether your real number is that number or the number with the big loss included. That's why we can't pay you more for the fact that you took over your boss's job. We have to give you the same bonus. I know you're disappointed. I am sorry.

Disappointed? I get another $350,000 bonus? Happy fucking days!

I was disappointed I was wasting my time fighting trash analysis from London. That part was true. I wanted to move our business forward, not have to fight with one hand tied behind my back. Live to fight another day, I always say.

23

Everyone was saddened and shocked to learn that Edson Mitchell had died in a plane crash during the holidays of 2000. He was the banker who Germany had hired in 1995 from Merrill Lynch to expand investment banking. At the time of his death, he was so high in the bank's growing executive ranks that his influence was not felt day to day any more. Looking back now, I think his passing was the tragedy that started the wheels coming off at Deutsche Bank.

Edson's death really shook things up. In the few months afterwards, there were no real changes at a desk or group level. However, there was a scramble by upper management to fill the leadership void. Let me translate that. Ten type A personalities with huge egos start to kiss as much board-member ass as they can, hoping to get appointed to take his place. We would hear the rumors on a daily basis of the games going on up top, and, like a horse race, we would hope our horse won. Human nature, right?

While the jockeying for position was played out, the year flipped from 2000 to 2001. About a week into the start of the new year I was doing some basic reconciliation of the daily profit/loss reports we would receive from Business Area Controlling (BAC-our accountants). Then I compared those numbers to the profit/loss report that was published in London on our internal web site. Well, will you look at that. I knew immediately and was astonished. Our numbers for 12/31/00 were adjusted lower by ten million dollars. No one told me. No one. Radio silence. Those fucking scumbags in London. They cut us over to the new methodology without even telling me. My old Repo boss knew and he was prepared when I marched into his office.

> Him: The adjustment was for last year. Take your pain and move on.
>
> Me: It's a reflection on me. I take over the desk and we have to take a hit of 35% of our revenue? And I can't even explain it because it was done behind my back. I really struggle to see how that can be acceptable.
>
> Him: We are getting all the numbers and analysis next week. We will finally be able to compare your numbers to London's and then we will try to make sense of it. London had a 12/31/00 deadline to change over the methodology.
>
> Me: And they didn't tell anyone this was happening?
>
> (I knew he knew and just did not want to hear my shit. Especially for something inevitable. Still sucked.)
>
> Him: Time for you to leave my office.

When we finally got all the numbers and methods from London, it was as I expected. Another incompetent job done across the pond. The methodology might have worked for London's business, but it was way off for our business in New York. I could not even be pissed anymore. I was just disgusted. Disgusted that in the limited contact I had with the geniuses that did this analysis in London, they were nothing but condescending. They probably knew I was a knucklehead. I still have feelings! Ha.

TEETH (192) MARKS

It did not take me long to understand what the problem was. While London had many more little nuances to the products they traded in their book, most if not all of their products could be converted in finality to a Libor swap or a cash deposit or loan. Our book in New York had those products, along with another two or three different products that would not translate into Libor or into a cash deposit or loan. Basically, the London methodology was the equivalent of taking Apple stock trading at $100 and putting it into an account with Citibank stock trading at $40 and then valuing that portfolio at Citibank's stock price instead of each stock at its own closing price. It was terribly flawed.

Not only did I now understand what the problem was, but I also knew what I could do to unequivocally prove to my old Repo boss that the numbers were wrong. As expected, when I explained it to him he did not fully understand what I was talking about. That was when I enacted my plan to show, in a way that could not be ignored, what was happening.

> Me: In the new methodology, theoretically on a day the market does not move, our profit/loss should be plus or minus $50,000 right?
>
> Him: Agreed. Theoretically.
>
> He knew he was being set up for a smackdown but he played along.
>
> Me: OK, can we meet again tomorrow?
>
> Him: If we must.

Now he's just being a smartass.

I went back out to the desk and went through our portfolio and found a 2 billion dollar Government Agency 3-year bond my cohort boss had bought before his unfortunate demise. It was still marinating on our books, collecting positive net interest (carry) daily. It was the perfect sacrificial lamb. I sold half (1 Billion) of that bond back to the Agency desk that day. If London's methodology was right, we might show a small gain or loss on the day. I knew the answer already but would have to wait to see what popped up on the web the next morning after London did the numbers. The next morning my old Repo boss calls me and sounds resigned to the fact that he will have to listen to me again that day. "You were right. Come in and explain this to me so I can get it fixed."

A three-million dollar profit had popped up on the web site under our desk after we sold that Agency position back to the Agency desk. That allowed us to "realize" the real numbers. Mark-to-market is theory, but once you actually sell something you own then it's cash in and cash out and it always nets to where it should be. He understood and it took another half a year but London finally started marking all of our products against the correct prices. They made my life miserable and cost me money in my bonus. The loss of credibility within our group during the fight was even more painful.

Just to show you what Deutsche Bank was turning into during this time, I will share this funny story. A guy from the Frankfurt Money Market trading desk shows up to spend a week in New York rotating to a few of the desks. Half way through the week, he gave my old Repo boss a private presentation. I did not know this. After the presentation my old Repo boss makes the guy give the same presentation to me. *What the hell is this?* It turns out the guy came over from Frankfurt to convince my old Repo boss to fire me and let him take over my desk. Apparently I was "lazy" and "unaggressive." Guilty as charged! So the guy from Frankfurt gives me the Powerpoint presentation and he has two windows up on the computer. One big window where the presentation is, then a smaller window where he is paging forward during the presentation. As he gave the presentation, I watched the little prick editing the forward pages so his criticisms of me would not appear. It was almost comical. My old Repo boss kicked his ass back to Frankfurt and shortly after he was forced into another group. This was my life. It was still worth it.

While in the middle of all this political and structural garbage, trading goes on. Got to pay for the lights and try to make some money. In early 2001, at some point I had the grand idea to buy $50 million face amount of Xerox three-month commercial paper because I probably thought I could sell it at some point and make ten grand or so. You can take the knucklehead out of commercial paper but you can't take the commercial paper out of the knucklehead. The bank had a credit department well built at that time, so I'd have to get approval from them before the purchase. Standard operating procedure.

Not more than two weeks after my Xerox purchase, newspapers start reporting that Xerox might shortly have to declare Chapter 11 bankruptcy. Oops! Ah, the classic phrase of my broker screaming at me comes back into play. *This trade is gonna make my ass look like the Lincoln tunnel.* When I bought the Xerox it was probably priced at 99 cents on the dollar, or the price of 99/100. After the first week the price had leaked down to 93 cents on the dollar. That means that the fucking idiot who bought that CP trying to make ten grand was now down three million bucks theoretically. When I called credit to get their opinion, since they had given me approval, I got the totally Deutsche Bank answer of, "We are neutral on Xerox but have taken it off the approval list." Translation: You are shit out of luck and on your own, moron. I was not surprised.

I had three options. At that point the CP had about 2 ½ months until it matured. At maturity if Xerox had not declared chapter 11, I would receive my full redemption value of 100. That was option one with five gold stars. The other two options remind me of the Lincoln tunnel. I could sell the paper and "realize" my loss, or if Xerox declared bankruptcy,

I was in unchartered territory and would probably be forced to sell my claim as a creditor to a group within Deutsche Bank called the "Workout Group." The Workout Group was made up of traders and lawyers known as the vultures. They had a tough job. They would buy distressed securities and then when they defaulted they would "work out" with the courts a price that was hopefully higher than they paid. It could take years. Tough job.

You would agree I had no choice, right? Options two or three could be fatal to my fairytale (career) so I wanted to stay away from them. I decided to hunker down for the next few months with my fingers crossed and hope for the best. Every day I scanned the papers for new information and tracked the Xerox markets closely. It was not pleasant. The big Australian in London was very understanding and he and I were starting to get on the same page. On the day the Xerox matured, I spent all damn day on the phone with my operations group after we put in for our money for the redemption. At 4 p.m. that afternoon, the $50,000,000 cash finally cleared into our account through the Depository Trust Clearing System. If I had a pipe in front of me, I would have smoked crack. I had no fingernails left and promised myself I would never put myself in that situation again. Lesson learned.

As I was immersed in my Xerox debacle, management was meeting in London to decide the forward-looking structure of Money Markets globally. This meeting was supposed to address the fact that when we bought Bankers Trust and were not able to fold them into the bank, it created a gaggle of problems. Between Money Markets and Treasury, we were very overstaffed and everyone knew it. In addition, since the brain surgeons who screwed up the merger had left us operating two separate banks under one roof, we had to address how all these moving parts were supposed to mesh. I was in charge of raising cash for Deutsche Bank in New York and we needed it badly. The Bankers Trust side reported to Treasury and had tons of cash they could not give to us due to regulation 23-A. They were in the markets selling cash and funding our competitors at the same time, and DB looked like idiots to the market. It was pretty clear that a change needed to be made and somehow these two groups needed to be combined and consolidated. That was the plan, at least. As in the best laid plans of mice and men, the big shots came out of London with a solution only Deutsche Bank could arrive at. Let's create a third group to add into this soup. Hooray, a new layer! Not only that, but the third group does not even address the real issue. Those fuckers in London all toasted with champagne. We rolled our eyes and thought, *You can't make this shit up.* It was after that meeting when I started telling anyone who would listen that if you took a group of people with 150 IQ's and put them in a room together, the decisions that came out of that room would be equal to a 70 IQ. Laugh all you want, you know deep down it's true. We watch it in the government every day.

A few months after the death of Edson, the horse race to take over for him was over and the guy who ran the global sales group had won. Let's just say he was not our horse. We were the nuts and bolts of banking and he had the reputation of being interested only in complex products that only the MBA's and MD's could "figure out." Storm clouds gathering.

24

My old Repo boss and Edson's successor butted heads and I think it was true dislike and lack of respect both ways. You can fight every day and still work with people, but the lack of respect can make it impossible to work with someone. For that reason, a few weeks later when my old Repo boss was summoned to London to go kiss the ring, I knew he was toast. He was toast all right. He was ready to call it a day and head out to the sunset, so he probably suggested his departure. I can't even remember if we had a party for him.

The good news was his replacement. Remember the guy I used to work with at JP Morgan who took over the Government bond trading desk at Deutsche Bank after it blew up? It turns out 007 was being groomed for very senior positions by the hotshots so he was being moved around frequently to get a flavor for managing every business. It was our turn now. I would report to the big Australian and he would report to 007. They were both based in London. I also had a dotted line to the guy who was running the whole New York trading floor; we will call him Commodity guy. The power base of the Core bank was still in Frankfurt but moving slowly towards London and the investment banking base was now fully entrenched in London.

My relationship with the big Australian was fully on the

mend and he was consolidating his power on the global group he was responsible for. I was his guy in New York so I was to keep him apprised of all things affecting our group, both trading and politics. To that end, there was some type of management meeting going on in New York that he could not attend. The big Australian said he was reluctantly sending me to this conference to be his representative.

>Big Australian guy: This is your chance with the big boys. Don't fuck it up.

>Me: I'll try.

I have zero interest being involved with the big boys or doing this boondoggle.

Did I say boondoggle? What I meant was a very professional conference of professionals discussing important structural processes to bring the bank forward. Just kidding, I was right the first time. It was a total boondoggle, an utter waste of time. It did not go well for me. These guys spent the whole morning trying to agree how to structure things within the groups to benefit themselves, while screwing the other groups within the bank that had not attended. I had the balls to ask how it moves the bank forward if our group takes fifty million dollars of revenue directly out of the pocket of another part of our own bank? Shouldn't we be talking about market share and new business and streamlining what we have? Silence. After the morning session, I was sitting in the reception area reading my notes when I see a pair of fancy brown French shoes in front of me. *Oh no, not this douche.* I look up and he shakes his head and says, "You just can't keep your mouth shut, can you? You made our group look stupid." He was some poser who ran one of the European groups. He then stomped off, probably to go tattle on me. In general, I do try to keep my mouth shut when I can. I know I can grate on certain people, or maybe all people, for all I know. I have to admit that certain people who I piss off, like this idiot, I take great pride in pissing off. It's kinda fun. I skipped the evening festivities of this boondoggle. I did not fit in and was happy to be out.

Here is the big Australian guy's critique of my performance:

> Him: I agree with you 100% but why did you say it?
>
> Me: It's the truth.
>
> Him: Young man, you need help. What am I going to do with you? That was your last management meeting.

Mission Accomplished!

About this time, the tech bubble had burst and everyone in the markets was dealing with the aftermath. A few of the bigger technology firms that had been very hot in the late 1990's with investors were now having major problems. One of those companies was Comdisco. Comdisco was some type of networking company. I have no idea and it's not important. What is important is that one of the traders on the Repo desk had bought some of their bonds as collateral for some type of funding transaction, and was now in the same position I was in with Xerox, only much worse. At least Xerox had a fighting chance to survive without defaulting. By the time I found out about the position in Comdisco, it was just a matter of time. I think the size was $100 million but it could have been twice that. I think they had owned the bonds for a few years but at that point it was probably six months until those bonds matured and that desk was repaid in full.

At that point the guy in the black overcoat, whose trading prowess when he was hired in 1995 had impressed me so much, was an MD and starting to move up in the world. At the time, he was in charge of the Repo desk where these bonds were owned. He had remembered that I had gone through something like this a few months back with Xerox, and also that I had a lot of experience with corporate credit, so he asked me to help them with the position. Once again, the sucker is happy to help. The first thing I did was find out if we had a banking relationship with Comdisco so I could get as much information as possible. It turned out a lot of Comdisco risk within the bank was already turned over to the Workout group. That was not a good sign. Many times after defaults the recovery rates are lower than 70%, so a default was going to cost the Repo desk at least thirty million dollars if not more. An amount that big reflects on everyone in the group. Not good. I set up a meeting with the Workout group to try to help our group make an intelligent decision.

It was at that meeting I learned about "going over" the Chinese wall. The meeting went nowhere at first because the Workout group was on the other side of the wall. The Chinese wall was a regulation keeping certain parts of a financial organization from communicating with each other. In banking, certain groups have inside information about their clients, so to keep that information compartmentalized, the Chinese wall is put up to separate groups that are entitled to that information from those that are not. I was not entitled, therefore I got nothing. As I discussed the situation broadly with them, it was a one way street and I was blabbing all my bond information to them and they were giving nothing in return. I'm sure they were hoping they could get me to turn over these bonds to them (at a major loss to us) but I was nowhere near that decision yet. Whether the loss was twenty five or fifty million bucks, at least five people were losing their jobs. And now I'm involved? Why do I do this to myself?

When these guys came to the conclusion they were not getting our bonds, they asked me if I wanted to "come over the wall." *Please translate that to the knucklehead.* "What does that entail?" I asked. They told me I'd have to sign a confidentiality agreement then they could share everything with me they had on the company. I could not discuss ANY of it with my management chain, and by going over the wall I could not ever trade in Comdisco again (no problem there). What was a group decision thirty minutes ago would turn into a Matt decision. I would be nuts to go over the wall.

Me: I'll sign it and go over. *What did Lucy just get herself into?*

A day or two later we had the next meeting, where we discussed the cash flow of the company and prospects for default as well as payout. It was worse than I thought all around. The lawyers eat up the recovery amount of the liquidation. It was virtually assured Comdisco was going to default; it was just a matter of when. The Workout group had compiled a list of all Comdisco bonds maturing and we overlaid their current cashflow on top of it. So we had a basic picture of the assets and liabilities the company would have maturing over the next six months. It was a close call but I (we) decided that it worth the chance to roll the dice, rather than locking in a multiple career-ending loss.

Those god-damn bonds were paid in full on their maturity date. God does look after drunks and fools. Comdisco filed for bankruptcy just a few months later, so we made it by the skin of our teeth. *NEVER AGAIN!*

A few months after my old Repo boss headed off into the sunset, rumors emerged of him showing up on other banks' trading floors. The working theory then was that he was interviewing at other banks to build the same businesses he had built at Deutsche Bank. He was like Elvis, he was seen so much in "secret" interviews. I heard the rumors but my old Repo boss had not reached out to me and there was no way I was going through all this shit again anyway.

Those same rumors must have reached Europe also because the big Australian and 007 were both soon in New York and asked me to go to dinner. As I remember it, the dinner was attended by myself, the big Australian, 007, and the big Australian's business manager. I had not really put two and two together and just thought it was a routine check-in get together. After a few pints of beer, 007 brought up that my old Repo boss was seen on the Barclay's trading floor. As a side note, don't you love the whole stupid spy aspect of who shows up where? How does the word even get out? People are a bunch of washwomen, aren't they? 007 then says Barclays would be a perfect place for my old Repo boss to start a business. *Oh jeez, this is no routine dinner.* 007 says that he wants to make sure our group at Deutsche Bank stays intact and he thinks I will be the first one contacted, if I had not already been contacted. He asked if I would be interested in getting "locked up" for the next two years so that they did not have to worry about it. I still viewed lock-ups as a swap of extra money to one guy which comes out of the pockets of the people who work for him. There is only so much money to go around, right? In exchange, that person becomes the bank's bitch for two years. *No Deal.*

> Me: Guys, I'm not going anywhere. I'm happy and I like working for you both. I'm not interested in moving somewhere else and I'm not interested in being locked up.
>
> 007: You will let us know if he approaches you?
>
> Me: I have not heard from him and doubt I will. If he reaches out, I will let you know but it won't matter. Deutsche Bank is my last stop in this business.

So we shook hands and that matter was tied up for the night. We then moved on to the important subject of the evening. The eating contest.

Most of these management types are type A, ultra competitive personalities. They will bet on anything and everything. It started innocently. We all ordered burgers. Big burgers with a huge heaping pile of skinny fries.

007: Holy shit, this is a huge burger.

big Australian: This is nothing.

007: I got $100 you can't eat two of 'em.

big Australian: Child's play. You're on!

007 asked about side bets. The big Australian's business manager and I both decided that whether we bet on our boss or our big boss, it was a lose-lose for us so we passed. Never underestimate how competitive these guys could be, even on a casual bet.

The first burger and fries went down too easy. I'm not sure if 007 knew it but the big Australian had a record of success in eating contests in Australia. For some reason I knew that little nugget, so I was not surprised. It was child's play so far. After 007 ordered the second platter for the bet, he excused himself to hit the men's room. When the second platter showed up we were all in shock. Well, all of us except 007. It turns out instead of going to the men's room, he went into the kitchen and gave the chef $40 to double the fries on the platter. They were piled at least a foot high. It was comical. I saw the big Australian look at the platter and take a dry gulp. He looked nervous.

The second burger and fries were a struggle. I could see the big guy concentrating. Pace, it was all about pace. That, and a lot of water. When he got about three quarters of the way through, he slowed down even more. It was quite a performance. Then he looked 007 in the eye and made the cockiest move I have ever seen. He started stealing fries off of all of our plates, slowly dunking them in ketchup and eating them while staring down 007. Classic. When he finished the second burger, he threw his napkin on his plate. Bet over. He looked pretty good overall. When the napkin hit the plate, 007 stood up and whipped a $100 bill down on the table and stomped out of the restaurant. He did not like losing. We did not see him again that night. When the big

Australian realized 007 was gone, he turned a strange white color and started sweating profusely. I thought the guy was going to keel over. Then he puts his head down on the table and moans, "I couldn't let him see me sweat." Type A. Very funny. He dismissed himself to go to bed and it was an early classic night.

The Toronto office was doing much better and the three amigos had a pretty good thing going on. The wee little man was the defacto leader of them and he and the big Australian had started to interact more in the global scheme of things. In the summer of 2001, the big Australian told me it would work better in his Global structure if the wee little man reported to him directly. I think he was worried I would be pissed off that my little empire was getting smaller. I am sure he was surprised when I told him I did not give a rat's ass. Hey, good for them to get some global love and for the wee little man to report to an MD instead of a knucklehead Director. I felt like a proud parent sending his kids out into the world well prepared. Corny, I know.

We all planned a weekend trip up to Toronto for a little ceremony to pass the torch to global management. I think it included the big Australian and a few Brits from the London office and we were also going to spend a night in Montreal after the business was done. It was my only time in Montreal and I hated it. I loved my time in Toronto and would always tell people that Toronto had all the same cool things as New York did except it was clean and the people were friendly. Our group in Montreal was one ugly American (me) along with two Canadians, two Australians and two Brits. We took a seat at the first bar we went to and someone ordered drinks and we started a conversation. After a few pops we were going to sit down for a dinner. In the meantime, I tried to get the bartender's attention to order our second drink. He ignored me. Walked right past me. It happened a few times. The Australian gets his attention and orders our drinks. One of the Canadians whispers over that they hate Americans in

Montreal and if the bartender had heard my accent there was no way I was getting service at the bar tonight. We tried it again a few times, and I was totally ignored. The Australians, the Brits, and the Canadians thought it was the funniest thing ever. I was beside myself. What a petty little fuck. If he knew how much I dislike the French, he'd be in the right to ignore me, I could at least understand that.

I am quite sure we went to the ballet in Montreal, but I was so disturbed I don't even remember it. Now to be clear, I am not a huge fan of the French, and Montreal is very French. I had had some bad career experiences with the French. Apparently, my family tells me I am part French but I refuse to believe that and will fight that rumor to the end. If anyone asks me if I have ever been to France I have been known to answer that the only way I want to see France is from thirty thousand feet looking through a bomb sight. I'm sorry. It is what it is.

We flew back from Canada into the United States that Monday afternoon. After we flew through Customs, the Brits and Australians caught their flight back to London and I went home. My Toronto management duties were over, but the three amigos and I had bonded and would stay tight. That day was September 10, 2001, and we had no idea that on the next day, the world would change forever.

PART III
9/11/2001 THE WORLD CHANGES

25

From September 11, 2001, to December 15, 2001, there is no way for me to separate fact from fiction, so I won't even try. It's all just a blur, but so real at the same time. There is no way to explain it rationally. A month or so after the attacks, I remember sitting in a funeral service at a church in my town, and actually visualizing tanks rolling through the church walls. Whose tanks? How the fuck should I know? Not ours.

On the morning of September 11, I'm pretty sure we all remembered what we thought was the loudest subway train ever running under our building. We talked about it later. It must have been the first plane screaming down 6th Avenue. Others said they were in the shitter and the water splashed up onto their thighs as the building swayed from the rumble. They thought it was a subway also. Who knows what's real? At some point early on, one of my brokers from the World Financial Center next to the World Trade Center screamed over the hoot & holler that a bomb had gone off in their building and they were leaving. We heard later it was not a bomb, but an engine that was thrown from one of the planes that hit the World Trade Center. I still have no idea.

We were all standing up, watching the first tower burning on TV, when the second plane hit. Watching the second plane hit may have been the single most traumatic second of my life. Because at that second everyone KNEW it was an attack. Knew it. I had also spent three months next door at 130 Liberty and had commuted through the World Trade Center for eight years, so it was a living, breathing thing for me.

After the second plane hit, people on the trading floor with me in mid-town started to panic. Many just left. Picked up a few things from their desk and hustled out the door. At least half of the trading floor did not show up for a week or two. I guess they went and huddled with their families or grabbed their families and drove out to the boonies where they felt safer. For the rest of the day hundreds of rumors of how many planes were hijacked and where they were heading were reported on the news, as well as through email and message systems. People were trying to make sense of the situation and regain control, and the exchange of information was how they tried to do it. Probably twenty percent of those rumors were true, the rest totally false.

> Fifty planes are unaccounted for.

> Seventeen planes coming across the Atlantic from Europe have been hijacked and are on the way to the East coast.

> Fighter planes have shot down six planes headed for the White House.

> A plane was shot down over Jersey City.

You get the picture. Chaos. Before that day, I had always assumed that fighter jets were always up in the air as a defense against this. Wrong again. As it was happening I would have believed fighters were shooting down planes left and right and some were getting through. Around four in the afternoon, when it was confirmed there were no more planes in the air, people started to focus on the next thing. Car bombs and suicide attacks.

The rumors shifted from one thing to another all week.

There must have been rumors of ten car or truck bombs in New York City in the next few days. Some of the rumors were very detailed too. Like this one:

Five suicide bombers blew themselves up at Penn Station an hour ago.

Penn Station was pretty close to us. It took at least a day for all the phone lines to come back, mostly it was cell phone service that was down. That probably made the rumor mill worse because of the extra stress of not being able to reach out and confirm your loved ones are okay.

A few hours after the towers went down, the people who were left on the trading floor tried to regain their senses and busy themselves by doing their jobs as best they could. Since my group had a huge part in the payment systems and funding of the bank, we were integral to the solvency and survival of Deutsche Bank. About this time the big Australian yells over the hoot & holler from London to our group. "Not one penny leaves this bank without my express approval. Not one wire goes out." He was still learning. That's the exact opposite of what banks are supposed to do in a crisis. I ignored him.

There is a Funding/Treasury group at every bank. I am sure we all feel the same way and we proved it through the 9/11 attacks. Our first responsibility is the survival of our own bank and our second responsibility is the functioning of the overall system and every bank's well being. It has to go together because all banks inevitably extend credit to each other in hundreds of ways each day. It is a delicate ecosystem where every decision is crucial and one misstep can touch off a falling line of dominoes. We always felt we were a finger on the hand of the Federal Reserve and our actions should always have the consequences of benefitting the system as a whole and that, in turn, would help our bank survive any crisis. Through every crisis, we would have tons of contact with the Federal Reserve; they would bounce ideas off of us and we would bounce ideas off of them. The Federal Reserve had a market operations desk which handled the nuts and bolts of the day-to-day functions and they also had an administrative side. Deutsche Bank was structured almost the same way. My desk was the market operations side and our Treasury Group was the administration side. Our combined job was to make sure when people went to an ATM machine that the damn machine spit out cash. We went to ridiculous lengths over the next week to keep those machines spitting out bills.

The Fedwire payment system is the main money system within the US. Each big bank has an account with the Fed and solvency is when that account is funded every single night when that wire closes. The Fedwire operated normally I think from 12:30 a.m. to 6:30 p.m. every business day. The 6:30 p.m. close could be pushed to later if a bank was having system problems or problems structurally making payments, but this was pretty rare. From the Tuesday of the attacks to Friday, the Fedwire stayed open until midnight and then was "turned over" and started the next day's operations a half hour later. It was insanity and the pressure on the people working at the Federal Reserve must have been enormous.

When the Fedwire closed the night of the attacks it was too late to get home and every hotel was already packed with people in the same situation. We were all going to sleep at our desks until Europe opened in four hours. As it turns out, 007 (our Global boss) was in New York for another big shot conference called to sort out turf wars over global or local control of the businesses. He sat at our desk the whole week until planes were allowed back in the air when he could fly home. He was a godsend to us that week. 007 was well connected and had friends all over. A friend of his owned a hotel nearby, so he set us up with rooms for the week. No questions asked, no bills. We even had the presidential suite. Too bad it was not to be enjoyed that week. We were all a mess.

All rules were suspended that week, so the bars that were open just stayed open twenty-four hours a day, until there were no patrons. My first real memory of later that day is standing at the hotel bar that night with a few of the guys from work after the Fedwire closed. We conjectured on how many people died in the tower collapse. We had thought ten thousand to fifteen thousand at least. I am sure we were all wondering how many of those were our friends. I know I was. We drank down some beers then went for a couple of hours' sleep and then got back in the office by 5 a.m. to touch base with Europe. At least we could shower, but then we Xeroxed. That term describes a person who stayed out all night and came right into work in the same clothes (hence copied from the day before), or Xeroxed. Smelly, bad breath and all, is a real Xerox. I had a few of them and was actually sent home early one day in the 80's, my Xerox was so offensive. Hey, I showed up for work on time though. I got points for that.

We were all concerned when we got in the next morning and saw what was happening in the funding markets. By the time the attacks started on Tuesday, Europe had mostly funded itself for the day. When European funding markets opened on Wednesday, they were a mess. We were so concerned the previous night with staying alive and solvent as the wire closed, we could not even look to the next day. We got our coffee and started calling around. One guy called the brokers, one guy called Frankfurt, and I called London. Confirmed clusterfuck. At the time the Fed funds target was 3.50% and 1-day funds were trading at 7% or higher in Europe for US Dollars. That was a bad sign. Even worse, when we canvassed those branches for their cash positions, they all came back with the same answer. "We are extremely short dollars." I'll explain how this happens and especially when the market is under strain.

Even all the way back in 2001, Deutsche Bank had a huge balance sheet of assets and liabilities. Most of its stable bank deposits were in Euro currency after Europe converted to the Euro. The only deposits the bank had in US Dollars was the twenty billion dollars that by law (23-a) we had to keep separate and could not use. Once again, thank you dumb fuck who missed that little detail when we bought Bankers Trust. Since the US has the biggest economy and uses the most debt to fund in the world, by far the best quality and most liquid assets are denominated in US Dollars. The bulk of Deutsche Bank's assets around the world were in US Dollars and therefore needed US Dollar funding. There was no way we could possibly source that many dollars as a bank on a daily basis. So every day Frankfurt would take their huge Euro deposit balance and use Foreign Exchange Forwards (F/X swaps) to swap their Euros into US Dollars. They would use these dollars to fund their own dollar assets and move the rest over to London to help them fund their dollar assets.

To refresh, an F/X swap is just a loan in one currency versus a deposit in another for the same amount of time. Other banks, such as US banks, might have massive US Dollar balances and need to swap it into Euro to fund their European balance sheets. So most days it was very liquid and easy to swap currencies in and out. Because F/X swaps are not a real market with real securities, but more of a cash derivative with many moving parts, they tend to freeze up first in times of crisis.

If the F/X forwards which Deutsche Bank needed desperately were not working, it meant that New York would have to make up the shortfall. So not only did we have no idea which companies were still afloat and which people at those companies were alive or dead, we would have three times the cash to source in a market that was frozen in panic in New York. The stock market did not even open up. It looks like I picked a bad day to stop sniffing glue.

One of the things that did not sit well with me all day was the fact that the Fed Funds target was 3.50% and funds were trading in the markets above 7%. Not only would the Federal Reserve want to get that rate back down to the target rate to settle things down, but from a patriotic point of view, I wanted that rate back down to the target because panic, disruption and chaos were all signs the terrorists had won. I was going to find a way to help settle things down. I was not alone in those thoughts, I was to find out.

By that time in the morning, 007 was in the office and he settled into a spot on our desk for the week. I'll never forget the cover photo of *The New York Times* that he brought into the office, which showed the second plane hitting the tower with the fireball shooting out. I am nauseous thinking about it now. From five in the morning until midnight we were all running around plugging holes all week. Not only was 007 running interference for the things I needed from our management, he made sure hot coffee and tons of food were delivered to our desk the whole time so we could focus on our task.

Many salespeople were not in the office, so we were even covering many of our clients directly from our desk. That first day after the attacks was just 100% winging it; we had no idea what we were supposed to be doing. Half of the clients we had trades with needed our attention, but we could not contact them. Were they solvent? Were they even alive? We had no idea.

That morning, the Federal Reserve tried to inject large amounts of cash into the market via Repos. It was mostly a symbolic move to calm nerves because the Repo market only very indirectly feeds into the Fed Funds (unsecured) market. The problem was not that there was not enough money, the problem was that no one knew *where* the money was or what currency it was in. Many banks did not even have systems working to track the money flow on a real time basis. Many banks had to rig up their antiquated Fed account direct link to figure out what their current balance was. It would be the equivalent of tracking your checkbook balance by using a register or excel spreadsheet to track deposits and withdrawals. You can keep a good idea of your balance by tracking which deposits/withdrawals/checks have hit the account versus your records. It works pretty well. What we had to do that week was react to whatever the bank balance said at the Fed, because we had no record of deposits/withdrawals/checks. All the banks were as blind as we were and so was the Federal Reserve.

More good news. We had to evacuate to the safe zones because bomb threats were called into our building. Then someone left a truck parked outside our building and it was deemed a threat so we were evacuated again. After the second time, our desk decided we were not leaving the floor again. We had too much to accomplish and whatever was going to happen was going to happen. We all knew we were the most vital front office group to the bank's survival and our back office payment people were the single most important group. No payments were made without them. Half the operations group was at 130 Liberty Street, which is right next to where the attacks took place, so they had to leave the day of the attacks. They regrouped in New Jersey at the back-up site on Wednesday and were absolutely heroic through the whole week. Those types of groups never get credit but they are the absolute backbone of any bank. Nothing gets done without them.

During the day I would call anyone and everyone to get help and to find information. We spoke with our Treasury group in New York all day long. Treasury and Global Finance had a rough relationship globally, but in New York we got along just fine. During these attacks we cut through all the bullshit politics and acted as a bonded team to keep the bank safe. I spent much time on the horn with the big Australian in London talking through my problems. Luckily he had core banking experience so he was up to speed on the bulk of my issues, which were different from most funding functions. I was worried about our London office. It was always every man for himself there and since the sales guy took over the whole shabang a few months earlier it was already less controlled. I asked the big Australian to make sure all the business units in London were not increasing their funding needs for the bank. I asked that everything be "funding neutral" until we can stabilize ourselves. I know he ran around like a madman that week in London trying to educate the other groups on the problems we were having in New York. Being the blunt, honest guy he was, he let me know he would do his best but had limited control over the inmates. Understood.

Most of the trading floor was barren by 6 p.m. that night. The wire was supposed to close at 6:30 but we knew it would be a midnight deadline again. The Federal Reserve said that no matter what, midnight was the deadline for the wire because systematically they could not turn the day over to the next day after that. As many people on the floor who could went home to be with their families. There was nothing they could help with by that time anyway.

We were absolutely guessing at what our funding needs were that day. The guys on my desk were on the phone all day with every US Dollar trading group, updating information and getting guesses. It was all guesses. I remember we bought our last five billion dollars (a massive amount) for our account at 10 p.m. and then decided we had to watch the account to see what happened. There was nothing more we could do. Whether the bank stayed alive or not was in God's hands at that point. Our emergency borrowing facility at the Federal Reserve had somewhere in the neighborhood of three billion dollars in borrowing power. Normally that was a plenty big cushion, but compared to the numbers we had to throw around that day, that number seemed small enough to make me want to puke.

From 10 p.m. to the midnight close we just sat and stared at our two fed account direct links. Thanks to the moron who was in charge of the Bankers Trust merger, we had two accounts and double the work and double the risk. I will never stop whining about that.

I wish I could remember the exact details of how the close worked out that night. All I remember is the six of us from Global Finance and Treasury standing around our rigged up fed links watching the numbers change until the midnight cutoff was reached. We were all exhausted and needed 100 beers. I can't remember if we got fully funded or we had to use some of our Discount Window buffer that night. On a big funding day we might source 10 billion dollars, but I remember checking the numbers that night and seeing a staggering 70 billion dollars sourced from the market. All I know is the bank survived and we survived. We were lucky.

We all huddled back at the hotel bar. We went over the day and shared what we knew about people who we found out were missing during the day. We were too busy and focused to discuss it during the day. Between us there were already more people missing than we could keep track of. We changed the subject to our clients who were in the towers, clients we could not contact that day. We just assumed they were all dead and we would have to decide what to do with their trades over the next few days. I made the decision on the first day that we would roll every loan we had with people we could not contact. A roll is a time extension of a loan that is now due. It was just easier to try to roll everything in place to keep things stable. We could work out the details later. After pounding about ten beers, we headed to bed and agreed to meet up in the office at 5 a.m..

Thursday morning, all the smelly ones got together again. The clothes situation was getting pretty bad. Maybe my smell at that point was why no one was coming into work? I'll have to think about that. Thursday was the worst day. That is the day the 15% rule started to come into effect. Since the markets had survived the first day barely intact, the 15% of crazies and slimeballs decided they could exploit all the havoc and make money for themselves. Agonizing. Management started to sprinkle its way back into the trading floor, so that was a hindrance as well. Seriously. I had assclown after assclown who did not even know who we were or what we did marching over to my desk demanding updates on the bank's health. After I told the first one to, "Fuck off!" (and I wonder why I never got promoted?), 007 told me it would be better if I just let him handle those inquiries. *Mission Accomplished.*

The markets Thursday morning were no better. Funds in Europe were trading at 7% again versus the 3.50% target and F/X swaps were still not working. To make matters worse, the F/X forward group in London had ignored the big Australian's plea and had lent out fifteen billion additional dollars to our competitors in London (other banks) and expected me to find that money for them. To put that in perspective, they decided that making an extra $125,000 in their account that day was worth putting a trillion dollar bank at real risk. And these are people with 150 IQ's. I was beyond furious. The big Australian apologized, said he did not have the power to stop it.

I called up our Treasurer in New York and asked him if I could ring up the German guy in Frankfurt who hired me and was now our big Global Treasurer. I was hoping he could knock some sense into these guys in our own bank who were arbitraging my desk as we were limping along performing triage on the bank's solvency. Our New York Treasurer asked me to please stay off the phone to the Global Treasurer and that he would make the call instead. I guess a lowly guy in my position calling the Global Treasurer would be a breach of military etiquette. I tended not to give a rat's ass about that stuff. Sometimes you've got to cut through the bullshit quickly.

By Thursday we had updated contact lists on clients and co-workers and had a basic idea of who was left and where they were and who was reachable. The Federal Reserve had a great call tree plan they executed to get every bank's contact information updated so people could contact those they needed to. At that point basic triage started to ebb and we could concentrate on a one or two-week strategy with the Fed to settle things down. We had many conference calls with the Federal Reserve, both their market desk and the administrative side. I felt Thursday was the day where the markets were at the biggest risk point. Money was nowhere near where it needed to be and yet market participants were trying to trade normally in Europe and it was putting even more strain on the system. The day before, not only did DB New York have to source 70 billion dollars to fund the bank, DB Frankfurt ended up having 40 billion in Euro balances they had to dump into the market or give to the ECB. It sure would be nice to swap that 40 billion Euros into 40 billion US Dollars.

Our conference calls with the Fed focused on two things that morning. Finding a way to get the F/X swap market back in operation, and also making sure the broker dealers had access to money. Since broker dealers like Merrill Lynch, Morgan Stanley, Goldman Sachs and Lehman were not banks, they did not have access to the discount window or other types of unsecured funding. They did have very active secured funding (Repo) sources and could raise money via the Fed by doing Repos. The problem was those broker dealers had no systems and they could not even figure out what collateral they had to give to the Federal Reserve. Not good. Someone had to fund them. I decided we would fund the broker dealers we had contact with on a daily basis. Goldman, Merrill and Lehman. I had called them that morning and said that after 5 p.m. I would give them as much unsecured cash as they needed at the Funds target of 3.5%, then I'd take the risk to find it somewhere between

5 p.m. and midnight. Most of the credit department was nowhere to be found so we had to make unilateral decisions that were over normal limits. Our group notified the Fed we would be helping the broker dealers. They did not comment. They never commented. You just had to assume that no comment was them saying okay without saying okay. Weird.

It was a few hours after this that the Commodity guy who was in charge of New York found his way to our desk (he probably needed a road map) and started to lecture me that we should not be lending to broker dealers and that management was worried about them. *That ship has sailed, Dickhead.* Clueless. I proceeded to tell him I was overruling him and we would indeed fund the broker dealers. Period. Unlimited. To get money moving again. I also told him we were self funding about twenty of our accounts we could not contact. We did not want other counter-parties panicking and liquidating their securities and putting those companies out of business so we provided cushion. The dude was not happy. He actually put his hands over his ears like he did not hear me and scurried away. *Mission Accomplished.* 007 saw the whole thing because he was sitting at our desk and Commodity guy had no idea he was there. 007 walked to my desk and asked, "Did I just see what I think I saw?" he asked. My reply was a simple, "Welcome to my life." He was speechless.

While we worked to get F/X swaps back in order, we were also trying to sort out some of our systems so that we could predict what our cash needs would be, instead of pulling guesses out of our asses. We begged the Fed to jumpstart the F/X swap market somehow. That is what we needed. It's not a terribly risky transaction, but it does involve four or five different parts. The Fed was good at figuring that shit out and we needed it bad.

At the same time, the fed funds market was still under pressure and that was also making things worse. The

Federal Reserve had added so much money, pretty much all they could, but the money was just not moving through the system correctly. Panic was causing spikes in the Fed funds rate. Not only did the spikes erode sentiment further, but a few of us were still hell-bent not to let the terrorists win by having the payment system unwind. The stock market had still not re-opened so Libor and Fed funds were what people were looking at to gauge the banking system's health. We needed to settle things down.

I trusted the Fed. They wanted the same things we wanted. Orderly markets. They had forcefully come out in support of the markets and were doing all they could. It was my desk function at every bank that had a duty to help the Fed do their job. We needed the Fed funds rate to start trading closer to the target. For the good of everyone.

I called a few of the banks out of the blue and told them in no uncertain terms that they would not see anyone at Deutsche Bank paying above 3.50% for funds. I may have even intimated to the NY banks that they had a duty as a US bank to help the Fed keep the funds rate at 3.5% and not above. I may have pulled the patriotic card; it was the least we could do to help during a nasty time. The funding desks of Bank of New York (BONY) and UBS were totally onboard. We even decided to call our clients and say we were "locking down" the Fed funds rate at 3.5% for the time being. We decided we would only transact at the rate the Fed had targeted both internally and externally. Our twenty biggest clients at Deutsche Bank were incredible about it. Totally onboard. If enough of us could band together to cut through the panic, it would give the Fed time to sort out the mechanics and legalities of what they needed to do.

The key was those god-damn F/X swaps. C'mon baby, daddy needs a new pair of shoes. By Thursday afternoon, a broad strategy to fight all the different fires was in the works but we had no idea what would work and what would not.

You just had to act and pivot from problem to problem to problem. Rinse and repeat. I had trained for this my whole career and the guys at my desk and in our Treasury were warriors.

To say we bent the rules would be conservative. We exceeded credit lines lending to broker dealers. We plugged unauthorized cash into client accounts that were at risk of being liquidated or overdraft. We roped in other banks and customers and agreed to lock down the funds rate where the Fed wanted it. Someone had to do it. We made sure the Federal Reserve knew everything we were doing and their no comment was assent. So what's one more little bending of the rules, right?

As both my group and the Treasury group were running around trying to get things in order, one other subject kept coming up. It was killing us that we had 20 billion dollars sitting at Bankers Trust that we had to get rid of in the market, while having to source 70 billion for Deutsche Bank. The risk of us making a mistake dealing with those types of numbers under this much duress was frightening. That situation in itself was adding to the operational risk of the whole market. Those were huge numbers. I begged our Treasury group to ask the Admin side of the Fed if we could combine those cash balances until things settled down. The Treasurer of our New York office did not want to do it and I did not blame him. Once we started to see the morning numbers Thursday, numbers that had gone higher from the previous day, he was swayed. F/X swaps were still dead in the water, so no relief there. Our numbers were going higher also because my desk was giving cash to others who had no access otherwise. After he changed his mind on the call, he said to me that, "I can't ask them, I need to tell them we are doing it, then beg for forgiveness." Politics. Weird.

He called the Federal Reserve and told them that the operational risk of all these different pools of cash was creating too much operational risk in the market. His words to them were, "We are combining the bank balances because I would rather be responsible for a 23-A breach that saves our bank rather than watch our bank fail and the affect that would have on the market." He said he might have heard a grunt on the line in response from the Fed, but that was it. I coulda kissed the guy. It took big balls to make that call. We called our operations department and set up the transactions we had never been able to execute since we bought Bankers Trust. Direct loans from the Bankers Trust main Fed account directly into Deutsche Bank's account. Now the trick will be to actually get that money moved over the fedwire into our accounts.

After the Bankers money was added in, we still projected another 20 billion dollars was needed before the close. We had zero confidence in our projection to boot. Good times. That night, the same eight people gathered around our two computer screens watching our Fed accounts, held together by band-aids. Despite all the cash the Fed was dumping in, there were still too many blockages in the system for it to filter through, so the Funds market was still tight. As of 10 p.m., we were nervous on the verge of desperate, because we were stuck. Then our prayers were answered when our friends at BONY (Bank of NY) called and offered us 20 billion dollars at the Fed funds target of 3.5% while funds were trading at 5% in the market. It was heroic on their part. Thanks fellas, I owe you one.

OK, so now our check register says we should be close to zero when all the money moves both ways. We had our fingers crossed because money had barely been moving and we still were waiting for 50 billion in contracted money to get in our accounts. Pass the glue, please. Word came down from Treasury upstairs that the Federal Reserve and the European Central Bank (ECB) were trying to get an emergency F/X swap facility set up for the next day that would allow us to swap our euros in Frankfurt into dollars for New York to use to fund Deutsche Bank's dollar needs. Those words were heaven to me and knowing the Fed, I was certain when I walked in Friday something would be accessible to us.

I still remember the relief I felt when massive blocks of money from Bankers Trust and BONY started pumping into our Fed account with only half an hour of wire time left. Watching the short balance go from "-50,000,000,000" to "-37,000,000,000" to "-18,000,000,000" to "+1,000,000,000" was cause for my heart to start beating again. We made it through Day 3.

BEER.

Not so fast, smelly. I really wanted to see my family and get new clothes. It was Thursday at midnight and I had not seen them since Monday night. I think the tunnels were only open out of Manhattan on restricted times, so I made the hour drive home that night and then had to get back in before the tunnels closed again. I was only home for ten minutes but I needed it. I threw some new clothes in a bag and asked my wife how she and the kids were doing. They were doing better than I was, so that was good. I kissed my wife, then kissed my sleeping kids and headed back to meet the guys at the hotel bar to decompress and strategize for the next day. At least I would not smell so bad the next day, at least in theory.

26

Friday did not get off to the start I was hoping for. When I got in at 5 a.m. I had an email that the European Central Bank and the Federal Reserve could not get the F/X swap lined up and running. We needed that swap line as the swaps in the market were still not working. As we started our morning duties of gathering information, I called the New York Treasurer at 6:30 a.m. when he got in. I wanted more information on this F/X swap line and wanted to see if maybe I could help somehow. He relayed to me that the swap line was all set up but that the European Central Bank needed to be paid fifty basis points, or ½ of 1% in order to do the trades. They had not been able to sort out how to assess that fee so they just said, "No, we can't do it." I had a shit fit on the phone and he was just as mad as I was. I'm sure as we hung up he knew what my next move was. You guessed it. Rogue Director Matt calls up the Global Treasurer in Frankfurt, the German guy who hired me back in 1995. I can't believe he took my call but he did.

> Me (incredulous): So let me get this straight. The ECB won't do this because they want to make 50 basis points profit on us? I'll pay the money, we just have to get this done.
>
> Global Treasurer: Matt, settle down. I'm more mad about this than you are. It's sickening that

they can't sort out the bureaucracy of this. I promise you we will do everything we can and I have calls into everyone in the European government I know.

He went on to explain to me that the Euro currency and all the mechanisms were only a few years old and they still could not figure out some of the legalities. Apparently, legally they had to make a profit on these types of transactions but they could not sort out how to bill the profit or how to set up the transaction. Fucking politics and legal mumbo jumbo.

I trusted him 100% and I knew he would get this done eventually. We were on the same page. It was the maddest I had ever seen or heard him. He was German but certainly knew every swear word I had ever used in English, maybe a few more. So Friday was destined to be another knee knocker without F/X swaps. More technology was slowly coming online and a few clients that had disappeared had contacted us either from their homes or their firms' secondary sites. We had a good rhythm going with our clients and our little band of banks so by Friday afternoon we were getting through the day with a little more support. We also planned on keeping that 20 billion dollars from Bankers Trust over at Deutsche Bank until things settled down. Unfortunately, the rumors in New York were still hot and heavy. Towards the end of the week rumors were making the rounds that the terrorists were going to use the chaos to move a nuclear bomb into Manhattan or into the Hudson River to finish off the city. We just wanted to get the hell out of there by Friday. The rumors were getting more scary instead of less. Finally, Friday night the payments system went a bit smoother and towards the end of the night the Fed Funds rate had started to loosen up. It was a relief because we had hoped that having the weekend to work on all the systems and figure out where people were would help things recover even more next week.

Mission Accomplished. Time to head home and see how the family is holding up.

It's interesting how the mind works. During the week when there was a job to do and a goal at hand, your mind stays focused. As I started to unfocus over the weekend, I was able to think about exactly what was happening and what the future would be like. At least for the next few years. It was disturbing. I also had time to think about all the people who were missing. I don't think the media was yet reporting names, it was all a little underground communication network of people emailing or calling with news about who never came home. I also started to get group emails from spouses and family members, asking if anyone had seen their loved ones. Heartbreaking.

It was that weekend when I started to realize that, despite my thoughts otherwise for many years, a man has very little real ability to protect his family. Loss of control and realization that I had no control. It was destabilizing. Matters were not helped when we started to get taped calls over the weekend that terrorists had a bunch of small planes and were going to be spreading chemical poison over the countryside of America. So bizarre. That did not help. Up to that point I just thought people in cities would be at risk but those crazy calls just raised more questions about my ability to protect my family. It's hard to explain rationally. It was not a rational time.

During the weekend I was getting emails and calls from work regarding the security situation in New York City, as well as updates on the progress of getting our systems back. It was also announced that the stock market was going to re-open that Monday the 17th. That was a morale boost. The best therapy at that point was everyone's effort to work towards getting things back to normal. The effort was the real therapy, not the results. Tough to explain but I will try.

Helplessness is a decaying emotion. Whatever it is, people

need to be doing something to move forward. I remember during the first Gulf war in 1990 when Iraq was shooting scud missiles at Israel. The people in Israel were taking plastic sheets and taping their windows closed and also taping plastic around their walls. I never understood it. I do now. I'm not sure that was a great way to protect from a falling scud missile or chemical warfare, but the act of taking action itself is empowering. It's all about hope.

On Monday morning, we had more systems and were able to monitor more of our payments. In addition, those F/X swap lines were nailed down so we dumped a massive block of euros on the ECB and got a big block of US dollars in return and happily paid the fucking fee. The stock market opened that morning and we all stood. Some cried. I might have too. I did not care whether the market went up or down, I just wanted the market to be open. It was all about getting back in service to not let the terrorists win. It was all about being patriotic. As small as our part was, we were still happy to have any role.

There were only enough resources available to get the most urgent systems running. Just enough to operate the bank. For that reason our risk reports and profit & loss schedules were not even calculated for a week to ten days after the attacks. Our desk and the big Australian had no idea whether we had made or lost money in the aftermath of the attacks. To all of our credit, it was the last thing we cared about. There was too much real raw shit going on to care about those details. I do remember when that first report was run a week or two after the attacks, it was a little bit like waiting for the emcee to open the envelope during the Oscars. We had no idea if we made money or lost money. I'd be lying if I said I was not relieved when the envelope was opened and our desk showed a small gain in the ten or so days after the attacks. One less worry.

There were still more rumors that second week. Every

day. We got immune to the rumors and the security scares. We laughed when they tried to get us to evacuate out to the sidewalks during bomb scares. That ship had passed.

Flights were back in the air so people were moving out and about and 007 flew back to London. A few days before the attacks, we had a new intern start for us in New York. She had been an intern for us in Toronto and was the best intern in the history of interns. When I had been up to Toronto previously, she had asked about coming to New York for three months. I was all for it and thought if anyone deserved it, she did. So we hired her in New York and she started right before the attacks. I was horrified for her after the attacks. What a terrible situation. I think she had some family in the area, which helped. As the flights re-started I wanted her away from New York. I explained to her that New York was going to be a terrible and possibly unhealthy place to be for the next three months at least. I wanted anyone who could leave to get the hell out. She refused. She insisted on helping. She was a warrior. I know I throw that word around a lot but it's the only appropriate word when people who are scared shitless fight through the fear and get the job done. At some point, I made her go back to Toronto against her wishes. I felt terrible for her.

That week as things were settling down the fear and paranoia started to creep in. We fully expected a car bomb or suicide attack any day. We were immune at that point. We were worried about the bigger threats. The nuclear bomb rumors were still making the rounds. My personal view was that if the bad guys had a nuke, they would have used it first. I did not believe they would have flown planes into buildings and then set off a nuke. After the initial attacks the guard went up, so a nuclear attack was more likely to be foiled after and they would not take that chance. What the fuck do I know?

My biggest fear after that initial week was a dirty bomb

attack. A truck bomb outside our building with a few ounces of radioactive material pulled from a piece of medical machinery. Spreading radiation over the city and forcing people out for years. Rational? Probably not but fear is fear. Since I seemed to be obsessed with that as the next shoe to drop I asked myself, *Can I do anything to prepare?* I had to feel like I was doing something. Anything. Being proactive sure as hell beats waiting for the shit to hit without fighting back. So I became obsessed with anti-radiation pills. Potassium iodide.

My father-in-law passed away from thyroid cancer way too early because the US government, in its infinite wisdom, decided to sail his ship through a nuclear cloud after a test of a bomb. This was the Marshall Islands in the 1950's. He was just a kid. Whose fucking idea was that? I got $20 a bunch of people with 150 IQ's went into a meeting and that was the 70 fucking IQ idea that the group came up with. Let's send our kids through a nuclear cloud to see what happens? Morons.

Sorry for that diversion. So I knew a little bit about that stuff from his experience. A person's thyroid is the biggest sponge for radiation. Once the radiation starts its work in body tissue, it's tough to reverse. Potassium iodide blocks radiation from settling into a person's thyroid. Medically, it's used for people going through heavy radiation so that radiation does not stick in the thyroid. This became my secret little obsession to protect my family and me. Since I view those I worked with every day as my family, I had a duty to protect them also. Deep down I knew it was irrational but it was my version of taping plastic around my house. I have to do *something*.

I found some website selling these tablets and went nuts. I bought about $400 worth of this crap. It had a shelf life of six or seven years. A few days later a big package was delivered and I was the proud but secretive owner of 1,000 Iosat anti-radiation pills. Good Lord. I stashed them everywhere. I was like a fucking squirrel putting nuts away for the winter. I had to have enough to give to my family, friends and co-workers if any attack ever came to fruition. I stashed them in my car, my kitchen cabinets, my home office, my work desk, and my briefcase. Enough for everyone. Just like in grade school. "Mr Connolly, you're chewing gum. Did you bring enough for everyone?" Yes teacher, as a matter of fact, I have anti-radiation pills for everyone!

I'm glad they still sit unused in my kitchen cabinets. You can take the nut out of the city but he is still a nut. Why throw them out, you never know, right?

As things were returning to normal, reports started to filter in of friends, co-workers and colleagues who died in the attacks. One of our brokers was in the first building when it got hit and made it out without a scratch. They had thought it was just an accident. He decided to go get a better view of the damage to his building. He took the elevator up to the top of the second tower to get a look. He was somewhere in the second tower when the next plane hit. Tragic. Sadly, his wife took her own life three months later, rather than live without him.

In our continuing attempts to be patriotic, our group decided we would spend two nights a week in the city doing our small part. Getting hotel rooms and buying booze. It was the least we could do. The city was deserted and bars, restaurants, and hotels were dying. The tourists stopped coming and people just sat inside from fear and I did not blame them. The trauma was very subtle but it was there. New Yorkers just soldiered along. I was slowly losing my shit.

My family seemed fine and I did not want to disturb that by admitting I was having mild delusions and paranoia. When Deutsche Bank offered trauma therapy, I jumped at it. It was secret too and no one would find out so I was all in. I needed to stuff this fucking genie back in the bottle.

As you can imagine, trauma counseling at the time was in very high demand. There were just not enough counselors to go around. There was four miles between my office and ground zero. I was not even close and I did not witness any real horrors that day, and I was in need. Can you imagine what the people who were in close proximity went through? The workers, cops and firefighters at Ground Zero? I shutter. The group the bank brought in was from Scandinavia. They mostly worked with survivors and witnesses of plane crashes. The theory they worked me through has since been debunked but it still helped me. At least temporarily, which I am still grateful for. They convinced me that the human brain views trauma in three-month increments. That it is wired to reset from trauma in close to three months and that it does this for continued ability to survive and function. I guess after a caveman saw his buddy ripped apart and eaten by a wooly mammoth, he needed to get back to hunting, so he had three months to forget about it. I'm not 100% sure, but I think that was even an example they gave me. They were performing emotional triage on people. They did not have time to do anything but get people going again. I went to two or three sessions then I was done, expecting to feel better in three months. I think convincing myself that I would feel better in three months actually became a self-fulfilling prophecy because by December the genie was back in the bottle. *Mission accomplished.*

By October things were starting to sort themselves out at work and in the markets. Clear sailing to recovery, right? Nope. In mid-October the next shoe dropped and it was not a dirty bomb. It was dirty bacteria. A bacteria named anthrax. The news reports were sketchy at first because no one was really sure what it was or how to look for it. I remember that it was unclear whether the first person who was in the news after contracting it was infected by natural or man-made means. Just like after the first plane hit the tower, people wanted to believe it was just a coincidence of nature and not man-made. Then envelopes started showing up with anthrax and more people started dying. When powder was found at multiple places in New York and one of them was at an office right near our building, it all started again. The panic, the fear, the unknown. Anyone know where the glue is?

As I had thought, another shoe had dropped, but as usual I was wrong about which shoe. It was not radiological but bacterial. Is there a pill for that? As it turns out the best treatment or hindrance to anthrax then available was an antibiotic called Ciproflaxin (Cipro). It stops the bacteria from replicating. Cipro pills started flying off the shelves. People could not get enough of it. In my state of mind I was sure that all of us in New York would be on Cipro at one point or another during the next year to ward off anthrax poisoning. Right off the bat many people found themselves Cipro one way or the other and started taking it. I was going to wait until I saw the whites of anthrax's eyes before I took it. Antibiotics are funny things. The more people use them, the less they work to ward off infection. I was worried that if we took too much of this stuff up front, that when we actually needed it to treat something, it would not work. It took another month or so, but when the new infections stopped and a few people were cured, the public was calmed somewhat.

27

When the US went after Bin Laden in October in Afghanistan and the Anthrax attacks occurred, the economy took another hit in sentiment. People were not going out, not visiting New York, and no one was getting back on flights yet. How could the knuckleheads do their patriotic duty, you ask? The answer: Las Vegas. We scheduled a trip in November of 2001 and it became an annual event.

The only thing I remember specifically from that first trip was airport security. The planes were empty but the security lines were still long because it was all new and bootstrapped together. I remember going through four or five security stations. We had a group of eight and most were just basic white bread boys. One of the guys, however, was very Mediterranean looking with olive skin. He got searched about ten times before we got on the plane. The white breads were searched once or twice. Every time on the line, when the cops stopped and searched him, they apologized profusely. It was obvious profiling, right? His response to their apologies was always the same, and we loved it. "Do not apologize to me. You are keeping me safe and that's all that matters and I should be thanking you. You can search me a hundred times, I have nothing to hide." On the way back to New York we sat on the security line in Las Vegas for three hours. Imagine. Eight hungover knuckleheads with no sleep and slouched shoulders (from losing at the casinos) trudging through. I'm just thankful I didn't puke on anyone.

We had such a good time it became a yearly trip in November with some fun stories over the years. The bulk of us would leave on the late flight Thursday and then come home Sunday morning. We packed a lot into just a few days. Since my desk always had to be staffed by at least two people from 6 a.m. to 6:30 p.m. on days the money wire was open, every year someone would have to take one for the team and grab the late Friday flight and join us a day late. We would usually draft an unsuspecting soul from Treasury to be the second body on the desk so that only one man would be left behind.

As December came and went, we were all thankful that our first-day estimates in the bar of 10,000 to 15,000 people dead were overblown. I had lost 12 friends, co-workers and acquaintances. We can all thank the Fire, Police and EMS departments for the huge number of lives saved that day. It cannot be said enough. When we are running away from danger, they are running towards it.

We started to hear from a few of those customers that our desk helped keep solvent by funding them or not liquidating them when money was not paid back. We just kept rolling loans along until we could contact someone. In one case it took a few weeks before our contact called to tell me he had made it out alive. His firm was decimated. He wanted to thank us for the risk we took helping to keep his company alive and solvent after the attacks. He said they would be Deutsche Bank fans forever and that the head of the company had relayed his thanks to Deutsche Bank's management personally. It was just nice to hear we could help anyone in any way. Our little part. We heard an article was written in the magazine *Euromoney* which included some of our exploits at Deutsche Bank after the attacks, but

I don't remember ever reading it or caring to live through it again by reading it.

Bonus time came and went and no one really cared. We were just happy to be alive. It was the quietest bonus season I remember. Our desk had a great year revenue-wise; we had pumped all that money back into our portfolio that the London accountants hit us with incorrectly at the end of 2000. The year 2001 seems like it lasted ten years. Our group's efforts on behalf of the banks and the markets right after the attacks were looked upon favorably. It all lined up well for our bonus numbers that year. The big Australian was still trying to get my numbers closer to where he said my previous boss was. I didn't care. The situation in the world and in New York was so uncertain and unstable that even though we made great revenue, it just did not make sense for the bank to dole out the big numbers people were expecting. I found it incredibly ironic when my boss apologized to me when he relayed my bonus of $600,000 for 2001. "You deserve more after what you did this year." *No one deserves a bonus this big. This is fantasy land.*

A few months later, I returned from a week's vacation to learn that the new CEO Ackermann and his security detail had stopped by my desk. They wanted to shake my hand and the hand of my Treasury co-head, in recognition for our efforts right after the 9/11 attacks. That was a nice gesture, but I'd rather not have the attention so I'm glad I missed it. The guys on my desk said his security detail swept onto the trading floor like secret service agents. Big guys in black suits with ear pieces. My guys all thought they were being arrested.

Let's talk about the Deutsche Bank trading floor at that time. It was an embarrassment. The floor was over capacity before we bought Bankers Trust and now it was simply teeming with people. About a month before the 9/11 attacks, we had purchased the 60 Wall Street JP Morgan headquarters I used to inhabit. After I left JP Morgan they had merged with Chase, so they did not need 60 Wall Street anymore. Our trading floor in midtown was so bad people were threatening to quit or sue over it. Not only was it crowded, but it became unsafe. The whole floor was infested by mice. Women who left their heels under their desks to switch into after commuting in sneakers would find their shoes chewed through. These damn mice even snacked on a few pairs of my high heels. Relax, I'm kidding. I never wore my high heels in the office, just at home. A few people contracted hantavirus from mouse droppings and spent time in the hospital. At mid-day almost every day, brown water would seep out of the men's room right off the trading floor. The toilets were always clogged and backing up. Can you imagine bringing clients into that mess? Neither can I, and that's why you never saw clients on our floor. The Connecticut people were up in arms about the extra fifteen minutes that would be added to their commute, were we to switch from midtown to downtown. It would be a much better commute for me from New Jersey and I always liked downtown much better than midtown. Everyone knew we needed a bigger building and 60 Wall Street really was the perfect solution. We moved into the new headquarters in 2002 and my desk ended up about twenty feet from where my desk was on the 3rd floor in my JP Morgan days.

Sometime in the first half of 2002, it was announced that 007 was going on to another job within the bank. It was obvious he was being groomed by the former sales guy, who was now the big kahuna, for much bigger things. He was in our group to get a sprinkling of experience before he was going up the golden escalator to executive land. I was very sad to see him go. He was replaced by some guy I did not know. He ran the bank's futures trading exchange business and now was adding our group on top of that. By that time the new regime's strategy of making everyone report to everyone – and having dotted lines to everyone – was starting to create massive infighting and confusion. I was stuck with the big Australian and I was happy with that. He dealt with all the garbage in London and I just had to keep the bank solvent and make some money.

One afternoon, one of the 14 people I had a dotted line to called me into his office. It was the commodity guy who ran the New York trading floor. There is no way this can be good for anyone. I'm just not a yes man. You ask me a question, you get an answer, good or bad. A lot of type A's don't like that. I then get frustrated. Rinse and repeat.

I walk into his office and it's him and the guy who runs South America for Deutsche Bank. *What the fuck could this possibly be about?* My first thought is always running back the tape for the last month to see who I had mouthed off to or pissed off. I had a habit of writing opinionated emails to people who did not want to hear my opinion. The aftermath of the 9/11 attacks emboldened me because it was then I realized just how little our management knew about how a bank actually ran. It always made my stomach churn. I felt I had to educate them on the realities. It got me into a lot of trouble and the big Australian had to run interference for me.

> Commodity guy: We are closing the Toronto office next month.
>
> South America guy nods his head.
>
> Commodity guy continues: You probably know more about that office then anyone in New York so you can help us do it. Thoughts?

By that time I was no longer responsible for Canada, but I knew they had turned the office around to break even and the wee little man was now in charge of the whole Global Markets in Canada. I thought it was time to expand the bank's business in Canada. They had a good base of business, Canada was growing, and they had plenty of leased space that they were committed to for another ten years. In my mind, it was a no-brainer they could turn a profit up there, as opposed to breaking even currently. I could not possibly tell commodity guy that in this situation. It would make him look bad and be suicide for me.

Me: I think we should be expanding up in Canada, not closing it.

I just can't keep my mouth shut sometimes. At the time Deutsche Bank was trying to expand everywhere. Why would you shut down a G-7 economies office when your not even losing money? For goodness sakes, shut the Tokyo office down, that place is a loser every year.

I don't think he was happy. The South American guy looked at me like you would look at a guy who was being marched to the gallows. I wasn't done yet, I had another card to play.

Me (again): Seth just met with the Bank of Canada last month and told them how committed Deutsche Bank is to the Canadian marketplace. I'm sure he would not appreciate being undercut like that.

Oh boy, I had done it now. The commodity guy turned bright red and dismissed me. Seth was the President of Deutsche Bank America, or North America, or THE Americas. No one could keep track. In the normal course of business, these executives would meet with central banks of different countries and check in and make sure everything was going well. The central banks would always then check back and make sure your bank was still committed to their country. It would be a massive scandal to shut an office down after an executive had just told a central bank how committed the bank was. In my mind, I had not only saved a bunch of jobs but also saved Deutsche Bank from looking like a band of idiots. I thought I did a good job. Later that day, the managing director who ran the Repo desk and was starting to take over more businesses in New York, and get more power, came over to talk to me. He was the guy trading massive size in his black overcoat the day he was hired in 1995. Remember?

Black overcoat guy: You managed to piss everyone off today. We all want to say the things you say, but we are smart enough not to say them. You need to get some polish.

I could never understand why giving your opinion to your superior could be so scandalous. Shouldn't a manager want every opinion and every piece of information before they make a decision? It is a sign of weakness in leadership to only want to hear what you want to hear. History is littered with the bad decisions resulting from not allowing opposing opinions into the debate.

The result from that day was that Toronto had a reprieve for now and that I had to take classes to "polish" myself. I'm not sure why I agreed to it. There may have been a threat involved. Or maybe black overcoat guy and the big Australian had an intervention with me. Ya know, like when a family intervenes to send someone to rehab. Only my rehab was polish school. I did it for my work family. I decided for me that to continue to piss everyone off was just going to hurt the guys and gals who worked for me and end up holding them back. I had to protect them so they could prosper.

The first step was a public speaking class. I was terrified of public speaking. I was often asked to go to a conference or do a presentation to a client's company, but I always refused. "If public speaking is now mandatory for me, you need to fire me and find someone else." I used that line to my bosses multiple times. I may be a little stubborn.

Speaking class was a disaster. I still have the tape of that day. They tape your sessions throughout the day to prove your progress but I was the same nervous, stuttering idiot at the end of the day as I was at the beginning. So embarrassing. I refused to go back. At least I tried. I was fine running meetings. No problem at all. Something about standing up and being the center of attention in front of strangers revealed some deep dark fears in me.

Later that year, the wee little man was summoned to New York to make a presentation about keeping Global Markets Canada open and his plan to expand it. All the hot-shit executives from DB North America were there. I was not invited and my feelings were hurt. Just kidding, I didn't give a shit about their stupid reindeer games and another conference where type A's beat their chests and tell everyone how great they are. My bullshit filter was very full by then.

The night before the wee little man's presentation, he flew down to New York. He was very nervous and worked up and asked me to join him for a few beers to try and relax. Me, beers? Don't mind if I do. He was a mess. We had a few beers (more like ten) while we watched a hockey game on TV in the upstairs of a bar called "Connolly's." No relation. I had been giving the wee little man a little good-natured shit to loosen him up and we were going back and forth. At one point there was a big fight in the hockey game we were watching. Big brawl. The wee little man loves his hockey. Gets him all fired up. The fight breaks out and the little bugger's hockey violent streak rears its ugly head. Before I know it the little bitch braces me with one hand on my shoulder and cold cocks me with his other hand on the side of my head. The little fucker just popped me one. *What the fuck?* I look up at him, and horror crosses his face. His eyes bulge wide and he starts shaking and apologizing profusely. "I don't know what came over me," he wailed. He was fighting for his career the next day and was pretty worked up. Another three pints and we were laughing about it. I have no idea how it went the next day, but I guess it must have gone well because Toronto stayed open and expanded.

On to our second annual trip to Vegas in 2002. Our desk and a few friends went to Las Vegas for five or six years. We packed in a lot of awake time in two or three days. I don't know why we decided on going to the Hard Rock in Vegas. It may have been because the guys on my desk and I were all music freaks and we knew the Hard Rock pumped rock onto their casino floors as well as the restaurants and hallways. I loved it. It was a much more fun environment than some of the other hotels that were more sedate and sterile. For the most part, we were not huge gamblers so we did not need a boring place to focus on gambling. We just wanted to drink and listen to music. Isn't that a big surprise? Every once in a while someone would drag us to one of the famous strip joints in Vegas. The ballet was low on our priority list and most of us never even wanted to leave the Hard Rock. The traffic in Vegas is a nightmare so those forty-five minute cab rides while drunk are more annoying than anything else.

In the early years, we would try to mix in a round of golf. By this time my second-in-command was the guy we brought up from operations in 1995 to learn the business. He was the guy we made go out and get drunk with the clients we hated, instead of us having to do so. Remember? He had moved up and spent a few years in Singapore. He was a seasoned vet by that point and I could trust him to get the job done because he was solid as a rock. He would set up the golf and since we were drunks in Vegas the golf had a twist to it. Teams of two were picked for the competition. We knew the teams beforehand but were not sure of the exact nature of the match.

The previous night, we all stayed up to five in the morning getting hammered and listening to AC/DC while playing $5 hands of blackjack. We would get three hours of sleep then take a van out to the golf course. None of us was in good shape. Whose fucking idea was it to play golf? Each team got its own cart and I was just happy we did not have to walk the course with caddies. If the cart was electric and quiet I might even be able to squeeze in a nap. It was too early to start drinking again. Wait, what is that red and white thing stuffed in the rack of the cart behind the seat? It looks like a case of Budweiser. It can't be, can it? Turns out the match was as follows: Each team of two had to finish a case of beer by the time their last ball hit the cup on the 18th green. Because the guy in charge was feeling charitable, he made the rule that the beer did not have to be consumed in equal parts. If a team member was feeling strong and wanted to drink 18 of the 24, then so much the better. The teams with one strong drinker had to put a plan in place of the best pace at which to drink copious amounts while still functioning in the match. If a team did not finish the whole case, they were disqualified. All fallen soldiers (empty cans) had to stay in the cart and be counted as proof. It was one of the best days I have ever had on a golf course. After we finished, we sat (or slumped) around the 18th green and watched everyone limp in. One group chugged six beers each on the last hole. They wanted to play good soberish golf most of the round and then chug in to finish their case. Did I mention most of us were in our 30's? I guess a normal person should be embarrassed, but you will never hear me apologize for acting like a kid or being human. Ever. One player teed off on elevated ground and was so drunk he stumbled backwards on his follow through and went ass backwards over a three-foot rock wall. Good times.

Then there was the Vegas moon year. We looked forward to our trip every year and would usually set it up four or five months early. One of the guys was a big gambler so he would call up the Hard Rock and get us free rooms, then we would each book and pay for our own flights. Usually it was during this process that we picked the sucker who would stay behind and work Friday. That person would be in charge of drafting someone from another group to help get through that day before the Friday flight to heaven.

After the arrangements were made people would get fired up for the trip. You know what I'm talking about. You go on the web before a trip and look at the pictures of the beach or wherever you are going. It's all part of the fantasy. We found these web cams of the Hard Rock and started watching what was going on there in the months leading up. There was a restaurant cam, a casino cam, a club cam, and a pool cam. By far the most popular cam was the pool cam. Boys will be boys. At random times when we had five minutes we would pull up the cams to see what was happening at the Hard Rock. We all had them bookmarked on our browsers. That was before the fun police frowned upon such activity. It was all PG rated, even the pool cam. Move along people, nothing to see here.

About a month into the process of getting fired up by stalking the Hard Rock cams, I came up with the best idea I have ever had in my career. I'm still proud of it. I blurted it out one day. "I'm going to moon that fucking pool cam on our trip this year." Brilliant. Of the many strange things I have decided were good ideas in my life, mooning things and dressing up in offensive outfits on Halloween are two of them. When my wife and I were first dating we were invited to a birthday party of a guy I barely knew from work. The rule of the party was that the present had to cost no more than three dollars. Somehow I decided my ass would be the perfect present. The fact that my girlfriend (now my wife) agreed with me was one reason why I married her. So I did the first moonfie on record and snapped a picture of my own ass. My wife said it was my best side. Always the wiseass. We proceeded to buy a two-dollar frame and then signed the pic, "Bottoms up from Matt & Beth." After it was wrapped, we were so proud of ourselves. Sometimes I just don't know my audience. He was offended when he opened it. Oh well. It probably did not help that there may have been a glimpse of my small Irish bean bag that photobombed the pic. Live and learn. OK, where was I?

The planning starts for the Vegas moon. By the time of the trip we had the plan all sorted out. What could go wrong? It was easy. I knew where the cam was, so I would just find it and pick a good time to expose my "better side." I would grab my cell phone and call the trading desk so they could pull up the pool cam and watch for my ass. The plan sort of built on itself and there ended up being side bets between other desks and the salesforce on whether I could pull it off or not. Talk about pressure. Billion dollar trades going against me? Nothing compared to this pressure.

As the trip got closer, the weather got cooler in Vegas and we saw fewer people using the pool while we stalked the Hard Rock. I thought that would make it much easier to pull off the Vegas moon without ending up in jail. When we arrived on Thursday, my second in command and I scouted out the territory. Problem. The pool area was closed for the year and was not accessible. Not good. So we took a full reconnoiter of the battleground and met at the Hard Rock bar to get our drinking caps on. Once Motley Crue's 'Kickstart my heart' started blaring on the sound system, I knew the plan we hatched would work the next morning. It was destiny.

After huevos rancheros for breakfast, we got into our workout gear for the gym. We had found a door from the workout room directly to the pool, which we thought we could get through with no one seeing. Then I would just have to maneuver through a small garden and a few hedge rows and I'd be home free. We synchronized our watches and I grabbed my cell phone. The first obstacle appeared quickly. It cost ten bucks to get into the gym. *I ain't paying no ten bucks for no gym.* My second-in-command saved the day by saying we had left a gym bag inside and just wanted to retrieve it. Always good on his feet.

After we got inside, it all starts to go quick and blur by. There was no turning back now. We run over to the door we found and I turn my cell phone on and start dialing the trading desk back in New York. My guy pushes the door open, then he is going to stand lookout for me and make sure the door stays open so it does not lock me out after the mission is completed. Ingress and Egress. I only tripped twice flopping through the garden looking for the cam. I got the trading desk on the phone and I hear the sucker who had to stay behind yell to the floor that I was on the phone and for people to pull up the pool cam. I heard a lot of hubbub in the background then silence. It's finally time for the skirt to be raised, so to speak. I find the perfect angle and pull my shorts down and am now bent over in the open with a cell phone to my ear. Still silence on the phone from the trading floor. *They should see me by now, something is wrong.* As I am sitting prone, my colleague yells from the door, "A security guard is coming!" Can you imagine what that dude thought, seeing some ugly fat white dude in the position I was in? I bet he thought I was doing a Cleveland steamer on the concrete. All of the sudden, I hear huge screams and an ovation from the trading floor in New York. *Mission Accomplished.*

On the way out, I told the security guard the truth. It was the only way out. "I've been planning on mooning that cam for four months. I had to do it." He gave a small smile, shook his head and replied, "Get the fuck out of here before I arrest you." Yes sir! It turns out it was not a live cam per-say, but snapped a new pic every twenty seconds, and that accounted for the delay. Live and learn. At least I hung out there long enough. The lesson here is: Don't bet against me when it comes to being a knucklehead.

Our days in Las Vegas were all eerily similar. Wake up and grab some sort of egg and meat breakfast at the Hard Rock diner, then go find a $5 blackjack table that is empty and pony up to it. Order drinks. The drink situation was as follows. I have a weak bladder and always have. By this point I'm the old man and getting towards forty. The more beers I drink, the more trips to the bathroom. On the casino floor, it's considered bad etiquette to get up during the hands as much as I would need to if I was sucking down beers. The solution is simple. Kettle One vodka and diet Red Bull. Breakfast of the mini-bladder champions. Diet because

I was chubby. Red Bull to stay awake. Vodka to get drunk. Very well thought out, wouldn't you agree?

If all went well, our group would take over an entire table and sit there all day with people swapping in and out. For a break, I would wander back to where the big gamblers hung out in the VIP section. I'd then track down my buddy who would get us our comped rooms and meals. It would be fun watching him whipping around $1,000 hands in blackjack while I was gambling all day on $100 at the $5 tables. He had some major wins and major losses in those years. Fun to watch but I could never do it.

One of these afternoons, as our group was sitting at the Hard Rock blackjack table, a big group plopped down at the table next to us. They were younger guys and gals, a lively bunch whooping it up and making noise. After one of my blackjack hands busted, I looked over and recognized one of the guys. It was the wiz kid, the young computer driven trader I sat a few seats from when I traded T-Bills in 1997. He noticed me at the same time and a look of horror flashed across his eyes. Then a little panic. He was not happy to see me. I was surprised because we always got along well and I had spoken with him even after I left that desk. This was years later and he had worked his way higher at the bank and was doing the same type of trading, but much more focused and client oriented. I decided I'd just ignore him. Life is too short.

A little while later, I feel a tug at my arm and turn around and it's him. He pulls me aside and then it all becomes clear. "I need a favor," he said. "Sure, what do you need?" He tells me he needs me and my guys not to tell anyone they saw him in Las Vegas. He borrowed the Deutsche Bank private jet to fly out to California to make a presentation to some of the bank's clients. He decided to bring his posse with him on the trip, and to stop into Vegas for a day or two of partying before ending up in California. What did I care? He wasn't hurting anyone and I ain't no nosy neighbor. "Absolutely, our lips are sealed," I told him. He seemed genuinely relieved, and was able to continue his partying.

Later on that day, his group got up and went to whatever the nightclub was at the Hard Rock. I don't remember the name, I never stepped foot in the place. Casino floor, Hard Rock Diner, Pink Taco restaurant. Rinse and repeat. Over the years I wore out the carpets to those places, as well as to the bathroom and the ATM. We used to call having to hit the ATM for more money the walk of shame. I did it many a times. Back to the story.

A few hours after his group leaves, our group starts to thin out and the few stragglers decide to get some late night diner food. As I get up from the table, a beautiful lady saunters up beside me. I wonder to myself if she is blind. She tells me to take her cell number and call her when I'm going up to my room for the night.

> Me: Sphincter says what?
>
> Her: Call me when you want me to meet you in your room.
>
> Me: I'm sorry miss, there must be a mistake. I'm definitely not in the market.
>
> Her: You don't understand. I'm yours for the night. A present from the group that was here before.

Ding. Ding. Ding. The bell goes off, I get it now.

I let her off the hook and she left. She probably was relieved she did not have to see me naked. Perish the thought. When I told the story at breakfast, the guys were pissed. Just like I was. Only they were pissed at me!

> Knucklehead 1: What a waste, you could have sent her to my room.

Knucklehead 2: That was rude of you to rebuff such a nice gesture of friendship.

Knucklehead 3: I always knew you liked men.

And on and on it went. It was a fun breakfast. Someone asked me why I was so offended. Was it an issue of morals? Hell, no. I am about as pure as the driven slush. I don't judge anyone. The best way for me to describe the feeling is an old episode from the TV show *Seinfeld*. Jerry's dentist converted to Judaism just so he could tell Jewish jokes. When Jerry complained about it to the dentist's old priest, the priest asked, "Are you offended as a Jew?" and Jerry replies, "No, I'm offended as a comedian!" I felt (rightly or wrongly) it was a bribe and a way to control me and make sure I kept my mouth shut. That pisses me off. I'm not even sure if the wiz kid knew about it. Maybe the plan was hatched by the posse. He didn't get fired, so I guess I kept my word anyway.

28

Let's talk about a very serious subject for a change. No one on a trading floor likes to talk about this, but we all had to deal with it. You ask anyone who worked on a trading floor and they will reluctantly agree it happened too often, and was very frustrating. Of course I am talking about "cropdusting." Cropdusting is when some asshole passes by your desk configuration and releases a silent but deadly fart. Also known as laying land mines. If the mine is laid correctly at the right time, it is impossible to figure out who did it. Sometimes it could be a minute or two since the last person passed by before the smell punched you in the face. The smart dusters would make sure they were in a group when they let loose. Then they would scurry back to their desk and stealthily watch the fireworks as the complaining started. I considered this a huge breach of fart etiquette. Gentlemen always claim their brand, it's just common courtesy. You don't have to go with the formal, "Excuse me," but jeezus have enough compassion for your fellow man to blurt, "I just blew one, you boys might want to take a walk." Is it so tough to do?

The year 2002 was another very good stretch for our desk and the group. I was probably the happiest I had ever been in a job. I had a great boss who ran interference for me so I could get the bank funded on a daily basis and make a little money. He had also worked his butt off to globalize our group so we were streamlined and efficient for the first time. Since 1999, we had more than doubled our revenue on my desk. The streamlining allowed us to cut our costs over that time so our net revenue was eye-popping. The previous year, after the attacks, no one really paid attention when the bonus pool for our group was not up to expectations. As time goes on, the focus changes and the big Australian is hell bent on getting our group's compensation where it should be compared to other, more sexy groups.

As well as being happy with my boss, I had a great group of people who I managed. Being a crappy evaluator of people during the interview process, I was lucky I had not had to hire anyone cold. Everyone who worked on my desk I was able to hire after watching them in other jobs at the bank. I had my second-in-command, who I had brought up from operations in 1995. I had two traders I had cherry-picked from the Bankers Trust merger after watching them for three months. I had also grabbed one of my old workmates from my first trading job on the Repo desk at JP Morgan. He was the grizzled vet who helped me out of my futures jam when I was a rookie. He had come over to Deutsche Bank and then found himself overseas. He didn't have a fancy college degree and that was looked down upon by the new regime, so he was at risk of losing his job after his stint overseas was up. That is a crock of shit so we grabbed him back to work for me in New York. He knew the business, was solid as a rock, and the salespeople loved him. Our group also consisted of a few others I had the pleasure of pulling in over the years. Make no mistake, you are much better off when you know the people you hire.

The big Australian had really put himself on the line. He made no bones about letting the group know he expected our compensation globally and in New York to increase dramatically. He did not fuck around or play games. Just a straight shooter, you never had to figure out where he stood. That's why I loved him.

When people visited from overseas, I hated to see them sit in a hotel room alone at night, so my wife and I would always ask them to have dinner and sleep over. The big Australian liked his cigars, so when he agreed to join us I made sure I saved a special Cuban cigar for him to enjoy on our deck. Someone had given me the cigar, and since the one Cuban cigar I ever smoked in London made me feel like I was on a bad LSD trip, it was a perfect gift for him. After dinner we head out to the deck and I open up my humidor and present my grand offer to him. He picks up the cigar and examines it closely. He then hooks his finger to me and leans in, signaling he has something to say. When I lean in, he proceeds to slap me. Not a big slap but one of those quick and cropped slaps that lets me know that he is offended. *Why does everyone hit me?* I was a cigar rookie and did not really know how to take care of them properly, so I guess there was a spot of mold on my special gift. His follow up to his slap was one simple comment. "You don't treat a cigar like this. You treat a cigar like a lady." And there he was.

When bonus conversations started, the big Aussie was agitated. Over in London, all the managing directors would gather and hash out the bonuses and promotions. I had always likened it to the scene in the movie Animal House when the fraternity is deciding which boys they want to pledge. Pictures of prospective pledges flash on the screen and then everyone has their say. When one picture flashes by, all the brothers boo and throw popcorn and beer at the screen. I always felt that was the reaction London had when my name came up for promotion. I may be a little paranoid. Or maybe not.

The big Australian had said I was due to be promoted and to get a big raise commensurate to where my predecessor was. He made no promises, but said it was time to try. I told him not to bother if it meant I had to attend the "big dick" conferences. Where the type A's get together and beat their chests and figuratively slap their dicks on the table to show how big it is. I despised that and wanted no part. I got my wish as he let me know a promotion was not coming this year. Maybe next year, he said. *Yawwwn.*

As the bonus conference was concluding, he would call me and tell me where I ended up, as well as my desk. He always gave me a fair say in my staff's compensation. Not so much on how much, but more the spread between everyone to make it as fair as it could be. There was not an ounce of bullshit or games in the guy. When he read the numbers off, however, I did have one glaring problem. The old grizzled vet who we brought back from overseas was getting stiffed. The big Australian said he did his best, but that was it. It was not acceptable to me. I was pissed they were throwing around all these big numbers and they were dicking around over $25,000 the guy totally deserved. Finally the big Australian got tired of my whining and said if it was that important to me, he would lower mine by $25,000 and give it to him. I jumped at the deal. Problem solved and all was fair.

My number was ludicrous. Gluttonous. It was that year or the next where if your bonus was over a certain amount, you got a percentage in Deutsche Bank stock that would vest over a few years. I thought that was a good idea as it would get people thinking about how the bank was doing, as opposed to just their own pockets. The big Australian said I should have gotten the upper end of the range he had previously said my position was worth. That would have been a $1,200,000 bonus. Crazy. He ended up agreeing in London to $800,000 minus the $25,000 we switched. $775,000 plus $150,000 salary. That was roughly 35,000 cases of good beer, just from the bonus. Of course, after taxes, the government got 12,000 of those cases.

The big Australian felt betrayed by management over our

group's global compensation. They made representations to him and then he made those representations to his group and it did not pan out. He did not take it well. I believe it was early 2003 when we heard about an incident that took place on the London trading floor that started big changes in motion. His support of his group (managing down instead of up) ultimately would stop his career at Deutsche Bank in its tracks. Nothing changed immediately, but we could all see the writing on the wall.

29

THE DESK WAS CLICKING ON all cylinders and I was just where I wanted to be. I think most of us on my desk agreed that the money and promotions were secondary to enjoying our job and being productive without politics interfering on a daily basis. We had our hands full daily funding the bank. We still were operating two separate banks. The Deutsche Bank balance sheet was still growing by leaps and bounds and we still had the "stranded liquidity" at Bankers Trust. I was a much better streamliner than I was an empire builder so I always kept our desk understaffed, busy and not worried about their jobs. Most of the type A empire builders hired any time they got the opening with zero forethought into how the big picture would blend together. I always thought fatness and excess people just caused infighting and low morale and lack of efficiency.

As every year passed, the core bank people I considered my allies became fewer and the investment banking people became dominant. I'm sure many of my emails to upper management begging for changes in the balance sheet contributed to the "sound of crickets" that was heard when my name came up for promotion. The bank had billions of securities hidden away that could be funded by unlimited amounts of collaterized funding or Repo, but instead I was funding that part of the balance sheet unsecured. Unsecured funding (with nothing but credit behind it) was a scarce resource and the investment bankers with 150 IQ's could not understand that. Sometimes, when I hit the send button, I thought maybe my emails were mistakenly converted to Chinese.

Towards the middle or end of 2003, the changes we suspected were coming started to take vague shape. I found out about it in an interesting way. The guy in the black overcoat from 1995 was in charge of Repo and gaining power in New York. He called me into his office in late 2003 to let me know that the wee little man from Toronto was leapfrogging me and being moved to London to take over the group there. He apologized, but said I was never a serious consideration because the futures guy said I was "not a good fit in London." You're god-damn right I wasn't. I guess they thought I'd be mad, but I was happy for the wee little man. He always wanted to go up against the big boys in London and see if his dick measured up. I already knew I had a small dick. He was scheduled to move to London and I was safely in New York under the radar. *Mission Fucking Accomplished.*

Is it bonus time in 2003 already? Thanks to the big Australian filtering out the bullshit for me and helping us sort things out, I could concentrate on the funding and trading while he was doing the politics as well as being a great trader. I liked it that way. My bonus was the same and I again moved $25,000 to the grizzled vet, who got hosed again because he was not a highly educated ass kisser. I had the opposite view of most of management. While they paid the squeaky wheels and posers whatever they asked for, the nuts and bolts people who just went about their jobs quietly were overlooked and treated like second-class citizens. So the incentives were backwards. Assclown posers would be rewarded for whining and self-promotion while the quiet people who just worked their asses off in their jobs found other places to work. The 15% crazies and exploiters were starting to take over the bank I loved. A little at a time.

More managing directors were moving to London so it was getting too crowded there and something had to break. We were worried for the big Australian. At least after inflation that bonus was worth 34,500 cases of beer. I had that going for me.

In early 2004, the big announcement was made about a huge restructure at the bank. People were flying all over the place. The management structure was always a nightmare to figure out at Deutsche Bank and this announcement made it insane. It's comical reading about it now. In order to simplify the bank's structure, four divisions were combined into two. As usual, it's all about perception over reality. The reality is the hundred moves that took place below that combination made everyone just throw their hands up in exasperation because now the bank structure was hopelessly fucked. As usual, decisions were half-assed, and six-month transition periods because no one had the balls to make a real decision just led to more confusion and infighting. My theory was that the former sales guy in charge of it all thought if he kept everyone at everyone's throats twenty four hours a day, they would not be able to focus on the fact that the emperor had no clothes. Deutsche Bank was becoming a bubble and bubbles always pop.

I was told that for the time being, I would have a new dotted line to the guy in the black overcoat in New York, as well as the big Australian guy in London. We were told the wee little man and the big Australian were going to share duties. Whatever. We were smart enough to see where this was heading. The net effect for us in New York was that we were reverting to local management as opposed to global. We knew the big Australian was about to get kicked to the curb. The guy in the black overcoat had always treated me very well and I knew it would be fine overall. His management style was more difficult for me because he was much more of a yeller and very intense, whereas the big Australian would just say, "Don't fuck it up" and you never wanted to disappoint him.

For the past few years, I had been dealing with back problems and knee problems that continued to worsen. I had been in a car accident as a kid and that, combined with being a lardass, explained my woes, I thought. I was going to a chiropractor and started eating salads at work for lunch, which made me a prime target for being salad shamed. By this time I'm forty and very much on the old side for the trading floor. The youngsters working for me all ate like horses every day. Pizza, burritos, burgers, cheesecake. Daily. My salad did not go over well.

At a routine visit to my chiropractor in 2004, he was surprised I had been getting worse and not better so he did a few more tests on my knees by grabbing them in a certain way. He grabbed the side of my knee and I jumped in pain. He shook his head and said, "Uh oh, you have hip problems. You need to see an orthopedist." How the fuck could he know that by grabbing my knee, I had hip problems? He was right as usual, and I was told I'd have to get both my hips replaced sooner rather than later as my mobility deteriorated. I decided to put it off for as long as I could and went on with my life.

Shortly after the black overcoat guy took over, he wanted to make changes in New York. The good news is he wanted to give me more responsibility. The bad news was that I had no ambition to take more on. Especially what he asked me to take on. The Money Market Derivative (MMD) group was the short-term swap desk in New York that resided in our group. When I took over my desk in 2000, that group had five people. A managing director who did one-month Libor swaps, a director who did three-month Libor swaps, a trader in charge of Overnight Index Swaps (OIS), and a swap option trader as well as a junior trader. They had gotten so much flow from my predecessor doing trades with them that they were doing tons of business and making tons of money. This meant promotions and good bonuses. By the time 2004 rolled around, this group was in shambles, caused by my decision to stop trading Libor products in 2000. The OIS trader had moved to another bank and the swap options idea was a bust so that trader moved over to trade OIS. That group was down to four people, and two of them were getting virtually no business in New York. There was no reason for me to accept and no upside and swaps (besides simple ones) were over my head. When offered to put that anchor around my neck, I declined so fast it would make your head spin. I wanted to make damn sure my new boss knew I had zero interest in having to sort out their problems. Selfish? Maybe. Whatever.

By the end of 2004, most of the changes went into effect and the other moves were made. The big Australian was being exiled to Asia for some regional job there. It was a bummer. By that time, our relationship with London, which the big Australian had worked so hard to repair, was fraying again as it became locale vs locale in a fight to the death. That's the way it would feel to me anyway.

30

The balance sheet continued to grow, increasing our funding needs on an unsecured basis. We had a committee in every region called the ALCO. I think it stood for Asset & Liability Committee. I'm not even sure. It seemed like committees were popping up at this point to discuss bathroom use, numbers of pens used, or anything else. I despise bureaucracy. Each region had their own committee and then there was a Global ALCO run out of Frankfurt. The global one was the one that all the big shots attended. The committees were formed to monitor the bank's health and make sure limits were being followed as well as discussing a few other bank issues. In our regional ALCO in New York, I could stay awake in maybe one out of five meetings. We met once a month. We all know those types of meetings. Put a big binder of flashy numbers together that mean nothing and then discuss them while nodding your head and softly rubbing your chin like you give a shit. There was always fifteen of us rubbing our chins and nodding, pining inside for the meeting to end.

I never kept track of when these Global ALCO meetings took place. No reason to. That committee was designed to monitor and control the bank's health via the balance sheet. The problem is that it had zero control over the asset side of the balance sheet. The asset side was out of control and the people in charge were making stupid statements like "upwards and onwards" and stupid-shit-sounding slogans like that. The various committees had no control of the asset side and only minimal control on the liability side. The liability side consisted of my desk in New York and all the other Asset & Liability desks worldwide in all the other currencies. For that reason we took the bulk of the harassment to try to control this growing beast of a balance sheet.

One afternoon on the day of the big global ALCO meeting in Frankfurt, I get a call from the Global Treasurer. One of the top five executives in the bank. If you remember, he was the German guy who hired me back in 1995 so I knew him and we got along well and were usually on the same page. That being said, he resided on the gold plated floors and I was ten rungs down the ladder in the trenches. Let's just say I knew I was not about to be asked out for a few Beck's with the guy. He started right in. "I want to tell you how disgusted the ALCO and I are with your management of the Commercial Paper Program." I was less worried about the message being delivered and more worried by how that message was being delivered. Frankfurt was five hours in front of New York so it was 8 p.m. where he was and he had obviously had about ten Beck's before he called me. He was slurring pretty bad and I was not having this conversation with him right now. It was a short call because I found a way to get off the phone without discussing the issue further. Why bother? It was my next move that is about the only thing in twenty-two years on Wall Street that I regret.

I marched over to my new boss in the black overcoat and told him about the call I had just received. He knew that when I got this mad there was absolutely no talking to me or changing my mind. My stubbornness when provoked can be quite irrational. It will never change. "He has forty eight hours to apologize to me or I'm resigning and going to

Human Resources with a complaint, not necessarily in that order."

Let me try to explain why I was so angry. He could blame me for the numbers in his binder not looking the way he wanted them to look, but those numbers were useless and out of my hands at that point anyway. On a daily basis a bank had three funding products available to it. Taking deposits (just a loan) or issuing Commercial Paper (under a program) or issuing Certificates of Deposit. It was marginally more expensive to issue CP or CD's, but not enough for it to matter. The investors and banks that kept us solvent by giving us large amounts of cash every day were in charge. If a money market client had two billion dollars to give us but that account could only do deposits and not CP or CD's, then guess what? They got god-damn deposits! It was simple as that and I was a slave to whatever product a customer wanted to give me money through. If a customer through a salesperson could do either product, I would always put them into the product that we were slouching on to make the ALCO people happy. It almost never worked like that, though. My feeling was that the ALCO not controlling the asset side had put me in that position, so now the dude who is supposed to run that process is gonna run shit over me? Over my fucking dead body.

The Global Treasurer called the next day and apologized. Not for being disappointed in the numbers or complaining, but for how he had done it. I gladly accepted. Since he was a long-time ally and our views usually aligned, I bet the pressure he was under was insane. Deep down he knew we were both being run over and he just needed to lash out. I am embarrassed that I threatened to go to Human Resources, that usually is not me. I wished I'd just used my usual threat to resign immediately. I had plenty of "fuck you" money sitting in savings so it was not an idle threat, I assure you.

Bonus season in 2004 brought a whole new process in the bank with the restructure that took place that year. Not surprisingly, committees were formed. Promotion committee, compensation committee, executive committee, piss in a cup committee, etc. Bureaucracy. It can only end one way. Black overcoat guy introduced his bonus process to my desk. Everyone got a piece of paper that was a template. We all had to fill in our promotion wish, salary wish, and the high and low of our bonus expectations. I was not a fan. I told him I would pass the sheets out to my guys but I would not be participating. It sounds great, but in my estimation it was just a lazy way of managing people. If a manager worked hard for his staff and made sure everything was fairly done, there was no need for this. It created so much more drama than just sitting down with someone and giving the honest truth. Treat people like grown ups and they will act like grown ups. Play games with people and they will get all twisted in knots trying to guess what you want from them. It was destined to morph into a game of managing expectations and smoke and mirrors. I just wrote "treat me fair" every year on my sheet.

Black overcoat guy was always good to me. I hated the games and the yelling and the lies but he respected me (I think). He put me up for managing director and when he was in London the promotion committee met. As expected, it was not to be. I was not surprised or disappointed to hear, "You have no support for promotion in London." I'm sure empty bottles of Beck's and bowls of peanuts were thrown at my picture when it popped up on the overhead. He was able to come through with good bonus numbers for me and my staff. I got another whopper bonus of $900,000, and with my $150,000 salary, had cracked a million bucks a year. I knew going forward that I would have less control over my staff's compensation and promotions due to these new committees, so I was very uneasy even with things still going well. Sometimes you just know deep inside things are going pear-shaped.

31

In the meantime there were more moves in London. Futures guy was shipped out to some other project in the bank and another guy was brought in to take his place and be black overcoat guy's boss. Squinty. I knew Squinty from New York. I knew of him, I should say. He worked in our group in New York for a few years. He was in charge of Structured Repo. I have no idea what that is. Still don't. He was smarter than everyone else. Just ask him. He never associated himself with the nuts and bolts people like us. Unless you had six fancy degrees, he was not interested. Sorry, that's just the truth.

Close to that time we heard about a big move in our group in London and a few other offices around the world. The seating arrangement was being changed so that the cash traders and derivative traders could sit next to each other. Efficiencies, I guess. No effect in New York, since we were much smaller and the swap guys sat back to back with us anyway.

Squinty moved fast and was very aggressive. Along with the seating move, we heard that certain traders had weaseled their way into "eat what you kill" contracts. That means that a contract is signed between a person and the bank that his/her compensation is calculated strictly as a percentage of that person's trading revenue, with no subjective input. In addition, proprietary trading groups were being set up and staffed in each location. Usually proprietary trading desks can trade any product they want while having no customer contact, and work under "eat what you kill" percentage deals.

I thought at the time "eat what you kill" deals were possibly the dumbest move ever made on Wall Street. It boggles my mind to this day that the group of humps that came up with that, with their 150 IQ's, were not smart enough to know what it would lead to. The incentives were totally backwards and counter to every strain of common sense I can think of.

One of the big mercenaries, or "eat what you kill" guys, was a swaps trader in our group in London. He had developed a reputation as being a huge trader in the market over the past few years and getting more press within Deutsche Bank. Let's call him the Gunslinger. Gunslinger was a regular swap guy with customer contact who had threatened to leave for a hedge fund unless he got an "eat what you kill" contract. What surprised us at the time was that we had thought a trader in one of those contracts had to be ring-fenced (separated) from customers and also from the flow business. We had no idea.

Things were a changin'. My boss in New York had an ultimatum for me. You either take over the MMD desk and sort it out so that we can keep up with the changes in London, or I will hire someone myself to sit above you and manage all the desks including yours. Uh oh. I had a decision to make. Take over a desk I wanted no part of that would probably mean more layoffs, or take the chance some dope comes in above me and then I lose all semblance of control and put my current staff at risk. I could not let that happen. I took over the MMD desk (short term swaps) knowing I had to gut it. I was never going back to hedging our book using Libor. I knew the managing director and director who had Libor responsibilities were going to be casualties because of me. I was in a no-win situation and my boss damn well knew it.

Sucker Matt takes over that desk and starts to try and get a sense of that whole business. I now had my second managing director who reported to me, and I was just a director. What was I doing wrong? It would be sad if it weren't so comical. I was told to start the process of documenting the business so that if we had to fire someone we would be covered legally to call the terminations "restructuring." In fact, that part was easy. The two Libor traders were both very competent flow traders and good guys as well. Neither of them lost money, they just could not make enough money to pay for their overhead if my desk refused to give them business. There was no chance I would go back to using Libor, so I started down the road to letting them go. Against the advice of Human Resources (as usual) I made damn sure they had plenty of time to be prepared for their termination. I also made sure they both got very favorable release payments, which we called packages. Right is right. It was not their fault so I was trying to give them as much time as possible to get their affairs in order so they could attain another job when they lost this one.

In the mean time, Squinty and the Gunslinger were shoving down my throat resumes of people they wanted us to hire in New York. It was a difficult situation. Not only did the Gunslinger have power, but he had ambitions of power. He wanted his crew in New York. We fought that happening at every turn. The Gunslinger would give Squinty a resume of one of his French buddies. Squinty sends it to my boss in New York with the message "hire this guy" and the resume ends up on my desk. I would usually do some due diligence in the market to educate myself on the prospect. I would slow-play the whole thing, moving in slow motion on all these resumes. If I could, I would have no mercenaries working for me and certainly would do everything I could to keep the London Gunslinger mentality off my desk.

Unlike me, the guys on my desk are smart. They see what's going on. They know of Squinty's reputation and they see me getting ready to fire two people on the Money Market Derivative desk we sat back to back to. Morale on the desk was dropping like a movie starlet's assets after the age of fifty. Goin' low.

Clearly our group was at a crossroads and I had to be very careful with how I handled things. I had to play it close to the vest and not do anything stupid. Squinty would drop me faster than you could say the word "go." I was about six fancy degrees away from being acceptable to him. I had to be careful but I had to pick up morale. I came up with the perfect answer. I called it the strip club review option. Maybe not the smartest idea I ever had, but I was trying. At that point most of my staff had been working for me for years and years. We knew each other inside and out and our review process was quick and painless. I did my best to communicate throughout the year so that reviews and bonuses and promotions were as well advertised as they could be. Everyone had a choice as far as a review environment. A normal review in a conference room (I had no office). No review at all. A review during a lunch at the ballet. I just thought of something that pisses me off, as a matter of fact. I worked on Wall Street for twenty-two years and would never be offered an office. Never. Actually, I'm proud of that. I could never be an office guy. I always wanted to be in the trenches duking it out. The strip club review option was short lived as new hires coming onboard made it less a fun option and more a risk for me. One or two years at the most.

I had mentioned that I liked to communicate on performance throughout the year. It was just a better way to do it rather than having a bunch of surprises show up during the review meeting at some strip joint. Awkward, right? I had come up with a brilliant idea to streamline the communication process during the year for my desk. I called it the "review on the fly." I still had this three-foot-tall stack of recycled paper on my desk. I would take old paper and rip stacks into fours, then use them for notes and messages throughout the year. At some point someone on my desk did something so monumentally stupid that they just had to be smacked on the nose. Maybe one of my traders had told a client on the phone that he "did not have time for this shit" when he thought he had placed the call on hold. I'm not sure how the first one was created, but it was for some boneheaded move like that. I'd take a sheet of paper and make a sad face on it with maybe a few-word reference on how they had "fucked it up," then I would lay it on their desk. Just a simple circle with two eyes and a frown. Below it would be a reference to the action they were being reprimanded for. If a trader had done a bad trade and lost money that day, they might get a sad face with, "Great trade, dickhead," written underneath. It's all about effective communication, people.

Relax, there were positive "reviews on the fly" too. They just weren't as fun. For instance, say I was taking one of my thousand pisses a day. During that piss some prissy French dude in a scarf comes over to ask some moron question. My second-in-command would shuffle him away from the desk and answer his question so I don't have to deal with him. He would get a happy face review on the fly with a +5k written on the bottom. The +5k/-5k was of course in reference to me giving them an extra $5,000 in their bonus or docking them $5,000 in their bonus, depending on the review. Of course that was all fictional, but we had a good time with the reviews on the fly. Or at least I did, and that's all that counts right? As long as the big dog is happy. In reality I was not happy.

It was roughly around that time when "take your daughter to work day" became a thing. My daughter was born in 1997 so at this time she was old enough to be curious about what "Daddy does at work." Emily had loved numbers and the concept of banking from an early age so it was natural to bring her in when the time was right. The first thing I had to do was warn my staff about watching what they said when anyone's kid was in the office. Swearing was like breathing at the office. Hey, using swear words makes damn sure there is no miscommunication about how someone is feeling. Emphasis in communication is key so I am all for it.

Anyway, Emily and I take the trek in on the train and then ferry and hit the coffee cart outside my building. I get my two twenty-ounce coffees and she gets a bear-claw the size of my freakin' fivehead. It was huge. Thank goodness I never got into the habit of having one of those puppies with my coffee in the morning. One of the guys on the desk was on vacation two seats away from me so I plopped her down in his seat and showed her how to get to the Internet to entertain herself. It was a pretty slow and uneventful day as opposed to other days. I was happy for that.

As the day ended I was relieved that she enjoyed herself and that no terrible incidents occurred. I had no interest in having to listen to my daughter recount fights and swearing contests to my wife that night. That would not have been good. So when I asked for her summary of the day on the train home, I was pretty sure it would be boring and PG-rated (at worst). I was surprised at what followed:

> Daughter (blurting out): I heard the F-bomb seven times Dad!
>
> Me (furious): You tell me right now who on my desk said the F-word.

I am gonna kill those guys. We went over this!

> Daughter: The man two to your left said it once and the man behind you said it once.

OK, five more to account for.

> Daughter: The other five were YOU!

TEETH (271) MARKS

Oh boy, how do I turn this into some special teaching moment? Surely I am adept enough to think on my feet to take care of this situation in a manner that Ward Cleaver would be proud of. I thought for a moment of the perfect thing to say to make it all make sense to an eight-year old. Then I forcefully said: "Do not tell your mother!"

Mission Accomplished?

Just when I had thought my test taking days are over, I found out that since I now had multiple desks under my purview that I had to get a regulatory license. The series 24. Just another reason to drink. Another test? Are they trying to kill me? If you ever have insomnia and need to fall asleep in twelve seconds, order yourself a series 24 binder off of Amazon. Guaranteed to put you to sleep within the first paragraph. I was just thankful that instead of having to wait a week for the results, like with the series 7, I'd know immediately after I pushed the button on the computer whether I'd have to commit hari-kari if I failed and had to do it again. So I crammed for a few weeks and passed the test. It was ten times more stressful than putting on some trade and watching it turn my asshole into the Lincoln tunnel. I hated school and I hate tests. On the way home, I stopped at Dunkin Donuts and bought a dozen donuts. Promptly ate every last one during my half-hour ride home. Let's not even get into my eating disorders. Not enough pages.

32

During 2005 there was much talk on our trading floor about the housing market. It was flying high and it seemed that every new product that was being created was mortgage-related. Since the bank's solvency rested mostly on my desk and with the Treasury group, we worked closely together to monitor the new products being invented to make sure they were not detrimental to our world. Treasury had official responsibility for this but we had a good informal agreement (between me and NY Treasury) to keep each other in the loop on developments. There were times I either got pulled into, or weaseled into, meetings on subjects where it was unclear whether Treasury was linked in, so I would link them in after or vice versa.

Let's talk Collateral Debt Obligations (CDO's). As we all know, I'm not capable of understanding anything more complex than the sequence of dropping a shot of Jaegermeister into a beer and chugging it. Forgive me if I screw this up. A CDO is just a group of loans packaged together like a bond. The CDO has a yield, so it looks like an attractive investment as compared to a government bond or something safer. A CDO might yield 6% versus 2% for a government bond. Since the CDO may consist of some loans guaranteed by Fannie Mae and other Government Sponsored Enterprises, as well as the houses themselves as collateral, what could possibly go wrong? Wouldn't a fund rather return 6% rather than 2%? It really was too good to be true.

The invention of the CDO in 1987 or thereabouts, and its popularity and eventual destruction, is a great example of the law of unintended consequences. I remember watching Alan Greenspan on television in the late 80's getting raked over the coals about home ownership and what could be done to make homes more available to all. The intent was absolutely heroic. Who would not want more people to live the American dream by being able to purchase a house? The Government Sponsored Enterprises such as Fannie Mae and the others have been around for a long time but were really just niche solutions. It was after these grillings over home ownership and a few law changes in the early 90's that the GSE's became a much bigger player in the broader market. As happens so often, the road to ruin is paved with good intentions.

Ask anyone who knows the history of banking and they will tell you banks have lived off lending people money to buy property for hundreds if not a thousand years. Giving out mortgages backed by property had been the safest and most profitable way for banks to be viable while safe forever. Take deposits from customers and pay them 2% for their passbook savings (the liability) while using those deposits to write thirty-year fixed rate mortgages at 6% (the asset). The house backing the mortgage can be sold if the customer defaults on the loan. Easy peasy and it worked for hundreds of years. It's just like that Christmas movie *It's a Wonderful Life* from 1946. That's where I learned banking, certainly not at college. Can you tell?

The advent of mortgage brokers and the ramp up in the GSE's effectively cut banks off from traditional mortgage lending and the big profit margins associated with it. People can write studies all they want about that not being the case, but those people with their 14 doctorates and 12 master's degrees cannot see the forest through the trees.

Banks had to recover the revenue that was lost as traditional mortgage lending shifted to non banks. Once the GSE's were able to raise unlimited amounts of money at much lower rates than banks, and started doing so, the rates consumers were paying dropped off a cliff and that was not a bad thing. But it did have consequences and those consequences were not understood.

Securitization was becoming much more popular at the same time the banks needed to weasel their way back into a market they were losing a grip on. The advent of CDO's was a natural progression to fill a void – revenue from traditional mortgage lending – by expanding a world (securitization) that was growing anyway. The concept made sense in that context.

By 2004/2005 that market was expanding by leaps and bounds. My limited involvement in the CDO world at that time was rooted in one thing and one thing only. Mistrust. There was information getting back to Treasury and myself that the CDO structurer/marketers at Deutsche were ambiguously leading some customers to believe that Deutsche Bank itself was guaranteeing parts of these CDO's. That was a huge bozo no-no in our world. The last thing we could afford at that point was to see some CDO that Deutsche Bank had guaranteed go belly up and default. That would obviously lead to the "Deutsche Bank defaulted" rumor and we could not afford those issues in the situation we were in. As soon as there is a whiff of a problem, all the customers pull back and before you know it there is a run on the bank. We could not even accept the hint that we were backstopping these products.

Internal groups would regularly request that DB issue a guarantee on these products. DB Treasury always gave a flat NO. NO. NO. So as this information started to get back to us, we (me and Treasury) would try to weasel or sneak into any meeting we could to make sure our views were represented. Trust but verify. That was our motto on that front.

The gentleman in charge of the CDO's was named Greg Lippmann. Let me just say this for the record. I knew of him and sat in a few meetings he was in, but otherwise I did not know him and I'm sure he would not know me from a container of General Tso's chicken. He was not my type of guy. Strutting around the trading floor in slicked back hair and expensive suits, hobnobbing with the bigwigs. Dismissive and arrogant in meetings. That might be unfair of me but it was certainly my take at the time. But let me give credit where credit is due. The guy had the best call of all time and the balls to stand on his desk and scream it out loud. He deserves respect for that.

Starting in 2004 or 2005, I remember reading research reports from his group that were available for both internal and external viewing. Those reports could not have been any clearer on his thoughts about the real estate market at the time, as well as his view on his own products. His group thought real estate was in a bubble and was due for a pullback. He was in a tough spot though, as his job was to structure and sell these things. In my view he did what he had to do. If clients want these products, products that he does not think will work well, he still has to produce them just in case he is wrong. If you make markets in Apple stock and think it's 50% overvalued, you still have to sell it to a customer if they come to you asking for a price. It's your job.

To that point, many of our clients thought he was dead wrong and were happy to take his products off the bank's hands. I remember sitting in a meeting where he told the client he did not think people should be buying this stuff at these prices. This client was another big bank and certainly a serious and sophisticated investor. The response from the customer was an arrogant smile, and "We know what we are doing. You just show us what you have and we will evaluate the economics ourselves." Another example of type A egos duking it out. I chuckled heartily when that bank sued Deutsche Bank years later for CDO's that went belly-up. That was total bullshit if you ask me. That other bank just called it wrong. Own up to it like the adults you are supposed to be. Accountability and principal in banking started a serious decline in the mid 2000's.

The year 2005 brought changes and stresses and our group had never felt so at risk and under fire. As the year came to a close, we were still wondering how this was all going to shake out at Deutsche Bank and what our roles would be. My staff were now openly questioning why I was not an MD yet and I could tell that most felt my lack of promotion was holding back everyone who worked for me. There was no way I would survive two seconds in that atmosphere without saying or doing something so offensive to the type A's that it would just boomerang back to hurt my staff even more. Getting promoted would just make me a bigger target and I said that often. Our desk had another good year in 2005 in spite of the struggling MMD desk. Struggling in that they made money but compared to the expansion of people and revenue in London, we looked like amateurs. So once again when my boss flew back from London after bonus and promotion committees had met, I got this:

> Him: I have good news and bad news.
>
> Me: Hit me. *I knew what was coming next.*
>
> Him: I think I got you guys a little more money but when your name came up for promotion Squinty shot it down, saying, "He is not a team player. I'm not sure why you keep him."

Mission Fucking Accomplished!

I am sure my boss knew what was coming next.

Me: You guys can fire me any time you want if you don't like how I do business.

I will give him credit though; he was intent on rehabbing me and getting me in the fold I did not want to be in. As a matter of fact, it was early 2006 when he told me the bank had hired an "Executive Life Coach" for me.

Me: What the fuck is an Executive Life Coach?

Him: He will polish you in all aspects of being an executive. Public speaking, communication and politics. Mandatory for you.

I did not say no because he told me I could not and he was my boss, right? So what I did was much more childish. I never took this coach's call or called him back. I just pretended he did not exist and after three months he stopped trying. I was never even confronted on it. I bet the dude still got paid a fortune. Good for him. Executive life coach, my ass!

My bonus was $925,000 with my $150,000 salary. Who needs a promotion? Keep me here under the radar and in the trenches. Probably a third of that bonus was payable in Deutsche Bank stock that vested over the next three years. Fine with me. The "fuck you" fund was growing nicely after I paid my taxes and tucked away the balance.

33

Toward the middle of 2005, I decided to get away on a vacation that did not involve showing my ass to a trading floor full of people from a Las Vegas pool web cam. Every August my family usually spent a week at the beach in New Jersey. They were there at least, and I was for the most part although I had to cancel or leave early on a few occasions and spent much of it on my Blackberry with work anyway. But it was always a good time and great to get away. My brother and I both played college hardball so we had talked over the years about going to one of those fantasy major league baseball camps. At that point one of my hips was bone on bone and I was struggling to get around. The dumbest thing I could possibly do was to play baseball for eight hours a day for five days. So of course I agreed to take the trip. Sometimes I think when god passed out brains I thought he said "trains" and I asked for a small set.

Here's the problem. I am a Yankees fan and my brother is a Mets fanatic. Since he is the big brother and refused to be involved with anything Yankees, I had to settle for going to the Mets camp. We booked our trip for January 2006. Three things came out of that trip. It was one of the best weeks of my life and I was a newly minted Mets fan (#2 after the Yanks, that is). I found out "a big guy like you can handle five Advil at a clip." That was advice doled out to me by the

Mets training staff as the week wore on. The third thing that came out of that trip was the total destruction of my hips. Full bone on bone on both sides. The Advil handles the pain but the bone grinding made me queasy then and the thought makes me queasy now. I had no choice but to bite the bullet and get these things fixed. That's when I started checking out surgeons.

By this point the Money Market derivative desk was cut from four people to two. We had one senior trader handling the bulk of it and the junior trader was now elevated and handled whatever long term risk that had to be dealt with. The numbers from a net revenue standpoint were fine. The two of them probably combined for the same $12,000,000 in revenue but we had cut two million in costs the hard way by reducing headcount and associated costs, so after expenses that desk returned to making a decent return on capital. While we downsized to be cost-conscious and reflect reality in that business, London was booming. The wee little man from Toronto who had taken over London was gaining power because his traders in London were knocking the cover off the ball. The London Money Market Derivative desk was probably ten strong and expanding faster than my waistline. Even though our net numbers were good, I was not empire-building so by this time not only was I in Squinty's doghouse but black overcoat boss was becoming less happy. The Gunslinger wanted his mitts on the New York business in a bad way. We had probably gotten four or five resumes of his cronies. Those resumes went from the Gunslinger in London to Squinty to black overcoat guy in New York. I would get a resume left on my desk with instructions to "interview this guy." I was doing a very good job slow-playing my boss. He was like the Tasmanian devil and would blow in and go nuts on a certain subject. For a week at a time I would hear Hire, hire, hire, hire. I'd ignore him and he'd go on to some other subject. The hundred million in revenue that was showing in the derivative world in London was making our twelve million in New York look like ant food. On the cash side we were still growing by leaps and bounds and the $25,000,000 in revenue when I took over in 2000 was probably closer to $100,000,000 but with less costs overall. It was never good enough and the pressure was now building in New York, not only from London but inside New York too.

The mercenaries in London were driving us crazy in New York. Inquiries would come in to our MMD desk in New York from that desk in London that were designed to put us in bad trades for their benefit. Those fuckers were getting paid 10% of their profits so they did not give a rat's ass where their profits came from. If they were able to increase their risk by trading with us and then strong-arm the market their own way, we would end up losing. They kept their 10%. Absolutely stupid incentives. If a trade done with us in NY made London fifty million dollars and cost NY fifty million dollars, they would still get paid five million bucks while the bank loses money after their pay. They also had a gaggle of clients they would trade with, so those clients would do the same thing and end up on our shit list as well. I actually was instructing my derivative traders NOT to do any trades with London or their clients that increased our risk. And this was my own god-damn bank doing this to us. Not only would undermining us make them money but it would increase the chances that Squinty and the Gunslinger would be able to get me out and get their cronies into New York. It was not supposed to work like this. The pressure on both of my desks at that point between the stupid revenue expectations and the funding problems was pulling us apart slowly. It was like water torture.

During that time my boss got himself named as the co-head of foreign exchange and fully in charge of F/X forwards (F/X swaps) in New York. He was moving up at a breakneck pace. The year before he had hired a guy into his Repo world on the same level as me as a marketer and paid him 50% more than I was getting paid. He said Squinty forced it on him.

In general, I did not care what people got paid but somehow the whole group found out about this dude's pay and low morale became lower. I was seen as not fighting for myself, and if I wasn't fighting for myself, then that was probably holding my staff back. My guys knew what was going on deep down, but if I were them I would be questioning my fight also. The fight was bleeding out of me and at Deutsche Bank it was imperative that you fought. It was the culture.

Trying to hold off hiring cronies of the French connection, I reluctantly agreed to hire two graduates from our intern program. I had hoped that I could put my boss off on hiring the two people I was supposed to hire for our new NY proprietary desk. I had no jobs for these two but the management regime at the time was intent on forcing these business program grads into every business so that older, less educated people were forced out during the inevitable number crunching. Who the fuck was in charge of this stuff? Take smart, seasoned, solid people and fire them because they don't have the required pedigree. Bring in overeducated kids who were brainwashed into worrying more about their career path and their neighbor's bonus than doing their jobs. Gee, I wonder how that will work out?

During bonus time, one of these grads who had not done a dang thing but sit and take notes was slated to get a $50,000 bonus when my boss came back from London. Over my dead body. There was no chance I was letting that money get taken from my staff that bled every day on that desk for someone who was in this business less than a year. I stomped and whined until I got my way. That money was sprinkled to my staff. Good. I was not thrilled to have to tell this guy he was getting no bonus, but right is right. You do not get a trophy for showing up on my desk. When the manager in charge of the grad program found out we were planning on giving one of her grads a zero bonus, she had a bird. After standing my ground, she actually took $60,000 from her group budget to give to my grad. Here is the funny part. Not two hours after I gave him his bonus, he asked for a meeting. He actually had the balls to complain to me that one of the guys in his Deutsche grad program in another group was paid $80,000, and why was he shortchanged? My response was two-pronged. I can fire you for discussing compensation because your code of conduct booklet outlaws that. My next comment was that I wanted to pay him nothing at all, and you should've seen the look on his face. A nice kid overall, but they were all brainwashed that they were more valuable than their work was. Call me an old squid but when I started out you worked your ass off and accomplished something before you looked to move up. Your work and your ability to make your boss's life easier, that's how you advanced. Not by flashing your diploma around.

I ended up hiring two people into our newly created proprietary group also. I found a guy that another desk in New York had interviewed previously but did not have the headcount to hire. That group handed his resume to me. The drummer. I called around about the drummer and everyone said he was a solid person with a good history. When I say good history I mean a "clean" history of not blowing up at any previous jobs and walking away, leaving a big loss on a bank's books. That's all I was interested in. I wanted no gunslingers or gunslinger's cronies to make my life miserable. It was already becoming miserable and money does not cure misery. He also agreed to my rule that he not trade any products that my desk was in charge of. He traded government bonds and currencies. He was my only "eat what you kill hire" and he never took a lot of risk or made a lot of money but he fit right in so I was happy. My old boss used to say, "Don't fuck it up" and at that point I was just praying, "Don't blow us up."

The drummer had been around the world and had done everything. He was very cultured, as opposed to myself and most of my desk. The brokers would ask us out for drinks and dinner and we used to never get to dinner. It drove most of them batty. Like normal people they want a few drinks and then to head off to dinner for some good food and wine. We were a bunch of beer drinkers. All food does is kill a good buzz so having a few bar sides dumped on the bar throughout the night was more our speed. The drummer was horrified by our lack of social grace and culture. He vowed to change us. He decided group tastings and educational sessions would be beneficial to us savages. His idea to do this was a surprise out of nowhere. He said he would reserve a conference room after hours in the office and be in charge of the curriculum. The desk was not very happy, but I made attendance mandatory. We can all grow. The first session was "Scotch Whiskey and Bourbon." The drummer dragged a case of different whiskey from his house all the way into the office. I loved his dedication. We all piled into the conference room a little after five o'clock. All seven of us. He had it all laid out. We learned the difference between scotch and bourbon. We sampled all and in their different iterations. There was neat, with water, and with ice. He used a little dropper to put just a few drops of water in to see how much that would change the taste. I'm not sure I learned a damn thing that day but when we stumbled out of the conference room we were all drunk and for some reason I remember our hair being all mussed up and being disheveled. So it must have been fun. A few weeks after that was wine and then we had a session sampling different port wines. We still drank our beer and had no culture but at least we knew where we could find some culture if we ever needed to.

The second addition to the prop desk, unplanned, at least took some pressure off of me for a year. The one-time New York trader who I later went to Singapore to visit was now on the outs in Asia. Once the big Australian took over Asia, it was just a matter of time because these two never saw eye to eye. The big Australian knew we were tight so he told me I had a few months to find a spot for him in New York before he fired him. It was a perfect plug-in to the spot Squinty was harassing us to create in New York. My black overcoat boss and I agreed that since we had sent this guy over to Singapore in the late 1990's with no choice, that the bank owed it him to move him back here to New York for another chance. If we had to let him go, at least he was back where he started and not stuck out in Asia. Fair is fair.

He was not on any type of "eat what you kill" or any other contract. Still, we sat him down and said he had a year to make money and pay for himself trading-wise or find a spot somewhere else. He was happy for that deal. Once again, I was just happy that the person I added I trusted, and I knew he would not put our desk at risk for his selfish gains. At the time many people were signing these contracts and showing up at banks and taking huge risk. It was a win-win for them. If they made a ton of money they would take home a percentage. If they blew up and lost huge sums of money, they get fired and go on to the next bank. Of course more banks would lose rather than win. It was absolutely insane and I wanted no part of it.

It was not long after my boss started to manage the Foreign Exchange group that another ultimatum was thrown my way. I had an inkling it was coming and that I would have no choice. My boss said I was going to take over the rest of his groups in New York for daily management as he was too busy with his new duties. In my perfect world I would be in charge of the cash desk only and could immunize myself from everyone else. Deutsche Bank was not a perfect world. My goal at that point was to fight all I could to stop the region and bank I used to love from being infected any more by the 15% crazy exploiters who were taking over. At this point at least running the group would give me more power in that struggle. The black overcoat guy and I had a long history together since 1995 when we both came in at the beginning. He did not like my ways and I did not like his ways. But I think he respected and trusted me because he knew I just wanted to stay off the radar and do my job. I had no ambition, so was no threat to him. That was a rare occurrence at Deutsche Bank so it added a little value to my presence.

The black overcoat guy did not drink and I never found out why. I'm not nosy. He was so intense and intimidating that I would be scared to see him after a few drinks. Maybe that explains it. His loss was my gain though. Even before I took over the whole group in New York I was defacto in charge of the group's morale. Black overcoat guy did all the politics and managing up for the group. Some of that was to help keep me around so I guess I appreciate that. Since I believed in managing down and taking care of the troops, I took it upon myself to help morale. What is the best morale booster to an old Irish Knucklehead? You guessed it. Booze and tons of group outings to socialize and quell problems before they start. Our traders and our support people were always invited. We would rent a hall (appetizers only of course) and get the troops together. Tracy, thanks as always!

It was at these outings that I perfected my signature move. The pee and flee. I was older than almost everyone else. They could stay out all night and operate the next day, but not me. After the wire closed at 6:30 p.m., it would be a beer sprint until 9 p.m. and then a cab would be waiting to get me home. I soon learned that saying, "I am going home" at 9 p.m. was frowned upon by the youngsters who would abuse me to no end. So I would excuse myself to hit the little generals room and then skulk out to my cab to go home and get some sleep. The pee and flee, my staff called it. Good times. The best part of the whole thing is that when I would hand in my $2,000 to $3,000 expense report that included a list of all the twenty to fifty people from our group and support groups who attended, my boss would thank *me* for doing it. He did not enjoy that stuff so he thanked me for doing something I loved. I thanked him for managing up and dealing with the politics because I hated that. Maybe that's why it worked? I always thought it was funny that he considered that I was sacrificing by doing that. I loved it, loved the people in my group and those who supported my group. We were all friends who were lucky enough to work together.

Back to me taking over the rest of the group. I had pretty much done all the jobs included in my new group, so it made sense. I now had the cash desk, the derivative desk, the Repo desk, commercial paper desk and equity stock-loan desk. Probably twenty-five to thirty people at this point and two hundred to three hundred million in revenue. In reality, the Repo desk I would never really own, and I was fine with that. The black overcoat guy was Repo through and through so he would never let that go. I just was a cheerleader for them while trying to jump in and help all the other groups.

34

OUR YEARLY JAUNT TO LAS Vegas that November was notable for two things. First, it was during that trip that I nailed down a date for surgery to get both my hips replaced. The surgeon I wanted had to be convinced to replace them both at the same time. The usual practice would have been to get one replaced and rehabbed for a year, then start the process over again for the second one. No god-damn way. So I set out to convince him I could handle both at once, was young enough and had enough support at home. It was during that trip he was finally convinced, so a date in January of 2007 was confirmed from the black jack table at the Hard Rock.

I also had a big forward futures trade in Europe that was making my asshole look like the Lincoln tunnel. My boss was not happy. I knew I had this monstrosity of a trade on that was going against me, but I thought I could monitor and manage the risk from Las Vegas just as well as from New York. As usual one of the guys on my desk stayed alone on Friday and got to the Hard Rock Friday night bearing bad news. Overcoat guy had freaked out when he saw my daily loss at the close of business Friday. "You will definitely be hearing from him this weekend. He had steam coming out his ears." Uh-oh.

I got a call to my cell phone from him Saturday morning, which I ignored as usual. I tried not to take his calls, I preferred to have our communication "on the record" so I had him trained to email me. I would get those messages on my Blackberry email and respond immediately so he would stop calling me and just email. He wanted me to get a conference room at the hotel and call him back later and give him a presentation on why he should allow me to continue with this trade. Ughh. Did that stop my drinking and playing black jack? Hell no. I used the hotel's conference center to access my Bloomberg terminal and print out a bunch of charts and also printed out the risk of this trade and all the other relevant information. Then I went back to the table until it was time for my call. I was not that worried. It was not his fault either. He was just doing his due diligence as a manager. I respected it. It was just bad timing on my part. My general rule of thumb on my desk was that I wanted people taking vacations unencumbered so they could relax and enjoy their family, wherever they were. I did not follow my own advice and it's totally on me. I'm probably lucky he gave me a chance to explain the trade to him. As it was, we had our call and I had him pull up the same charts I was looking at and asked him for approval to double the trade. To his credit, by the end of the call he was totally on board. When European markets opened up a few hours after I flew home from Vegas on that Sunday night, I started putting more of the trade on. It took a week or so before it turned, but it was probably the most profitable trade I ever put on. His trust in me and his trading acumen allowed that trade to happen. I vowed I would do a better job managing my time out of the office because I did not enjoy this experience at all. Live and learn.

 It was bonus time for 2006 and New York had a blowout year revenue-wise. Still, London was kicking our ass and my boss heard about it every day. He told us that Squinty was all over him about getting rid of "dead wood" in New York and upgrading our staff to more aggressive and better educated people. Sometimes it was tough to know if the criticism you were getting about yourself or your staff was real or not. Many of those messages were delivered as, "I think your doing a good job but so and so hates you." You always had to wonder if it was real or just a game being played to motivate someone. Either way, I had vowed after letting the two Libor traders and my friend from Singapore go that I was done firing people and was not going to cut into the core of my staff, all of whom were thriving.

The times were strange. We were making great money but it was not good enough. While feeling under fire every day and threatened, we kept making more money. Maybe that was how we were being manipulated? For some reason, the new guy who was now working for me and making 50% more than me on his guarantee was a sore spot for everyone. My staff viewed my not complaining about it as a lack of fight or letting us be abused. Or maybe that is how I perceived their view. It was pretty fucked up at that point, that is all I know for sure. Since I was in charge of all the groups, I now got a peek at the numbers during bonus time. I told black overcoat guy that I had no problem paying someone who worked for me more money than I got paid. As a matter of fact I did it during a few years. I was a manager who traded but I had a few people who were just revenue machines and if their counterparts in London or Frankfurt were making way more than I was, then they deserved it too. I tried to limit my whining because I didn't want any more life coaches or presentations or hobnobbing shoved down my throat. This guy was getting 50% more than I did while not producing a damn thing. Good guy, yes, but he talked to clients all day as a liaison with our sales force. I did not hire him and would not have. As we were going through the numbers I said to black overcoat guy, "You know everyone on the trading floor knows about this guy's contract. What happened to people keeping their mouths shut? What do you think my staff thinks when they hear this and know damn well none of them or me are even sniffing this type of number? Do you have any idea how bad that is for morale?"

Our whole group got a bump higher when black overcoat came back from the revenue/promotion/coffee/paperclip executive committee meetings in London. It helped a bit but things were careening out of control in all ways. We all should have been happier than anything and yet there were so many undercurrents running through Deutsche Bank at that time that no one was happy. I was paid $1,250,000 in bonus, of which roughly 40% was in Deutsche Bank stock that vested over three years. After I gave the government their 40% the rest was quickly added to the "fuck you" fund. It was during this time that my view of that fund changed. Things were so bad that I was now viewing that fund as a personally funded pension plan. If I could get that fund big enough after twenty years in the business, then I could retire like a teacher or a cop and live off the revenue it spits out while I go find something else to do. My guys thought my promotion to MD was a no-brainer that year. I knew it was not to be. It was never even brought up and the paranoid side of me wondered whether Squinty had a plan to drive the people he wanted out so his people, like the Gunslinger, could take over. Good times.

35

WHILE THE ADVENT AND ABUSE of the CDO has had much press regarding its role in the world's financial woes during this time, if you ask me a bigger culprit was the Structured Investment Vehicle (SIV). The SIV was the equivalent of a casino texting a crack addict with a gambling problem the following message. "A casino car will pick you up in fifteen minutes and fly you to our casino and give you as much credit and crack as you want. You just can't tell your spouse." Let me explain.

As we discussed, banks were being slowly cut out of traditional mortgage lending and for that reason they were always looking for ways to get back some of that revenue and market share in new and more complex ways. For the last thousand years banks would lend long and borrow short to make money. Thirty-year loans with houses as collateral funded by very short term demand saving deposits. For multiple reasons, since the 1980's the banks were being cut out of this business. In theory it was a great idea. The government tried to help home ownership by making mortgages cheaper and easier to get. Then the law of unintended consequences takes over.

I won't go into the history of the SIV because I don't know and don't give a crap but I will discuss why they were created and what they morphed into as human nature takes over and loopholes and laws are exploited. SIV's exploded in the mid 2000's as banks and others figured out how to exploit this complex structure to keep their gambling and crack addictions away from their spouses, in a figurative sense.

Many banks and investment banks would just buy certain parts of CDO's or other high yielding mortgage securities right on their balance sheet. But by doing that, they had to report the numbers on the balance sheet, compute all the risk, figure out how to fund those assets and then explain to the board why those assets are on the balance sheet and what purpose they served. That's a lot of work. Wouldn't life be better if we could hire a bunch of lawyers to exploit the rules and laws so we can do all this stuff secretly? And while doing it secretly and raking in all this revenue we can also boost our market share penetration numbers because we can incorporate many products into the scheme? How can a gambling addict resist? It was just too good to be true.

I will explain a simplified bank structure incorporating an SIV. Of course this is the simplified version because I won't be able to understand or explain it any other way. Even this structure was overlaid with many more complexities as exploited laws were then exploited again. It was a rinse and repeat operation. At the time I barely knew any of the details of this stuff. I learned the hard way in 2007 and 2008 as it was all exploding.

A bank creates an SIV, which is fully separate from the bank. They come up with some stupid name that is totally unrelated to the bank's name. They inject cash into this company to make their ownership "look" a certain way and reap the tax consequences (to pay less of course). Then they take a few employees from their bank and transfer them to the SIV. The SIV also uses the bank's infrastructure to operate. The bank then uses its clout with the ratings agency and a very complex structure to weasel out a good credit rating. What ratings agency wants to piss off one of the big banks that fed them deals to rate? Oh, it gets worse.

The SIV then goes to its own bank and buys all the assets the bank doesn't want on its balance sheet. Then the SIV hires the bank to issue commercial paper (for a fee) to fund those assets short term. The SIV also manages its interest rate exposure with its own bank's derivative desk. Oh, and when the ratings agencies get worried about how incestuous this relationship seems, the banks enter into reciprocal business arrangements with other banks to swap business so it seems at arm's length. Then the bank gets the revenue from the SIV in the form of ownership dividends. Let's recap how the bank benefits. Assets they don't want to show are off balance sheet so they can create more of the same. The risk numbers are not on their books. They get revenue and increased market penetration in the commercial paper, derivative and securitization markets for the bank directly. Oh, and they get back the lend long/borrow short revenue in the form of dividends. It's better than traditional mortgage lending, isn't it? It's unlimited crack and credit lines to the addict. What could possibly go wrong?

There were also many shortcuts being taken in this realm. For instance, collateral assurance in the derivative world. In a normal swap (ISDA) contract there are safeguards to protect both parties from abuse. Since a derivative is a bet and sometimes those bets can last ten to thirty years, there are periodic payments built in. For instance, if you and your neighbor have a bet on how many games your team will win over the next ten years and it's $1,000 a game on the difference, you might have the loser deposit the balance every year to your third buddy for safekeeping so the loser did not take off after five years owing you $50,000. Those periodic payments when the balances were big kept people honest and were important. The SIV's hated those payments because they never had a lot of cash on hand and they also did not want to spend the overhead to track them. They always lobbied the banks to deal without those periodic catchups. Since Deutsche Bank was famous for 70 IQ group decisions made by people with 150 IQ's, the bankers and credit department decided many of these SIV ISDA agreements would not be collateralized. I fought hard against the SIV's looking for these types of agreements but was overruled many times. I would tell my swaps traders not to be aggressive on the accounts that did not have the correct agreements. Inevitably the call would come from the Deutsche Bank banker to my trader or to me, saying the SIV is complaining about our prices and we are costing Deutsche Bank other business. The SIV would not buy our assets if we were not more aggressive in our derivative pricing. It went round and round and was the most ridiculous threat leveraging I have ever seen. It could only end one way. The SIV had no risk. It was structured so if it blew up everyone could just walk away, leaving its debtors holding the bag. This was just one example; there were many other structures all exploiting the same weaknesses. Where the fuck were the regulators? I did my part to end the madness.

By the time January 2007 came, I was actually looking forward to getting myself hoisted up on a machine and getting a hip joint cut out and replaced and then being rotated on the spit like a chicken at a Rush concert and doing it all over again on the second hip. That's how bad work was. This was not worth it, no matter how stupid the money is. Cut me, Mick. I went on short term disability and was out of the office until mid-April, when I was rehabbed and could walk without it looking like I had a telephone pole up my ying yang.

Besides getting pissed on at two in the morning – at some creepy rehab center – by a tragic fella with three personalities fighting with each other, my experience getting bionic hips went pretty smoothly. By late April I was back in the office. My first day back, I found a resume on my desk with a note attached. The note said Squinty was sending a guy over from

London to work in our group in New York. "Find a place to put him" was what the note said. This was an escalation. Squinty ran the group globally so it was his right. I thought it was the beginning of a terminal infection. We stuffed the guy on the other side of the floor in the group least involved in our core banking stuff.

Two weeks after the new guy arrived in New York, I got called into a meeting by two very serious people from Human Resources. I didn't know what it was about but I knew I fucked something up. I tried to stay away from HR at all costs. It usually meant someone was being fired. They asked me if I knew that one of my staff had just sued Deutsche Bank. *I only remember sexually harassing the guy next to me but he seemed to enjoy it.* Relax, I'm kidding. It turns out the new guy from London filed suit against Deutsche Bank, or filed an "intention to sue" document, over some obscure pension bull shit. This was now my life. Can't I just go back to being a clerk?

"What does this have to do with me and what should I do?" I asked. They wanted me to be careful around him. I guess it was a good heads-up. Just to be clear, he was an American who worked in London. I had a problem with only the London business culture, not the people. If you put people in a cutthroat culture, even the good ones can get caught up trying to impress people or succeed for their family's sake. That's why we have people supposedly watching over us.

Sometime in May there was some kind of hot shit hot shot executive committee meeting or whatever they were in New York. Thankfully, I was not invited but I was asked to attend the dinner afterwards with about ten people. I will give black overcoat guy a lot of credit. He was a persistent little bugger with his attempts to domesticate and politicize me. So far it was an epic failure but he kept trying. At the dinner, I tried to stay on the outskirts of the conversation and not say anything stupid. By that point, I had decided it was not worth being the sand in the gears. I had tried often to change things and each time I had fallen on my huge foreheaded face. It was getting worse, too, because not only had I lost the big Australian, but the Global Treasurer (the German guy) had either pulled the rip cord or been pushed out earlier in the year. He was replaced by an American who seemed to have zero core banking experience and had spent his career in investment banking. Alone and uneasy.

Back to dinner. I was sitting as far from the table as possible and chugging red wine to make it bearable. Then I got a close up look at Squinty's view of the world. I was horrified but not surprised. By that time clearly his two most valuable staff were the Gunslinger and the wee little man who used to be in Canada. The wee little man had succeeded in taking over the world and the Gunslinger was making more money for the bank and himself than I had ever heard of. To say those two were in stressful positions was a colossal understatement. The wee little man was so stressed he had a heart monitor alarm in his suit pocket that went off if his heart raced over a certain number. Nuts. The Gunslinger was at his desk eighteen hours a day and it seemed like more. Here was Squinty's take on the matter. About the Gunslinger, he said he had to get as much revenue out of him as he could before he dropped dead of obesity. As far as his thoughts on the wee little man, he said he just hoped when his heart gave out he dropped dead at his desk so his insurance payment would be higher. He was probably joking but I did not think it was funny, especially because in typical fashion those two were not even at the dinner. These were two people he liked. I could only imagine what he said about me. I was probably not even worth commenting on.

By mid 2007 it was pretty clear that housing prices for the country had topped out and were starting to retrench. As of yet it was not a big deal to us because we were not experts and it was billed as a healthy retrenchment until prices starting to rise again.

Part of our Repo desk function was to finance the hedge funds that were investing in mortgage backed securities. There was good stuff and bad stuff we used to make loans against. I didn't know the nuances of mortgages then, and I still don't. The hedge funds would buy CDO's and other high-yield instruments, then hand over those securities to us for a loan. They would then use the proceeds of that loan to buy more garbage. Rinse and repeat. It was leverage city.

We had a group that was in charge of topping off our collateral every night. That meant if the price of our counter-party's collateral dropped, that group would make a collateral call and the counter-party would have to true up the value of the loan or else. Or else what, you ask? Or else we would legally be able to seize their collateral and sell it in the open market to recoup our money. It's like the Repo man you see in the movies. You don't make your payment and we take back and sell your car. It really is that simple. At least in theory.

As the housing market indicators declined and we started making collateral calls on these hedge funds, our contact with the obscure support group monitoring this activity went from twice a year to five times daily. Our desk needed to know immediately when we were defaulted on so we could grab "our" collateral and sell it. Just like when the bank forecloses on a house for non payment.

When two Bear Stearns hedge funds went belly up in mid June, this process heated up. Up until then I had heard of only one time in the Repo market, twenty years previously, when collateral was foreclosed on and sold. There were not many of us (including me) who really had a clue. This was black overcoat guy's specialty and expertise so he took over the process of liquidating these securities to recoup our loan proceeds. It was insanely busy for the three of us involved internally, but very oddly ignored by the market as a whole. The market tried to view this as an isolated failure and a mismanagement of securities and leverage by the hedge funds involved. The markets did their best to shrug it off and go on. We kept a close eye on all of our collateral calls because something was amiss but we could not put our finger on it. It was with uneasiness that the markets entered the summer of 2007 and market participants started their well deserved vacations.

36
PANIC OF 2007

I'M SURE IT'S A VARIATION of Murphy's law. Whatever can go wrong will go wrong. And at the worst possible time too. The first two weeks of August are generally the quietest of the year. Even more quiet than the week between Christmas and New Years. The bulk of vacations in the financial markets are taken during these two weeks. What could possibly happen?

It's 5:30 a.m., and I'm on the train into work when an email pops up on my Blackberry. It was from the wee little man describing the funding markets' condition in Europe that morning. The wee little man had sent his update to Squinty. Squinty sends it to black overcoat guy in New York, then he forwards it to all his direct reports, then I forward it to my group with the following note. "And so it begins. Please do not forward." See, shit *and* information both flow downhill. Whenever the markets were shaky, I was careful about what information got passed to anyone. I was a paranoid son of a bitch and had to be. As worried as I was about what information and rumors flowed about Deutsche Bank, I tried to be mindful of never spreading rumors or other information about other banks, lest I inadvertently hurt their funding efforts. It reminds me of the movie, "Fast Times at Ridgemont High." Sean Penn's character calls the teacher a "dick" in the morning and by lunchtime the rumor was being spread that Sean Penn's character stabbed the teacher! That's funny because we all know it's true to life.

That email was the most disturbing work email I ever received. Basically, every funding market was totally shut down. The only market that was working was the government bond Repo market. No F/X swaps. No commercial paper, no unsecured funding, no Repo for mortgage, corporate or equity collateral. This was the beginning of the end. All the crazy complex and non-sensical products were now going to come back and destroy the markets. It was that email that confirmed that every single part of the market was now infected by the housing market, one way or the other.

What I knew immediately was that this was going to be a more dangerous time in the markets than even the 9/11 attacks. During the 9/11 attacks, besides the few groups in London that were more interested in arbitraging us to make a shitty buck, Europe and Asia were there to support us in New York. They were functioning normally, so they could help us through until we stabilized. In this instance, the whole world was frozen. Virtually no funding market was working and there was no counter-party trust at all. By that time it was realized that almost every company in every walk of life was infected somehow. The global tangle of inter-workings of companies was now infected with the housing virus and no one knew where the next shoe would drop so there was no credit trust. Lack of credit trust causes runs on banks. Period. Since that was my main function, my groups all went on high alert. Virtually every part of this 30-35 person group I had just taken over was in distress and I was responsible. Not good. Where is the fucking glue at???

Once I got that email, I would start calling everyone at Deutsche Bank I could get my hands on to get an update on the situation. Since my funding desk had some access to the Federal Reserve Discount window, I was the funder of last resort for the bank. If other groups around the world could not fund on their own, they came to me. We had to call everyone everywhere to get updates on the situations as well as a rough estimate on how much cash we might have to raise in the worst case scenario. My desk were all seasoned pros so they knew the drill and we all just did our thing. It's go time.

There were still other complications which had me reaching for the glue. It was all happening during the least staffed time of the year. August vacation time. That made things much more difficult. Both the market desk and the admin side of the Fed desk were short-staffed. Our calls to those areas were met with a lot of "…I'll track them down and we will call you back." We knew the Federal Reserve market desk could add a lot of cash via the repo market, but that was like putting on a scuba mask in front of a tidal wave.

The other problem I had at Deutsche Bank was the total lack of experience in crisis up and down management levels. The only ally who understood what was now going to happen was the Treasurer in New York, who was always getting cut off at the knees by the investment bank people up the chain. In London, Squinty, the wee little man, and the Gunslinger would be rubbing their hands together figuring out how they could exploit this whole thing to make money. That was a risk to me in many ways. Part of my running around calling anyone who would take my call was education. Senior management needed to be a help instead of a hindrance. I felt like my job had morphed into being the fucking sheriff of a city in the wild, wild west.

For some reason, I remember more about the daily occurrences during the 9/11 attacks than I do during the three weeks of the panic of August 2007. It was instance after instance of having to jump in to make sure things were being done properly from the bank's perspective. You find out who is for real and who are the posers in a situation like that. I already knew my staff were the real deal. They did not disappoint me. Unfortunately, what I came up against at that time showed me in vivid detail that the business had come apart and was not to be rescued. It was not just Deutsche Bank, it was the whole business. Infected. Want some examples? I barely remember the details of any of these, I have just pieced them together lately from other memories. No wonder I blocked some of this shit out.

> * The new Global Treasurer forbid me to speak to the admin side of the Fed. Great, we are in the middle of a crisis and he is worried about his turf. Bravo!

> * Somehow I got thrown into helping with Canada issues. Technically, I wasn't even in their chain. Their whole market was 100% frozen and they had many instances of defaulted commercial paper. Some of that defaulted CP that was owned by Deutsche Bank ended up in customers' accounts. I had to sort that. I didn't even remember at all. About a year later, I got called at home by someone who had a message for me from the lawyers at Deutsche Bank: "After listening to the tapes between you and Toronto, the lawyers said Wall Street's reputation would be much better if more people did business like you." A nice compliment. I didn't remember.

> * As Canada was falling apart, black overcoat guy found out the President of Canada was out of the office and he could not reach him. He tasked me to track him down to make sure he knew what was going on and to get back in the office. The president knew what was going on. He had more important things to worry about. When I got him on his cell phone he told me he was at his six-

year-old's funeral at that very moment, and he would be back in the office in a few days. I was in shock and apologized to him. I could cry thinking about that conversation. I was told later that black overcoat knew and that I was set up to be the bad guy. Can you imagine?

* After a few days of craziness, a massive loss in our derivative book emerged. It was just a left over vacation position but when black overcoat guy found out about it he flipped out and screamed at me in the middle of the trading floor. He threatened both my job and the trader who had the position. The loss was somewhere in the ten-million-dollar area. That's a lot of money for sure but it was less than 5% of my group's revenue so I thought he was being a big pussy about the whole thing. He was scared of having to tell Squinty we had a loss. Fucking ego. Being humiliated in front of the whole group definitely triggered some deep dark feelings from my childhood. Primal feelings.

* We also had one of our derivative clients who owed us a huge receivable default and declare bankruptcy. It was an SIV, a client that the bank decided it did not need to make collateral calls on. So our loss was going to be much higher than it would have been if the bank would have not folded to the client like a cheap card table.

* Since the Fed adding cash through the Repo market was doing absolutely zero to help, they had asked for other ideas to get the cash moving. In daily conference calls that first week I said the same thing every day. Unsecured cash. Term unsecured cash. "Term" just means a loan longer than a day or two. The longer your loan is, the more breathing room you feel you have until you have to pay it back. I was fully on my soap box internally, and externally lobbying the Fed to provide unsecured term liquidity.

* During the second week the Federal Reserve was asking banks to take money from the Discount Window to help stabilize the system. In the past, use of the window was discouraged as a sign of administrative or credit weakness. The Fed was trying to change that by pressing banks to use the window as a source of liquidity. While I totally agreed with that effort, I was worried that if Deutsche Bank did anything unilaterally, it would somehow wind up being misconstrued or used as an excuse to blast us. In banking the key is to NEVER stand away from the herd. Banks that stand away from the herd get shot. Period. So on the 17th of August we argued about it all day. My view was clearly only to borrow from the Fed if five other banks were going with us. Safety in numbers. We could not afford to be singled out. I was overruled. I was angry and worried as my desk borrowed a token hundred million dollars from the Fed Friday afternoon. Management decided to be heroes and to kiss the Fed's ass rather than to be smart.

Since my desk always bore the brunt of stupid decisions made above me, I was worried that if somehow our borrowing from the Fed became public and we were the only ones that borrowed, the bank would be left holding the proverbial bag. I was worried about leaks that whole weekend, especially after management refused to contact the Fed or the other banks directly to make sure we were not alone. Little did I know.

I was worried about mistaken leaks to the press. Haha.

Someone did me one better over the weekend. Someone from Deutsche Bank or the Federal Reserve leaked our borrowing to the financial press and when the article hit Monday morning in Europe that we were the sole borrowers from the Fed, the shit hit the fan and Deutsche stock was down 5% in pre-trading. In addition, some clients were shying away from giving Deutsche Bank cash in London. The road to ruin is paved with good intentions and stupidity. That morning was the closest we had ever come to a run on Deutsche Bank. By the time I got in, I had messages from fifteen brokers/customers/banks demanding clarification and numbers on our health before they would give us money that day. Good times.

I and the New York Treasurer spent the next few days trying to undo the damage. I insisted that we were screwed and told the Fed that the banks should borrow in a group from the window and announce in a group they did it to take the pressure off us. A group show of strength. No unilateral hangings. On Wednesday the banks borrowed from the Discount Window in a group and announced it as a group. My fucking idea from the first day.

I never found out who the assclown was that leaked the Discount Window borrowing to the press. I have my suspects, either someone from the Federal Reserve or two specific people from Deutsche Bank. I bet they are proud of themselves even though they almost caused a run that we had to stop in the trenches of New York. I'm glad I never found out because that person would have been eating through a straw for a while.

I don't remember the exact time in that two-week span or which of these issues broke the camel's back. My wife just remembers me coming home one day in August and saying I needed to resign, and that I could not keep doing this shit. Thank goodness for "fuck you" money. I knew I could never stomach another job in this business either, so it was career change time. My wife thought I was insane for just walking away with a 13-year-old and a 10-year-old. I understood that. I dragged her from financial advisor to financial advisor that September to convince her we could survive if I walked away. We also broke out two separate chunks of money from the "fuck you" fund and finished funding college accounts for the kids.

After she was on board, I decided I would resign the last day of September. If I had to, I would sacrifice my last bonus for 2007. It was that bad.

During September, one of the staff from the Repo desk who lived in my town asked to meet with me privately. Over wine on my deck, he let me know he was entertaining a job offer from a hedge fund. I really think he was hoping I would talk him out of it. Going from a bank to a hedge fund back then was a big move. Bank jobs were viewed as safer. I knew better than that, I knew it was over for the banks. Their greed and stupidity combined with no oversight was a game changer. Since I had already decided to pull the rip cord on Deutsche Bank, how could I be a hypocrite and lie to him? I told him I was not a believer any more and that he should make this move because he was talented enough and young enough to make it. I'm glad he made the move.

Black overcoat guy could not have been more shocked when I pulled the rip cord. I asked if I could come see him in his office the last day of September. I told him I was resigning and all I was asking for was my unvested stock. I earned that stock and was not leaving without it. I refused to give details, only that my decision was irreversible. At first he tried being nice and then it was the guilt. "If you leave now you are screwing me and your guys," he said. When I asked him to explain that, he said it would undercut him and make it look like he had no control over his guys (me). Weird, right? He said if I left with no notice then Squinty would bring one of his or the Gunslinger's cronies in immediately. "Do you want your guys working for them?" he asked. He had me there. My family (staff) working for one of those guys had nightmare written all over it. He told me he would slowly ease Squinty into the notion that I was leaving due to hip problems and starting in November I was to start handing over the reins to the senior guy on each desk. He could not believe I had let him know and had risked my whole 2007 bonus. Most people wait for their bonus and as soon as the check clears, they walk out the door. I could not do that. I needed to feel the relief immediately that I was pulling the rip cord. I would have chewed myself up waiting for a bonus and acting like everything was okay.

We agreed in that meeting I would quietly limp away after he had put a plan for New York together over the next few months. He wanted to let Squinty know I was leaving and provide him with a plan simultaneously so that nothing got forced on him. He also needed to make arrangements for someone to take the Series 24 duties in my place. He said if I did that, he would try to get me some type of bonus for the year, since we had done well. I knew he was going to slow-play me to stay so I made sure a six-month deadline of 3/31/2008 was written in stone.

Holy shit, I was relieved.

I started letting my staff know unofficially by October, so they could start doing whatever they needed to do to plan for my departure. They would all be fine. They were doing all the work and knew all the ropes, so they could easily live without me.

As I was moving things off my plate in December 2007, the Fed announced the creation of the Term Auction Facility, or TAF. This facility would use the Discount Window to auction term cash out to banks. Technically it was secured cash, since a bank had to give collateral to the Fed to borrow against. By that time rules were so relaxed on the collateral a bank could pledge to the Fed that I'm sure you could borrow against a set of hundred-year-old coffee mugs if you could get them over to the Fed. They made it easy. Well done.

I considered the TAF my baby, since it was my lobby from the beginning. So I decided that running that first auction for Deutsche Bank in December would be my last duty. We did not win any money in the auction, but I enjoyed the process and felt proud to be a part.

Now it is time for a reality check on my part. I take no credit for the TAF being enacted by the Fed, and I will tell you why. In Deutsche Bank it was my lobby. Period. It was easy to see from my perspective this facility would be a great help to the markets. However, since every bank has a person doing my job, I am sure they were lobbying the Fed as well for the same thing. I am also sure that staff inside the Federal Reserve were lobbying for this as well. That made fifteen or twenty individual efforts within the banks and the Fed leading to a successful group solution. That is the way the markets are supposed to work. For those people who think the banks were so scared of the Federal Reserve that they never collaborated on solutions, I scoff at you. You will never read about funding desks and Treasury departments working as close as we did with the Federal Reserve in any research report put together by the Fed. That is their bureaucracy. I get it. We treated the market desk at the Federal Reserve as a peer and that is how they treated us and that is why it worked.

Black overcoat guy did me a solid and did not screw me on my last bonus. He made sure Squinty didn't either. That was the risk I took resigning in September. Even if they begged me to stay until March, they could have given me nothing and there was not a damn thing I could do about it. Why waste bonus money on me if I was leaving? The flip side of that is that we had another great year overall, so I felt it was deserved. I got the same as the previous year of $1,350,000, with roughly 1/3 in stock that would vest over three years. Once again, after giving the government its 40%, the rest was tucked away.

Once January of 2008 arrived I had packed it in and was coming in only once or twice a week. I had given up all responsibilities by this point except the series 24 stuff and making sure our back-up trading desk in New Jersey was good to go and fully operational at any time.

They did not think I would really walk out the door. My deadline stood at 3/31/2008. By March my "old" group's revenue for 2008 was already huge. Good for them, but I didn't give a shit. I had no hand in it. I was told by black overcoat guy and his business manager that I was insane for leaving. If you stay, you're a shoe-in for managing director and a multi-million dollar bonus next year, I was told multiple times. I could not get away fast enough.

By March I was deciding how I wanted to spend my last week at work. I wanted no send off parties and none were offered since only my staff knew I was dead set on leaving. A few months after I left we had a small dinner with some of my staff and their spouses. Others above me refused to believe I could pass up the gold. They didn't know me at all. I decided that since I am a drunkard knucklehead who was truly blessed by the people I had met over the years, I would do something to tie it all together.

Every day during my last week at work, my wife drove me to the train station. When the bar next to our building opened at 10 a.m., I was standing outside scratching at the door. I put my credit card down and opened my tab and had given an open invite to everyone I knew in the business to come and have a drink, or just hang out, or not to come at all. It was a great week. So many wonderful people from my past showed up and snaked in and out all week. By 6 p.m. every day, someone would pour me on my train and my wife would pick me up from the station and nurse me into bed until the next day. Rinse and repeat. A fitting end.

I left Deutsche Bank a very happy, very relieved, and very destroyed man.

PART IV
LIBOR

37

Just because I am paranoid does not mean they are not out to get me.

The saying is, "In like a lion, out like a lamb." It started out in a lamb sort of way. My wife is sitting at my daughter's swim meet in early 2013 and her phone buzzes. She digs it out of her pocket and sees a 212 area code, so she lets it go to "missed calls." A few hours later, the same number calls back and my wife answers "Hello?"

"Hello, this is the Deutsche Bank Legal department, we are looking for Matthew Connolly." Interesting... "This is his wife's phone, maybe you want his cell phone number?"... "It's 908-xxx-xxxx." And so it begins, again.

At first I tried to convince myself that maybe it was just a call to sort out my contact information for my pension, or some other innocent reason. After all, I stopped working for Deutsche Bank and pulled the rip cord on the whole fucking business five years before, had no real contact officially since then. But I had a nagging feeling that something else was afoot. I had read a few of the articles in the WSJ and other papers about the Libor debacle, but it moved along like a fucking 2000-square-mile glacier so I had figured the whole affair was over.

From the time the papers had started to run articles on the investigations into Libor from bank to bank in 2010,

I vaguely recollected that one of my traders would have had reason to communicate with our London office on the subject, and I had thought it would have been at my direction. However, that is about all I remembered. From the few occasions some of my old trading desk guys got together, I knew the bank was poring through communications from that time, between 2005 and 2011. Sometime in 2011 or 2012, I found out that the trader who I thought might have had contact with London had left Deutsche Bank, with all of his vested stock and pension accumulations, and I was relieved. In my naive mind, that meant Deutsche did their due diligence, checked correspondence and records, spoke to him and others, and declared him free and clear so he could get what was due him and go on with his life. What a freaking dope I am.

Let me back up a bit. After the articles about the Libor antics (mostly in London) hit the paper in 2010, my former colleagues (on the rare occasion we spoke about work) had told me it had cast a pall over the whole business. At that point they had just started talking to the Deutsche lawyers on the subject. My advice was always the same: tell the truth and let everyone worry about themselves. It's the lying that destroys people, either legally or internally. I knew deep inside we were fighting the shenanigans, not part of the shenanigans.

Sometime in the summer of 2011 when the investigation was in full swing, I got a call on my cell phone from a former colleague. His message was quick and simple. He said, "Deutsche Bank Legal is looking at some of your emails from way back. The legal department is in such disarray right now, they will probably just go away if you don't talk to them." OK, thanks. Goodbye.

The problem was, as usual, I didn't give a crap about anything but making sure all "my people" were okay and not getting raked over the coals for anything I had directed them to do. So I would have been happy to talk to the lawyers at that point if they called, I was just waiting to see what happened to the one guy I was worried about. Once I found out he left (maybe Dec of 2011?) and was free and clear, I thought it was over. It was probably not too long after that he and I had lunch and I apologized and made sure he was okay. Besides a few jibes at London, we kept the conversation to the family. He was running a lot at the time and my daughter was big into cross country, so he suggested he drop a book off at my house for my daughter about "running barefoot" or something like that. The next day, he knocked at my door, I took the book, and he was on his way. So that was it, it was December of 2011 and I thought the whole thing was over, except maybe our London office getting microscoped up their ass and a fine from the government.

OK, now that you are caught up, here we are back in early 2013 and Deutsche Bank now has my correct cell phone number and I have a nagging feeling. A few days later, sometime in the late afternoon, I am looking at some trading charts and sipping on some Evan Williams bourbon (never drink and trade people!) when my phone rings and it's a NY 212 exchange and what looks like a Deutsche number. I pick up the phone and walk into my sunroom and say, "Hello."

> Caller: Hello, I am looking for Matthew Connolly, this is so and so from Deutsche Bank legal department (a professional sounding lady).
>
> Me: This is he, what can I do for you?
>
> Her: Matthew, as you know, we are looking into Libor at Deutsche Bank and we have some of your emails and audio tapes from taped lines we want you to come in to discuss.
>
> Me: But I left the business five years ago, subpoena me if it's that important. (Side note:

I really am a fucking moron, how can a bank subpoena me?)

Her: I know and I apologize. We suggest you come in and talk to us.

Me (in a panic): How many emails and tapes is it?

Her: Less than a handful.

Me (I'll explain this in a second): Was I at least professional sounding?

Her: For the most part.

Me (relieved): Thank you, goodbye.

So... Surprise, surprise, I am not the most politically correct and appropriate person. I speak my mind, I talk plain. I had some epic work battles (mostly with other branches of Deutsche Bank, but also with some of my brokers) over taped lines that I can only imagine how they would sound being listened to or read in the paper. I think it was at that moment that I was coming to grips with the fact that this was not over yet and my compulsive urge to document things might be used for nonsense (translation: to screw me). From the get-go I was never worried about any real legal troubles, my main worries were 1) my guys and 2) How can Deutsche Bank make me look bad to get themselves out of the jam they created.

I was left for another month or so to ponder all the different scenarios going forward. Most of those scenarios ended with me looking like a fool (or worse), but I also tried to convince myself that they (DB) really had no reason to keep contacting me and were just doing their due diligence and dotting i's and crossing t's at the end of their inquiry. Ahhh...the bliss of ignorance.

A month or so later, late afternoon again (I guess late afternoon is when lawyers get hopped up on caffeine and start calling people), my phone rings again at home. I was reading a book and sipping on a bourbon (you starting to see a trend?). I walk into the sunroom with my phone.

Me: Hello?

Her: Hello, Matthew Connolly please?

Me: This is he.

Her: The is so and so from the Legal department of Deutsche Bank (same lady), we spoke a while ago.

Me: I remember.

Her: I'm just calling to let you know that people from the Department of Justice (transfukkinglation: FBI!) just left and they requested your contact information and we provided it.

Me (PANIC!): (Pause)… WHAT THE FUCK DOES THAT MEAN?

Her: It means they may or may not contact you. It could be two days, it could be six months, it could be never.

Her: I suggest you get a lawyer.

Me (getting pissed now): There is no fucking way I am spending one penny of my money on a lawyer for the shenanigans (not a legal term) that Deutsche Bank let go on in London!!

Her: I understand, I just wanted to give you the heads up.

Me: OK, goodbye.

Now looking back on it, the paranoid Matt would not be surprised to find out the DOJ was in Deutsche Bank's office, and instructed them to call and were listening to my response. But that's just me.

Another week goes by, and at this point my mind has filled with more scenarios of me having my nails pulled out on my fingers and toes. I really ain't fooling myself that this is over.

Afternoon, cell phone rings, can you guess what I am doing? fooled ya! I was actually sitting in the office of a driving school setting up my daughter's learning permit, NOT sipping bourbon.

Me: Hello?

Her: This is so and so from Deutsche Bank.

Me: I remember.

Her: We have been discussing it here and if you will take a lawyer Deutsche Bank will pay for it.

Me: Just a moment, please.

Throughout the last week, I have been in a rage. A fucking RAGE! Pissed at the scumbags in the paper, pissed at Deutsche Bank, just pissed. But god damn it, I'd be damn happy to talk to the FBI or anyone else in the Government without a lawyer. I knew the truth. The government was more apt to be interested in the truth than Deutsche Bank, so bring it the Fuck on! However, if Deutsche Bank was paying, and I could go in and get all this anger off my chest, it would be well needed Deutsche Bank therapy! It was the best of all worlds at that point since I really am not that smart, go off half cocked, maybe some advice along with the lawyer therapy would be good.

Me: OK, I accept, what do I need to do.

Her: We will be in touch with a few suggestions.

Me: Thank you, here is my email address, goodbye.

Within the next few days, DB sent me a few resumes of lawyers to pick from, but I really wouldn't know shit either way, so I just let them pick one. Yeah, okay, I am going start reading lawyer's resumes and figure that shit out? I can barely read a menu and all those resumes are full of total bullshit anyway, spare me the time. My bullshit filter is full.

That night, I call the lawyer they suggested. He called me back the following afternoon. He was expecting my call and said he had to leave the country the next week, could we meet in about three weeks. By that time I was chomping at the bit to figure out what the hell was going on, so I pressed him for a sooner time and we agreed that I'd meet him in his office in NY four or five days hence.

The very next day, I am doing my usual thing, get up, check the markets, do a little trading (I probably lost again), work out, take a shower, etc. I decide to take a run to the bank and liquor store (hard to believe right?). I jump in my car, pull out of the driveway and what do you think I see? A black Ford sedan with Virginia plates driving slowly by my house. Can't be... can it? Dude inside is clean cut, wearing a suit, obviously a government guy. No way. Coincidence, right? Down the street he pulls over and lets me pass and I go on my merry way.

I just cannot register that it can be for me. It makes no sense, but at the same time, it is what it is and not that many cars drive down my street. So after a few hours, it leaves my mind.

Fast forward to that night, around 5 p.m.. This time, I am NOT enjoying happy hour. The phone rings and my wife answers it (I only hear her).

> My wife: Hello?
>
> My wife: Yes, it is.
>
> My wife: Just a moment.
>
> My wife (to me with bug eyes!): It's the FBI.

My wife told me later the man calling was very nice and very professional and said he was calling because the Department of Justice was investigating "Matt's colleagues" in London at Deutsche Bank and wanted to ask me some questions. He did a very nice job of putting her at ease, which was greatly appreciated.

>Me: Hello?

>FBI: Hello Matthew, we'd like to ask you some questions about some correspondence you had with your London office regarding Libor.

>Me: I am very anxious to speak to you, but DB recommended I get a lawyer and I just got his name last night and made an appointment for next week. I really think it would be stupid of me to speak to you before I speak to him.

>FBI: Well, don't drag it out or it can become a problem. We are just starting our investigation and want to move forward. It would be a shame if we had to make a visit to your house.

>Me: OK, me or my lawyer will contact your office ASAFP.

>FBI: OK, goodbye.

JUST STARTING THE INVESTIGATION??? How is that possible? It's been three years since this hit the papers. I really am clueless sometimes...

I called my lawyer (who I had not even spoken with yet) and he took the DOJ contact information and said he would call tomorrow in the a.m. to let them know he would re-contact them after he had a chance to speak to me in more detail. The next morning he called me back to say he spoke to someone handling the investigation and they agreed he would contact them back in due time. He mentioned that the woman he spoke to was businesslike and accommodating, not angry. He thought that was a positive sign. I needed a drink!

I found out later that the same very day the FBI showed up at the house of one of "my guys" who lives in the same town as I. I guess they also thought he could help them. Lucky him, they actually knocked on his door and he "had coffee" with them. I am happy he did, maybe I should have done the same in retrospect. I was pretty confused and dumbfounded thinking, like the assclown I am, that the investigation was in its later stages or even over with. I try not to second guess myself too much.

By this time, most of the people who worked for me had extensive consultations with DB Legal department while they were working, so they had not only seen copies or heard tapes of their correspondence, but they probably had a better idea than I what the next steps were and how the process would work. Sometimes ignorance is bliss, sometimes it ain't! I think it was probably worse for the people who used to work in the departments affected because every day they had to go into work and deal with this crap. Not only the DB legal fiasco, but the strange pall of suspicion that most likely was hovering over our trading floor at the time. I was probably lucky to be out of it all and not know what was going on behind the scenes. That being said, I think the fact that I was clear out of all the bullshit for a full five years probably made it tougher for me to try to remember all the crap I was supposed to remember. I am guessing that sitting on the trading floor day after day, seeing their correspondence (from DB Legal) and having a year or so head start may have helped "my guys" remember more than I was able to. I welcomed as many people as possible in my group speaking to the government as I was (and still am) convinced, the more my group talked, the better picture of how we fought against the craziness that was DB London on a daily basis would emerge. I still don't know who besides my one colleague they had spoken to. Selfishly, I hope they spoke to them all. At the same time, I did everything I could to clarify it all to the government so none of "my guys" would HAVE to speak to them. I guess I will find out once I read the government's report that came out a few weeks ago regarding the whole affair who they spoke to, and what the hell was actually going on behind the scenes in London. Since the report came out I have read nothing at all in the press except for the first headline that was emailed to my email inbox from the NY Times under "Headline alert"... But we are not done with the story, not by a long shot.

The next week I met with my lawyer. I drove in and paid the $12 toll and $25 parking. Being the cheap SOB I am, I was pissed that not only was I dragged into this crap, but I had to take the expense of it also? "That's bullshit," I stashed in my memory.

I don't like lawyers. I have had bad experiences with them in general, and in general I think a lot of them stand in the way of economic efficiency, being "glue in the wheels" just to pick up their fees. They say they are protecting their clients and in some circumstances that is certainly true. However, they get paid by the hour so guess what? The more they slow things down, the more they get paid. Where do I sign up for that? It seems the trick as a lawyer is to slow it down as much as you can until people just start to get pissed....then finish the job off.

Anyway... I ended up liking my lawyers. There was a more experienced partner, and a younger junior lawyer. My first session was a three hour Matt bitchathon with my lead lawyer (the partner).

Remember, I had no idea what emails or audiotapes that DB had given the DOJ. Libor was 1% of my life during my eight years running the bank desk and I had only very vague memories of anything.

My first few hours of ranting and raving were pretty

basic. There were a few details regarding how Libor worked that I gleaned from a trip to London in 1996 when I rotated around the DB London bank desk. I remembered thinking that it was a very imprecise index and even at that time there did not seem to be enough bank to bank trading to make it a robust index. The translation of that (in my paranoid mind) is that I needed to be wary of that index considering New York had no Libor setting responsibilities at all.

The next block of time was spent bitching about how regulated NY was compared to London. Not DB NY vs DB London, but I always felt we were much more regulated in NY as opposed to London in general. I spent so much time on "policies and procedures," which is the document we always had updated so if we took a bullet or were hit by a train or dropped dead, the desk could still be run step by step by an outsider (theoretically). In general, London was the wild wild west, and I felt we were the stuffy, formal, outsiders.

Next on the docket in that bitch session was the times we had to fight against what London was doing. For instance, after 9/11/01 when we were staying alive daily by the skin of our teeth from a bank funding perspective, our desk in London and more prominently, our F/X swap desk in London, was arbitraging the shit out of all the markets, making money while transferring all the risk back to our Dollar funding operations in NY.

I was not happy about how making "the quick buck" came before making sure the bank was run safely. I was disgusted. Our desk in London was also in charge of some internal global rate settings. Basically, DB London would set internal Libor settings and those rates were passed to London, NY, Frankfurt and Tokyo. These were internal trades between the DB money markets desk and DB Treasury and the rest of the bank. DB London was the sole decider of those rates. Sometimes NY, Frankfurt and Tokyo were on the same side, sometimes we were on different sides. On those rates, a big move from day to day would be .003 basis points, or say a move from 4.03% to 4.00%. That kind of move could result in gains or losses for the various DB branches running to hundreds of thousands of dollars. The rate London was supposed to set should have mirrored the cash market in London during their morning. There was one morning they moved the setting .017% (17 basis points) when the cash market moved .001% (1 basis point).. That move cost my desk in NY 1.5 million dollars, as I had (obviously) a risk setting opposite theirs. That means they probably made an extra 1 million dollars, and I lost that much or more, and I had NO control. Talk about fucked up. That kind of crap sent me out of my mind. I just wanted smooth and fair and always felt I had to open my mouth and fight for it. It was after that day that we started to send to London our "internal settings risk," so that they knew in no uncertain terms that if they played games and "jammed the rates," they'd be screwing us over, and I would god-damn well be watching. I have no regrets.

It was the same thing with Libor. I had no idea what the hell was going on over there, but I damn well felt that it was ripe for shenanigans, and if I did not act, their shenanigans would end up putting me out of business. So we did the same thing for Libor. But during my bitch session I had no idea I had documented that exact thing: Me getting them to post the right rate. Take it from me, I spent 18 hours a day ducking punches from the markets as well as my own bank, so Libor was very low on my radar in a typical day at DB.

Once my first session was over, my lawyer said he would mull it all over, educate himself, and get back to me. Just a side example of what a clueless dope I am: throughout the process, my lawyers kept talking about this guy, Paul Weiss. "We need to see Paul Weiss," "Paul Weiss has to get the documents together"..."Let's talk to Paul Weiss"... "I'll call Paul Weiss"..."Paul Weiss says the documents will be ready tomorrow." I thought this fucking lawyer Paul Weiss must have been the hardest working dude in NY. He was involved in everything. I was thoroughly embarrassed when the name of the law office that we visited to see the documents and listen to the audio tapes that DB gave the DOJ was named "Paul, Weiss & Whateverthefuck".. It was the whole firm's name! Clueless me.

The next week we visited Mr. Paul Weiss (see above) to see what emails and audiotapes DB gave the government to talk to me about. My lawyer and I go into a conference room and a junior lawyer from Paul Fucking Weiss is running around with three-ring notebooks and fiddling with an iPad to get the audiotapes lined up. If my memory serves, there were two short email streams and two audiotapes. I'm not sure I remember exactly but I think we listened to the audiotapes first so we could release the junior lawyer and have some privacy. The junior lawyer from Paul Fucking Weiss (sorry, it's still just too funny) left the room and we got down to business.

The first tape is of me and a clerk from another department discussing a bookkeeping issue they had. They would have to plug every day's Libor setting into their system to calculate their own "profit & loss" for the day. We would send the official day's settings via email to that group and then they would input them into their system. It was a 100% clerical call in nature and could not possibly have anything to do with the Libor investigation. My first thought was: what a stupid shitshow this whole thing is. What a waste of time. NEXT!!...

The second tape was a bit more interesting but I could not remember for the life of me what it was about. I knew damn well though that it was not about Libor because I don't think I would ever have occasion to talk about Libor settings with the guy who ran all of London, who was on the same level as my boss from NY. He was a friend of mine, he worked for me for a while when I was overseeing our Toronto office, then he went on to a big job in London running the whole branch for our division. The wee little man. The call started out with him calling me, "Captain fatass," which was a salutation of love between us. He told me a story about a strip truck that pulled up outside their office. A strip truck is an advertising tool in London where a strip club hires a truck with windows and a few strippers dance inside the truck in plain view of all passersby. Sounds like brilliant advertising to me. Anyway, fun stuff but nothing to do with Libor. At the end of the tape he says, "Just keep that thing we talked about on the call in confidence," and I said (on the tape) that I would. After I listened, I had no idea what we were talking about and still this day I'm not 100% sure. However, the conference call he was talking about was attended by probably 30 people in our group every Monday and I don't ever remember talking about Libor on those conference calls anyway. All those calls were listened to by 30 people so nothing could or would be a secret anyway. In addition, they were all taped. So I'd assume DB would go back and just listen to the conference call. So we get through the audiotapes and I'm wondering what the fuck am I doing here? What a joke. On to the emails we go!

 I chuckled to myself when I read the first email. It was classic Matt. Passive-aggressively calling someone out. I could tell by the wording that I was pissed and trying to prove a point. It was all about protecting ourselves, that I know. I had sent an email with the positions (Libor risk) of one of the hot shit big shot traders who was in an unrelated group in NY, but traded some of the same products, to the head trader of my equivalent group in London. They were short, curt emails back and forth two or three times. The last mail was a reply from London that they would "go in neutral." Neutral means not skewed, and that was all I wanted. THE RIGHT RATE. *Mission accomplished.* I still felt pretty good as the wording was vague and professional and definitely within the parameters of what I was supposed to be doing as far as communicating with London.

The last email was just a general email to London with basic and vague details of our Libor risk positions in the next few weeks, so it took all of eight seconds to discuss that with my lawyer and be done with Mr Paul Weiss for the day!

38

As I thought about the audiotapes and emails over the next few days, trying to piece my memories together so I could tell the government everything I knew, I vaguely remembered the "neutral" email being tied to one of the very few conversations I had regarding Libor with my colleague in London. He had told me cryptically, "We set the rate where the bank will make the most money." Since NY was small fries compared to London, and also many times on the opposite side of London position wise, this was disturbing news. Since we executed trades with London daily, this would put us on opposite sides of the risk spectrum, especially for the Libor fixings. So if London skewed their settings (which they had led me to believe was SOP in 1996), MY desk was always going to be on the wrong end of the spectrum. This was not good, not acceptable, and if I could not fight back from a position of economic strength, I could at least make them squirm a little bit if they were going to "screw us again." But still, at this point it was not all pieced together in my brain.

Regardless, I felt much more at ease now that there was nothing controversial or inappropriate or unprofessional besides being called "Captain fatass," which was true so it did not bother me a bit.

As far as my overall feelings about Libor, I really wanted those fucks in London (not just DB London, but in general) to pay for the misery their shenanigans plied on me over the years. I did not want everyone to get screwed, but those who I was reading about in the papers who were doing all the crazy shit and trying to "fix" the markets and collude with other banks. I wanted them to fry and anything I could remember to help with that process the government was welcome to. So I was anxious to get this over and unload all I knew on the government.

At this point, probably 2-3 weeks had passed since the FBI call. I instructed my lawyer to call and set something up as soon as possible to get this over with. We briefly discussed the conditions that I would speak to them under, and I was confused. Conditions? What conditions? I'm just gonna go tell them the truth ASAFP, why conditions? He said to me: "Listen Matt, don't be stupid. Regardless of the circumstances, if we can get you protection, it's stupid not to do it." Being a dumb, thick bastard, I still did not get it. He was talking about a proffer agreement, sometimes known as "queen for a day." Theoretically, this agreement infers that the government will not use anything you talk about directly in your interview against you in a proceeding. However, if you lie to them or something you say leads them to your guilt in another arena, all bets are off and they can come after you.

It took me about 2 seconds to say "Yeah, whatever, fine"... let's just go get this done.

He called me back a few days later and he said that his call was basic, the government agreed to the proffer agreement and we would all set something up soon. He also told me that the FCA (Financial Conduct Authority) from the UK wanted to listen in on the interview. My immediate reaction was the more the merrier, let's roll. I will say, I am thankful for my two lawyers. They were very good about taking a step back, slowing me down, and explaining the pros and cons of every decision I wanted to make. So okay, two good lawyers out of the twenty that had wasted my time and money over the years in bullshit matters. I certainly did not have to let the FCA listen in, but it was theoretically possible (he explained) that they could subpoena their way in to me one way or the other. Once again, why bother fighting, invite them to listen in. He mentioned that they could not tape the interview or write notes on my answers. What did I care...I guess the US government was not supposed to tape my interview either... but again, who cares? In addition, my lawyer told me the CFTC (Commodities Futures Trading Commission) and a few other entities wanted to be there. Jeez, some party this was turning out to be.

We met one or two other times in NY at my lawyer's office before the interview to go over whatever updates my lawyers could find about other peoples' interactions with the government. We also went over the strategy. To my two lawyers' ultimate credit in my eyes, there was no coaching at all. All they said was that I should stick to the facts, do not guess unless I asked the interviewer if they wanted me to guess...etc, etc. So just little tips to have everything in the interview crystal clear. My lawyers were very much on board with me getting shit off of my chest and just telling my story. I very much appreciated that because I left DB damaged and needed to have my say and good or bad, I was not going to be denied. I think they realized that and to their credit, just let me go.

So it's time to blast off and light this candle. I was always taught in the business from the beginning of my career that if your name is in the paper or investigators speak to you, you have failed. So in my mind I really struggled with what I could have done differently to avoid this, and what it all means to how I should view how I did my job, which I was still pretty sure was something to be proud of. Walking into an interview with a big group of investigators, regulators and random people looking to second guess me in some office really was one of my worst nightmares come true.

TEETH (332) MARKS

The Interview: Embarrassed, then confused, then angry

I will set the stage and go into the highlights of my interview. When it was all said and done my interview was seven or so hours, not including breaks. The transcript my lawyer produced was 69 pages. There was no official written record, but my lawyer as well as one of the FBI agents had a computer in front of them and were typing as fast as they god-damn could for seven hours to get an accurate picture of the day's festivities. I never got to see the FBI notes, but I went over mine the next week to fill in names and go over details with my lawyers for full accuracy. I am hoping I can get a copy from my lawyer to attach to this so if you need to fall asleep one night you can read the boring details. Otherwise, I will summarize here:

We met at 7 a.m. at the lawyer's office in mid-town. We hopped on a subway (they paid the fare) and headed downtown. Before you get worried about my lawyer's cash flow, I'm sure they expensed that ride back to DB plus every other thing (as they do). We were heading to lower Manhattan to a block of federal government buildings. I'm not sure where exactly, but I think it was an anti-trust department building in the complex. We went through security (I was wanded separately when my metal hips set the alarm off), and we grabbed an elevator. We were ushered into a dingy reception area/waiting room. We were the only ones there, and were told "they" were just getting ready. A few people wandered in and out and in 15 minutes "they" were ready for us (ME!!!). I spent the time waiting checking the markets on the Bloomberg app on my phone. I was ready, anxious but not nervous.

We (my two lawyers and me) were shown into a conference room, and I was startled by the number of people from the government. We introduced ourselves, they gave us their cards, and the people on the open conference call line were vaguely introduced ("Financial Conduct Authority is on the line") etc, etc. Not individuals on the call, institutions. There had to be 15 people in the room from the government, plus who the hell knows how many on the open line. My first thought was, "What a waste, I don't think they will be happy when this is a dud." That really was my first thought. I just wanted to make them happy and I did not need any more enemies. As best as I can tell their lineup was:

> 2 FBI people
>
> 4 anti-trust prosecutors/lawyers
>
> 3 or so from the Commodities Futures Trading Commission (CFTC)
>
> 4/5 various others from god knows where
>
> plus FCA in London and whoever the fuck else hacked in to the conference call.

A big crowd. Each person had loose leaf notebooks filled with papers in front of them. Filled with papers. They all seemed professional and cordial, no one was smacking a wrench into their fists while glaring at me. I considered that a good start.

The Government started with the basic ground rules, which I already knew, and they also let us know which one or two lawyers would be responsible for the main interview. Others could speak up with questions as we went along. I had thought the people from London were supposed to just listen in and not speak but maybe I was wrong about that. Who cares?

The first three or so hours was just basic information, starting with my family information and what I was doing now, then moving on to my whole career starting in 1987. Where I worked, what I did, who I worked with. I worked at JPM for 8 years, then DB for 13 years, did a bunch of different jobs. This took a long time. They wanted every job description, every person in my group at the time, what my responsibilities were, etc. I found myself running in circles in my mind because I had never gone through it before and had to really think about who I worked with, in depth. They also asked about why people left, where they went, and how I moved up the ladder.

When that was done we talked in basic terms about my time specifically at DB. Not only details about the groups I worked in that were in NY, but every person I could remember in London, Frankfurt, Singapore etc., even Toronto (for a few years I oversaw the Toronto office of our division). That maybe took an hour or so. I really am a shitty networker, I spent most of my time avoiding DB snake pits, so I don't think I had a very thorough knowledge of who worked where. Then the questions started about my compliance training at DB. Was I trained about Libor settings (hell no!, we had no Libor in NY at all), was I trained in how to speak to my other branches at DB (are you kidding me? hahahah), was I trained in that, did DB compliance guide me in this? What were the policies on my desk regarding communications with the people I was managing and other people. Then we had a discussion on "policy" vs "guidelines." I tried to explain that a policy was formal, a guideline was informal. For instance, external chat rooms were the norm at work after 2002, almost every group at every bank used them. I did not allow my group to use them, and we never did up until I left. However, it was a desk guideline, not a policy. Since most groups used chatrooms, I was not about to make it a policy within my group that would create discipline if broken. The guideline was: Have all correspondence in writing or on tape, and be able to defend it. No chat rooms, no work texts, no un-taped lines. For Christ's sake, I would not even pick up work cell phone calls, even with my boss, because I wanted a written record and so I responded immediately to all emails on my Blackberry, but very rarely picked up my cell phone for anyone. When I did not answer my phone, I'd usually get an email from that person and I usually responded immediately. It was like training a dog sometimes: Call Matt, no answer, email Matt, immediate response. So I got many more emails than calls on my cell phone and I wanted it that way. Paranoid? Your god-damn right.

Then we got to the fun stuff... the audiotape and the emails.

<u>Embarrassed</u>

They played the audiotape of the guy who used to be in Toronto who now ran London. It was only a minute or so long. I must have turned bright freakin' red when he started the call with "Hey Captain fatass, how are you?" After the tape played, the young woman prosecutor looks at me and says, "Just for the record, I don't think you have a fat ass." So I got that going for me! (apparently). I don't really think I laughed but there was a chuckle across the room. In general, I thought the environment was pretty cordial. There was definitely some fighting between the people from the US government in NY and the people from the UK government on the conference call. A few times the main interviewer cut off other people who were saying stupid shit. I had a lot to get off my chest about how lax the compliance and regulations were in London, how in general I thought the London business environment was rife for corruption and shenanigans. Let's just say I don't think I won any friends in the UK government that day. The truth is the truth. Certainly most of everything I said was borne out from some of the stuff we have found out since my interview. Collusion between the London banks as well as other shit they were pulling over on the rest of us who were just trying to make money keeping to ourselves. I definitely felt more victimized than anything else. But who cares, right? That's life.

Anyway, I guess they were looking to see if any of the vague language the London head used was regarding Libor. He had said, "Just keep what we talked about on the conference call confidential." I very much doubted it was, because I don't remember talking about Libor on the weekly risk conference calls. But it was probably a six-year-old tape at the time and I didn't remember any of the tapes or emails. They asked me to guess what it was in reference to and I said it was probably some type of personnel issue or a credit issue of one of our clients. If there was a personnel shift going on at the time, and someone was being moved and did not know about it yet, we would want to keep that quiet. If it was a credit worthiness issue with one of our clients, we would want to keep that quiet also so we did not get accused of spreading rumors about our clients. Those were my guesses but after six years, how the hell was I supposed to know?

The first email they showed me and asked me to explain was the email where I gave them another trader in NY's (not in my group) risk position as far as resets go. I gave them my explanation that I was told on the one Libor conversation I had with London (on a taped line), that they set Libor where the bank makes the most money. I did not know squat about how they set Libor, but I knew that NY was dead in the water and screwed if that's what was happening. So getting someone from NY with much bigger positions than my desk in NY was a good way to get them to not screw us. At the end of this email chain, which was short and had about three back and forths, London agreed to set the rate neutral. In my mind, I just FORCED them into setting the RIGHT rate and if I did not send the email they would have screwed us and set it their way. For me, this result was the best case scenario. They would never set it our way, but maybe if we let them know in a passive-aggressive way that we were "watching," they would just set the REAL rate. This email chain from 2005 become the precedent for NY's strategy to let them know our positions so we would not be victimized. It was all done on recorded emails and taped lines and I wanted it that way because I would have been thrilled if our compliance department was doing their jobs and called London on the carpet for their settings. That never happened because our compliance department was a big lie. They would say in the yearly refresh meetings that all work correspondence is monitored. That turned out to be a lie. It was saved to be searched later (six years in this case), but never monitored. During this question and answer, the government never gave me any idea either way whether they believed me or not. This was strictly a one way conversation. They asked the questions, I told the truth.

There were also one or two basic one line emails (that were never responded to) that were shown to me but there was not much to say about them. They were all explained by how I described sending our settings risk over to London, since they were in charge of the setting process. So I thought we were winding up since they had asked me about all the audios and emails that DB told me they handed over to the government. I was wrong and it got weird.

Confused

The lady interviewing me then got a little smile on her face and pulled out another sheet of paper and slid it over to me across the conference table. I think it was from the summer of 2007 when the financial crisis started. It was the same as the others, one line, just basic position information that I sent over to London regarding setting risk that a trader on my desk had for the next day. The only thing I thought was strange is that DB did not show me this email when we went and visited Paul Fucking Weiss. So I was a little confused, but explained it in the same vein as the other couple of emails between 2005 and 2008. Then the fun really started although I had no idea what was going on until the day after the interview.

The next email was an email from a trader involved, to me (on the same day) saying "we agreed with BAC to project Libor at 53 for tomorrow." Again, first time seeing this email (from 2007) until today (2013). They asked me to explain. The truth was easy! "BAC" was our internal accountant group, they did our position administration and also produced reports to our management regarding how much money we made or lost. BAC stood for Business Area Controlling. Our accountants. This email was strictly internal and totally useless regarding the investigation. Why the fuck would this be here?

> Her next question regarding this email: "Do you trust XX (the trader involved, the same one the FBI saw the same day they passed by my house)?"
>
> Me: (confused): I'd trust him with my life, he's an ex-marine and totally trustworthy.
>
> Side note: I found out later he was an Army Ranger, but I'd still trust the guy with my life.

At this point, I was totally flummoxed. I had no idea what was going on.

She slides another email over the conference table. This email is London's reply to me from my email from the previous day with our setting risk. The reply is coming from a Junior trader on London's desk. The reply says: "It looks like Libor is coming in at 53." His email was sent at roughly 6 a.m. NY time or 11 a.m. London time, right about when the settings are being posted officially. Okay? I'm thinking why the fuck does this matter? He's telling me where the setting came out.

The next email she slides is my reply and it says: "You're the man, James!"

Then about an hour later I let him know that we got out of the remaining setting risk we had for the next week. None of this shit is ground breaking. I'm still confused, I have no idea what they are getting at. They keep peppering me with questions that I keep giving them the same answer to. I just don't see what is happening here but I am really trying to remember the situation if I can to help the government get to the truth. There was just nothing behind these emails but the government would not let up and I kept looking at them like a cartoon guy with the bubble coming out of his brain conveying his thoughts...??????????... It was then my lawyer called a break. At this point it must have been seven hours in (we had a shitty government cafeteria lunch that may have been a stale bagel and a soda that my lawyers probably paid for) so it would have been 3 or 4 p.m.. We retired to a side conference room and it was just me and my two lawyers. The main lawyer shuts the door, turns bright red, looks at me and yells: "I AM SICK AND TIRED OF YOU SITTING THERE TRYING TO ANSWER EVERY GODDAMN QUESTION WITH THAT BLANK LOOK ON YOUR FACE." Holy crap!... This really snapped me out of it. He softened: "Just do the best you can and let's get out of here." He said I was doing more than anyone could ask and that it made no sense sitting there forever when it was obvious I had no idea what was happening. We then made our way back to the conference room. I have no idea how all the government people could not have heard him screaming at me. Funny now, not so funny then.

So I'm sure the fine people from the government were at the end of their ropes as much as we were. It seemed like this was winding up. There may have been a few more questions, I don't really remember in detail. The interviewer ended with a little spiel about how if I remember anything more I should contact them, that this was not the end of the conversation. She also threw in a little comment that paraphrased as, "If you lied to us, you are at risk and we still have a lot of people to talk to." As we were ending and people were thanking me for coming in to talk to them, the FBI agent that called my house introduced himself. He seemed like a nice guy and I thanked him for putting my wife at ease. Then the conference call line with London crackled..."Uh, excuse us."

TEETH (340) MARKS

<u>Anger</u>

We all stopped and said, "Yes?"..

> London: "It seems to us that for all your comments about having a bad relationship with London, that you guys were pretty tight."

What a bunch of overeducated idiots. I was furious immediately and maybe they just wanted to lash out at me since I was not so favorable to the London side of our businesses.

The funny thing is, out of the audiotape and the three or four emails, what they were talking about was the head of London calling me "Captain fatass" as well as me telling a very junior trader in London he was "the man." To this day I will bet that DB and the government missed a taped conversation early that morning where the junior trader "guessed" to me that day that Libor would come in at 53. So when it came in at 53, I'd be a good mentor and say "You're the man" to the Junior guy. The truth is I really liked the Junior guy and was fine with my counterpart in London and especially the guy in charge of London. My problem was the lies that always accompanied a conversation with London. So the only three I chose to speak to and could deal with out of twenty people were these guys. And there was not a lot of trust but that was just business.

Anyway, I was furious. What kind of morons would try to categorize 10 years of emails and daily conversations with one audiotape and three or four emails? There were probably 10,000 emails and 5,000 conversations regarding hundreds of subjects between me and London between 1998 and 2008.

My final words of the day: "You can't categorize a ten-year relationship in a few emails and an audiotape."

Man, I wished I had the set of peaches to really say what

was on my mind. That was my only regret of that whole god-damn interview.

We left the building, my lawyers told me to go home, have about nine big bourbons, relax, and we would touch base in a few days. Sounded good to me. God I was relieved, they told me it went very well. I answered every question they asked, answered honestly too, and there was nothing at all legally troubling to me or anyone else in NY that we spoke about or they showed us.

Just to be clear, because I know what you are thinking. I LOVE LONDON and the UK. I really do. I made two or three trips there and it's a wonderful place with wonderful people. My problem is with a small sampling of financial people who were the snake pit of those markets. In the Money Market and F/X arena, I thought throughout my career that those businesses in London were corrupt. Not just DB London, but London center for those markets. It's hard to argue with me after reading all the stories in the paper, before or since my interview. I also think that the disgusting corrupt market in NY and the US is the equity market. You will see things in the next few years (investigations, etc.) that I bet will bare this out. It's not the people in London or NY, it's the environment and I will stick to that generality because it's been proven right so far.

Two days and 20 bourbons later, it hit me like a ton of bricks. The government took three separate conversations regarding the same subject and tried to create something that was not there. I want to believe they wanted to try and shake me up so that if I knew any more or was hiding something, I'd give up the ghost and tell them. I think that is a valid strategy on their part, just to make sure they are getting the full truth and that people are not holding back on them. If that was the case, Bravo. There was nothing to shake up because I told them what little I knew, but I can respect that.

TEETH (342) MARKS

If they really believed the line of shit they were selling, I'd be disappointed. That would mean they truly were pretty inept at investigations and their jobs, and I really don't want to believe that.

My theory on that last email chain is the following. I think the fact that DB provided that last email chain to the government but withheld it from Paul Fucking Weiss (so it was never shown to me before my interview) means something. I bet they told DB not to show me those emails so they could try to ambush me, without me having time to come up with an explanation. DB has to cooperate with the government, right? So they just do what they are told and I never get to see them. I respect that strategy if they are looking to shake me up. I get it. However...

The email that referenced "BAC" (our accountants) was patently unimportant and I explained why to them. I was too dumb to understand at the time that they were trying to figure out if "BAC" meant Bank Of America Corp, whose stock symbol is BAC. So, in retrospect, they were trying to find out if we were referencing Bank of America when my trader said "BAC projected Libor at 53 tomorrow"... The thing is... for my whole career, Bank of America is "BOA", not "BAC".. Get it? Money Market traders are simple. BOA is BOA and BAC is Business Area Controllers. So NO, we were not speaking to Bank of America. I didn't know anyone on the Bank of America desk and I'm guessing my trader did not either. That's probably why they asked if I trusted him. Nuts man, nuts.

I also think that when I told the junior guy in London that he "was the man," that maybe they thought we had some big secret deal and he was running around changing rates on my behalf. Poppyfuckencock. Not happenin'. I'm guessing at that stage in his career he had no firepower at all so it was even more unlikely. But one of my favorite sayings when people are lying is: Never let the truth stand in the way of a good story. It was truly scary in retrospect that people can take a few emails and piece them together to create whatever little story they want. I will never forget that lesson, even though I have zero regrets on the whole episode. Flawed strategy? maybe. Pure intent? Absolutely.

I still have not read the report from the government. It came out three weeks ago and besides the first headline I have not read anything other than DB was fined 2.5BB dollars. The fine amount shocked me because from what I saw at DB, versus what we read about other banks when the government released their reports on them, I honestly thought it would be more isolated at DB. Apparently I can be incredibly naïve. I can't wait to read the report to confirm how absolutely stupid I am. Without any inside knowledge, I just assumed the DB settlement took so long because the bank was fighting the fine lower because there was not too much happening other than the two shit-for-brains we read about in the paper for Euro and Yen currency Libors.

To wrap it up, just a little anecdote on how sheltered (stupid) I can be. I was under the impression that I would go in, give my interview, and the government would cross check and speak to everyone else at DB about my story. Then I figured I'd get the all clear or some comment from them. Turns out the government don't say shit, nuthin', zilch in that circumstance. My lawyers said to go live my life, chances are I'd never hear back. They made a cryptic comment to each other that, "For various reasons, I'd probably never hear back and they would probably cease the NY inquiry." I guessed that if they got nowhere with me but thought I was lying, they would talk to all of the guys working for me to catch me in a lie so they could go after me. Conversely, if they thought I'd told the truth, it would make no sense to talk to anyone else. After all, the more people in NY that swore we were trying to do the right thing, the LESS likely the government could use our emails and audiotapes to get a massive fine out of DB. So I'm anxious to know at this point if they talked to anyone else in NY or if they dead-ended us because that will probably be all I get. I have no doubt that any email I wrote or anything I said would be used against DB. Regardless of the truth or intent, if the government can show an email to DB that "looks" bad, they can easily get DB to tinkle in their pants and pay a bigger fine. Standard procedure, who am I to judge? I guess when I read the report from the government I can cross check what they put in the report versus my thoughts.

Stay tuned!

39

Between my interview with the government in 2013 and the release of the report on Deutsche Bank in April 2015, my original lawyer had taken a permanent leave of absence to fight cancer. Sadly, he passed away soon thereafter. The junior lawyer at that firm had reached out a few times with basic updates, but when he left that firm for another one I was fine giving up any representation. I had no need for it, as it had been two years since I had heard anything from the government.

Or so I thought. In September of 2015, I got a call from my junior lawyer who said the government had reached out to his old firm to "talk about Matt Connolly," but since I was not represented no one could talk to them on my behalf. I told him that if I needed to re-up with a lawyer, I would want him to speak on my behalf. He knew my case and I was not worried. So he sent me the paperwork and I signed my representation over to him at his new firm. In the few days that process took, by the time he returned the government's call they said they did not need to talk about me any more. I thought that was a bit strange but was just happy not to be involved. I had speculated that maybe they wanted me to testify against someone at Deutsche Bank. That I did not need. So I was happy to stick my head back in the sand.

I did decide it was time to read the government report

from a few months earlier to see what could have attributed to the $2.5 billion fine levied against Deutsche Bank. So one night I poured myself a brown belt and loaded up the DOJ report as well as the CFTC report to see what all the hubbub was about.

As I started perusing the report, what struck me first was how scattered all the information was. It was tough to keep track of the story. Oh, there were plenty of terrible sounding snippets, that's for sure, but it was not put together solidly so it was tough to follow. I needed to pour another one so I could really concentrate on reading this. In the reports no names are used; they are replaced by monikers. My moniker was Manager-2. There was a "Submitter" moniker, as well as "Trader," "Senior Manager," and so on and so forth. So I was stuck trying to decipher who was who. I think I was able to piece together about half during that first reading.

When I finished reading the two roughly forty-page reports I was very happy and proud. All I cared about was New York's role, and specifically my desk. We were barely mentioned compared to the other major centers at Deutsche Bank. In addition, the report was clear that our communication with the Libor rate setters in London was encouraged and consistent with bank policy during those times. That is why they started moving the cash traders closer to the derivative traders in London and other places starting in 2004. I also saw three or four things I mentioned in my interview where I could not remember the specific details. It sure would have been nice if they had tried to refresh my memory beforehand instead of ambushing me. Whatever.

I saw examples of London soliciting our positions from us. I saw examples of traders in London "lobbying" the Libor submitters to skew the rate against us in NY and others. Insane. What a clusterfuck that place was.

The only worrisome thing I saw was what happened after I left the trading desk in March of 2008. It seems that those fuckers could not even wait until my body was cold before they started the London invasion of New York. My main swaps trader in NY, the XX guy, ended up reporting to the Gunslinger immediately after I stopped managing him. That would have happened over my dead body, and apparently it did. When I left in 2008 my interest in Deutsche Bank stopped cold. I was scarred by it all so did not track what changed after I departed. I talked to the guys as much as possible, that bond would never end, but I had no interest in details, only their well-being and when we could meet for drinks. Surprised?

I was bummed at what happened after I left but I was damn proud of my effort to fight for my staff in New York and the lengths I went to in order to be above-board. After reading the reports I felt great about our role while being a bit worried about XX guy and what happened after I left. I had no control over that. I also thought I did a pretty damn good job in my interview, allowing the government to put the vague picture together when they added all their other interviews and documents to the mix.

Less than a month later it was announced that the manager in London in charge of the Libor settings pleaded guilty to manipulating the rate from 2003 to 2011. I was not unhappy. I did not think he was a bad guy but I still was holding a grudge at the energy I was forced to expend to stay out of their shenanigans. They made a choice and were paid immensely for that choice, according to the papers. I made the opposite choice and it forced me out of the business I used to love and cost me millions in the process. Complaints, none. Grudges, you god-damn better believe it.

My lawyer called me to let me know that the dude in London pled guilty and he seemed a bit worried. I was not. After the London guy's plea, he agreed to cooperate with the government to prosecute others. My lawyer was worried about what damage the guy could do to me. I didn't think he could do any damage if he told the truth. He was my counterpart in the funding department but I always ring-fenced myself as much as possible from London and others. I did not know how the system worked but still believed in the truth over everything else, so I hung up after that call not having a worry in the world.

For the next few months things were pretty quiet and I thought again it was probably over, at least for me. I had come to the conclusion that the government reaching out to my lawyer in September was probably to see if I would answer questions about the guy who ended up pleading guilty. I figured him pleading would mean they would have no further need for me and I was relieved.

Both my kids were in college at the time and we had not had a "go-away" vacation in a few years, so in February we decided to book a family trip to Cancun for the end of May of 2016. We figured the kids could use relax and unwind time at the end of their school year. We were really pumped up to get away for that trip. The drinking age in Cancun is eighteen so it meant we could all have a few drinks together (legally this time) at the resort during that week.

It came out of nowhere. The call I'll never forget. I'm in my bedroom changing out of my golf clothes and my cell phone rings. I have the still picture in my mind. Standing half naked (gross, I know) watching my lawyer's name pop up on my phone. I accepted the call and put the phone up to my ear thinking I'd be receiving another generic update. Wrong again! I could tell immediately something was wrong. It was April 28th. He said he had very bad news. I still was not getting it. He had received a call out of the blue from the government and they informed him my status was now "Trending towards Target." A phrase I had never heard.

> Me: What the fuck does that mean?
>
> My lawyer: It means this is the start of a long process, three months to three years.

Since I still did not get it, he tried to explain further.

> My lawyer: It means they want to charge you with a crime.

I still have no fucking idea what a trending target versus a target is. Typical stupid mumbo fucking jumbo. Talk about shocked. I had never been more shocked in my life. I could not comprehend what possible crime I could have committed. After I told my wife, who immediately went into self defense denial mode, we went over the whole thing to try to figure it out. There was no explanation. Even my lawyer was shocked. He had said my name had not come up in the investigation in 2 ½ years. Sleepless night number one commenced.

The next day my lawyer called again and said he was turning my case over to the best trial defense lawyers in his firm. He relayed that this team was the best in New York and the "real deal." I never thought I'd need a trial lawyer, that's for god-damn sure. I was introduced to my new team the next day over the phone and they said they would get to work. They had to come up to speed and then contact the government to try to see what this was all about. I had to take my old lawyer's word this new team would be able to sort it all. I think my old lawyer felt bad. It seemed abnormal that something like this would just come out of the blue three years after running in there and fully cooperating. Maybe they had made a big mistake?

To say there were many undercurrents in this whole affair would be an understatement akin to saying that 9/11/2001 was just another Tuesday. Many governments involved. Everyone hates Deutsche Bank. People hiding in countries where they can't be touched. Political pressures and agendas. Even articles on how Deutsche people involved in the Libor cases are dying mysteriously. So the theories of what was happening behind the scenes are absolutely endless and impossible to figure out.

I guess during this "trending to target" phase a few things can happen. Your lawyer can meet with the government to see what is happening and try to gauge the case they may have against you. Then you can negotiate for immunity in exchange for cooperation, negotiate a plea deal, or go underground and hope you never get indicted and charged. Option number two, negotiate a plea deal, was not fucking happening and I made that clear from the start. No fucking way. I was alone and it was totally up to me because my lawyers were not up to speed and the government was not forthcoming on information. To boot, this had to be shit from nine or ten years ago that I still barely remembered. *A fucked up situation you got yourself into, Mrs. Connolly.* Agreed.

The other problem I was going to be bumping up against is that there were rumblings that Deutsche Bank was not going to be paying any more legal bills. If not, that would throw a huge monkey wrench into the plans. The Federal legal system is totally fucked up. The government's main strategy is to bleed people to death so that even innocent people have to plead guilty because fighting is so expensive. But maybe it's all a mistake and I won't be charged, right?

Sitting in limbo for the next month was the worst of the whole thing. Telling my kids, who were both away at college, was not fun. They both were amazing, as I had no doubt they would be. At least I knew I was a pretty good parent because I helped turn out two well grounded kids who were fast becoming adults. There was not much to do during that time, just sitting in limbo not knowing a god-damn thing with every terrible possibility going through my mind. I was getting about two hours of sleep a night and otherwise just pacing and bleeding off nervous energy. My new lawyer was saying this could last up to six months just sitting in limbo before more information was received. Well thank the good lord I have my trip to Cancun with my family to look forward to in late May. That will be a welcome piece of heaven, spending a week alone with my wife and kids.

When I asked my old lawyer if I could still take the trip to Cancun I had already paid for, he said absolutely yes. I was not charged with anything, it's not like the government would be sitting at the border waiting for me. I was relieved, I needed that god-damn trip. I decided when I met with my new team of lawyers the first time in early May that I would run it by them also.

In my first call with my new lawyer I asked him what I could do to prepare for this, what to do while I am in limbo. I told him I hated people blowing smoke up my ass and that I just wanted straight talk. He did not disappoint me. He told me to take my passport and the deed to my house and have it ready by the front door. When I asked him why, he said that if the FBI comes to your front door at 6 a.m. to arrest you (as apparently they like to do), you will have your passport, which they will confiscate, and you will have your deed, which we can use to post bail to get you out of jail sooner. I asked for it straight and appreciated the candor, as much as it really put things strikingly in reality. He said he hoped it would not come to that, but that I had asked what to do to prepare. Since I am generally a good instruction follower, I had my deed and passport in a box by the front door the next morning. What a good boy I am.

The next week I dragged my sleep-deprived ass into New York to meet my defense team. The meeting for the most part was a rehash of the same information I gave the government in my seven-hour interview with some new details that emerged when the DOJ and CFTC reports refreshed my memory. It was good for them to get some added color on some of the reports and the interview transcript provided by my old lawyer. I was still so surprised by the whole thing and openly wondered in the meeting how I could even be indicted, much less charged. As I learned in that meeting, the government can indict pretty much anyone they want, including a dirty sweat sock if they so choose. That ain't comforting! The government figures out their strategy and then puts up for indictment who they choose to. Not how I thought the system worked at all. I was learning the hard way.

As the meeting was ending I asked if I could still take my trip to Cancun. After all, this could still be a mistake or a scare tactic, right? My lawyer gave it to me straight, just like I asked him to. He said by all means take my trip to Cancun. That is, if you want to be arrested in front of your family at the airport and spend forty-eight hours in jail while they formalize the indictment against you. Holy crap, seriously? Seriously. That's some crazy shit right there. Okay, I guess my trip is off. I immediately dreaded having to break that news to my family. Bummer. So I cancelled my trip and was able to get about half my money back. My family took it like the troopers they are. Not a word was said. Love 'em.

The waiting and the speculating continued. Hey, you know that fifteen pounds I was trying to lose? It came off like melting butter in that month. I was so upset I could barely even drink. That's the real crime, I tell you. The one thing that went through my head is that the government could not make me wait that long. After all, I had left the business nine years ago. The statute of limitations was supposed to be five years but I knew the government could exploit loopholes in certain laws to extend that to ten years. Those laws are on the books to prosecute banks themselves, but the government has 1,000 lawyers looking to exploit every crack to accomplish their agenda and prosecute individuals. Tiring but reality. Whatever was going to happen, the sooner the better.

<u>40</u>

THE CALL CAME ON THE afternoon of June 1, 2016. It was my lawyer. He said that the government reached out to him and said they would allow me to surrender myself the next day at 8 a.m. in Manhattan. If I did not show up, they would come and get me. Rude. When I asked what the charges were, he said no more information was relayed. We agreed to meet in the park by the FBI building the next morning. He told me to make sure I brought my passport and the deed to my house. The bail, he said, would most likely be $500,000. That's a lot of my "fuck you" money! His final pieces of advice were to wear shoes with no laces and a tie that easily can be taken off and retied. No laces and no ties because they would prefer to suck the life out of you slowly, rather than have you commit suicide under their care. That is extra paperwork after all. He also told me if they sit me in the "box" between my processing and arraignment just be cool and keep to myself and I'd probably be fine. The box (apparently) is a big jail cell where all the arrested people wait until the court gets to them. I wonder if I can smuggle some glue in for the day? Sounds like a fun day, don't it? He ended the call by saying with any luck we should be on the way home by noon or 1 p.m..

June 2, 2016 – My world changes forever

In the morning, when I put on my suit it did not fit. In

a good way this time. I had not worn a suit in years; they were all too big. If I had to take my belt off my pants would drop to my ankles like a rock off a rooftop. That would not be good for anyone. I had no choice so I put on a suit that I was swimming in and one of my ten-year-old yellowing dress shirts. I don't really clean up well. A couple of the tassels were missing off my shoes with no laces. I was a prize. I kissed my wife and hoofed it into the city to meet up with my lawyer.

There was not a lot of talk while we sat on a bench waiting for 8 a.m.. My brain was fried and blank from the last month. We walked over to the front of the building where the FBI was located and my lawyer called to tell them we were downstairs. What a weird feeling waiting for them to come and get me. My kickass lawyer was not sure they would let him up, but he said he would try to spend every second he could with me throughout the day. I appreciated that. He was not sure how the day would progress. All surrenders are different depending on the circumstances, he said.

They came down and out to meet us. There was an agent from Washington, DC who was in charge of my surrender. There was also a New York agent. We shook hands and they led me in the building to pass the security checkpoint. Without a word, my kickass lawyer barreled in behind me. I gathered my phone and cash clip and belt on the conveyer as instructed. While walking through the metal detector feverishly holding my pants up around my waist, I waited for the inevitable. Beep! Beep! Beep!... There it is. My hips setting off all the alarms. Luckily it was only a five-minute search and wanding from a hand-held detector. During those five minutes my mind flashed back to the first flight I took after I got my hips replaced. It was 2007 and I was traveling with my family. My surgeon issued me a bright green card that identified me as a hip implant recipient. I flashed that god-damn card as I was told to, thinking it would get me the keys to the kingdom. Instead, the TSA agent smirked at me. "That card doesn't mean anything. Anyone can get one of those cards and try to smuggle a gun on a plane. I'm going to have to pull you to the side and do a manual search." I hadn't thought of that but of course he was right. Before I knew it I was stripped down to my tee shirt with my pants pulled down. All in public, and with my wife and kids laughing at my travails. Yup, everything's funny until someone gets an eye poked out. Bastards. Thank goodness I had briefs on and not tightie whities. I was also old enough at that point to worry about leaky pee blotches but when I checked I was dry as a bone. Thank god for small miracles. I threw the green card in the garbage after that but we had a great vacation. Where was I?

So I struggle through Security with my escorts and we head up to the FBI offices, my lawyer still in tow. They sat us in a room that looked like a combination of a doctor's office and a sitting room. Padded bench seats and medical equipment. They told me this would just be the initial processing. I took my tie off and stuffed it in my jacket pocket for later. Name, height, weight, eye color, surrender of passport (I think), family members, where they live, identifying scars, properties we own, cars we own, etc. After playing a thousand questions, they took a DNA test, fingerprints and a few pictures. It took about an hour. The agents were very professional. I appreciated that. Next they would escort me across the street to the courthouse for the next step which would be either pre-trial services or to see the US Marshal service. Pre-trial services is basically a parole office that makes sure you make it to the trial as healthy as you can be. As we were about to get up to go my lawyer said, "No cuffs, right? He can just walk over." The DC agent said, "We are all civilized, there is not reason to cuff him for the walk." I appreciated that. The walk over is usually the perp walk you see on TV. I could do without the perp walk in cuffs right now, thank you very much.

The walk over was uneventful. Just four guys taking a

stroll. The agents actually took a different route than expected and we ended up going through an auxiliary entrance so there was no hoopla. Thankful. With minimal obstacles at the security station, we checked in our cell phones and the agents decided pre-trial services would be the first stop. As the NY agent left, I thanked him for treating me so well. The DC agent would be my escort for the rest of the day. He dropped me off at pre-trial services with my lawyer still in tow. The agent left me in their custody and said he would wait outside for us. I was assigned an officer and we sat down in an office and answered the same questions all over again. Plus another bunch of questions on prescriptions, details of financials, medical conditions. The works. I found out later pre-trial services provides all the information to the judge so your judge knows how much bail a person can afford, as well as other pertinent information for your wait before trial. They also took a few pictures of my ugly mug. I'm sure I broke many government cameras that day. Their fingerprint machine was not working, so they said I could come back later in the day for that. That process took about another hour so it was around 11 a.m. by now. I still had no idea what I was being charged with and no one had said a word. We pick up my FBI agent escort and head over to see the US Marshals.

The Marshals were a bit busy so we waited a half an hour while my lawyer and the DC agent chatted. My lawyer was a trooper, still marching me around. Man, I was thankful to have him there. He very easily could have left until the arraignment to get work done but he held my hand throughout. They took his phone at the courthouse too, so he was truly detached. Alone, I was brought into the inner Marshal sanctum by an officer. He instructed me to put my hands behind my back as we walked. This guy looked like he could rip my heart out by flicking a finger so I just said, "Yes, sir." These guys are serious dudes. It was about a thirty-foot walk to an office and there were other officers milling around. They all looked like badasses. My officer was very professional, not an extra word said. He sat me in this dingy office with my hands still snugly behind my back. I looked around this "office" as he was getting his papers ready, and I noticed a few disturbing things. Firstly, the floor was done in a heavy duty tile that ran a foot or two right up the wall. Strange. Then I noticed dark maroonish/brown smudges on different places in the "office." Do you think that was what I thought it was? I was not giving anyone any reason to create a Matt smudge on that tile. I was quiet as a mouse. Have I told you what badasses these guys are?

Officer ready with his pen, time for the thousand questions. I still had my hands behind my back after I sat and it was a little uncomfortable. Not a word from my mouth. After I answered the first twenty questions like the scared little bitch I was, he told me I could put my hands in front of me. I thanked him. Then he looked at me and asked, "Do you know what your charged with?" I answered, "No, sir, I have not been told anything." He grunted, looked at me and said, "Wire fraud." Okay. Then the next batch of questions and another picture and more fingerprints.

The Marshal's questions were all geared to one thing. Finding my ass in a hurry if I skipped bail or disappeared. Do we have a dog? What do my hip scars look like? Where do all my family live? I do not want those guys on my trail, that's for god-damn sure. I was very uncomfortable. Not physically. I can't explain it fully but you just know when you are in the presence of people who will hurt you and then go have a meatball sub. I was impressed. He led me back out to my agent and my lawyer.

After finding out the fingerprint machine would not be fixed until later in pre-trial services, I was worried I might get stuffed into the "box." The holding cell where arrestees wait until they are arraigned. My lawyer's previous words kept playing in my head, "Keep your head down and keep to yourself and you will probably be fine." It was then that the DC agent said that he was taking me into his personal custody to wait until court and we would wait in the cafeteria. I coulda kissed the guy. What a human thing to do. The three of us headed to the cafeteria to bunker in. The agent went off and sat alone and my lawyer and I grabbed a bite to eat and got a table by ourselves. I knew I must have been indicted but the indictment was under seal still so none of us had a clue what was happening. The agent said when the indictment was unsealed he would let us see a copy on his phone and then get a hard copy sent up for us to read. Time clicked by second by second. We still had no idea who, what, when, or where, as far as my charges. It was probably 12:30 p.m. now and we still did not have a time or a judge for my arraignment. I know my lawyer had a lot of work to do and was hoping to be out by now but he was so patient. I thought we bonded that day.

An hour or so later the indictment was unsealed and the agent let my lawyer peruse it on his phone while he had a hard copy sent up to us. After he was done I got to scroll through it too. My brain is still stuck on seeing these words: *The United States vs. Matthew Connolly*. That was the name of the case. Words cannot explain the emotions of seeing those words. Let's have a moment of silence.

OK, back to the regularly scheduled program. I read the rest of the indictment. I had no idea. It might as well have been written in Chinese for all I understood of the legal stuff. I recognized some of my emails, though. I was surprised to see the man charged with me as a co-conspirator was a UK National who I never met and never corresponded with or did trades with. I knew who he was, but a total stranger otherwise. Weird.

A little while after that, a time and courtroom were set for arraignment. 3 p.m. I believe. At 2:30, I went into the men's room and put my tie back on and tried to clean myself up for court. We made our way to the court room in the building, can't be late. Judges don't like that. I thanked the FBI agent from DC as he released me outside the court room. I was thankful for his humanity and professionalism. As I sat on a bench by the court room door I had no idea what to expect. I just hoped it would go fast. I was starting to drag ass and wanted to get home to my family. Fifteen minutes before the assigned time, the prosecution team shows up. About six of them. Mostly young and spry. A few shook my hand, a few would not look at me. Par for the course. Everyone has a job to do. I figured there were at least another hundred lawyers working on this case against me behind the scenes. A hundred government lawyers versus little ole me. David versus Goliath.

As we shuffled into the court room a few minutes later, my first thought was that it was smaller than I expected. The judge appeared and my lawyer waived our right to have the indictment read out in court. Why bother, mumbo jumbo and filler. Let's get the hell out of here. She asked how I plea and we stand and my lawyer says, "Not guilty." Then we talk about bail. Bail was agreed at $500,000 and secured by my property deed. I guess a lot of these financial cases are about a lot more money because the judge seemed surprised that I only had one house. I guess multiple pieces of property are the norm. I'm too lazy. I don't even want to take care of my one house. So a lien was placed against my house and bail was agreed. Until the trial my travel was restricted to New Jersey and Manhattan. My lawyer tried to fight for the whole USA but the judge shot him down. For some reason the guy from the UK was not present and they talked about it taking a year to extradite him to the US from the UK if he fought it. The judge set the next court date for three months hence to see where we were in the process.

She also instructed the prosecution team to hand over the discovery documents. The judge noted that my charges were from nine years ago and she instructed the government to make sure no games were played in the discovery process. Discovery is a set of documents and files the government uses to put their case together on you. Theoretically, at least, a defendant is supposed to have access to every single thing the prosecution team has. It's supposed to make it more fair for people to defend themselves. Their team handed over a binder and a flash drive with all that. See ya in three months, court dismissed.

Before I could leave we had to go get my bail processed and go back to pre-trial services to finish my prints. I wanted to get it over with, I had no interest coming back into the city unless I had to. While I waited in some obscure office full of people waiting for my bail to be processed, my lawyer left me to get his phone and go outside to check-in with his office. What a strange hour that was. Behind me, the youngsters in the prosecution team sat, also waiting for some documents they needed. These were the people trying to put me in jail. They actually seemed like a nice and professional bunch. Civilized. The more senior prosecutors were not there. Jury out on them, so to speak.

My lawyer came back in and pulled me aside. He said that a bunch of articles had been released in the press as the indictment was unsealed. Ah, the media games start. Reporters were asking him for comment, as he expected. He asked me what I wanted him to say and I left it totally up to him. At that point, he knew me for only two weeks and barely knew my case. I did not want to put him in a bad light by having him say something he was not comfortable with yet. If it were up to me, my response would have been a big fucking drawing of my middle finger. Alas, old habits die hard. He went back outside to get his phone and respond. I continued to wait.

Right as he came back, my documents were ready so we grabbed them and I hustled off to pre-trial services to see about getting my fingerprints scanned so I could leave. My lawyer waited for me outside so he could retrieve his phone and keep monitoring the press stuff. All I ever wanted to do is stay off the radar and here is where I found myself. They say a cat will always find and cozy up to the person that does not like cats. I now understand.

It was after 5 p.m. when I pulled in to pre-trial services. The good news was the scanner was fixed, the bad news was that the operator had left at five. Shit outta luck. I told my officer I would schedule a time to come back in whenever it was convenient for her to get that done. She also gave me the instructions on my weekly "pre-trial supervision reports" that I would submit over the Internet every Tuesday. Basically they just need to know you are alive and functioning and if you have had any more run-ins with the police. I also asked if I could go to the US Open golf tourney in Pittsburgh in three weeks that I had already planned. She said I would have to get permission from the judge and my lawyers would have to submit the paperwork for the approval. Got it. Okay, get me the fuck out of this place.

I handed in my chip and got my phone and money clip back. I found my lawyer on the sidewalk on the phone. After he ended his call, he asked my how I was doing and if I was cool to get myself home. "I'm fine," I said. We agreed to talk the next day when things settled down. We separated and I started my walk to the ferry as I fired my phone back up.

As I was walking, I realized that I had gotten away that day with no perp walk and no pictures of me that would be flashed in the papers. I have always held the view that the fewer pictures of me and my nasty mug in the world is a good thing. I have this big bump on my head that looks like a second head growing out. My kids long ago named it, "Kenny." I did not need any pictures in the paper and neither did "Kenny." That was the positive I pulled out of the day.

I called my wife to let her know everything was fine and

I was on my way to the ferry to come home. She said a ton of articles were out but no pictures. Good, Kenny was still anonymous. She told me she loved me and was proud of me, and then I got on the ferry.

As I found my seat, I looked at my phone and saw that my emails and texts were going nuts. I had a bunch of emails and texts from people I used to work with who had seen the news and wanted to wish me well, offer their support, and vent their anger about the process. That really helped my morale. Word sure does travel fast in the financial community.

On my drive home I briefly checked in with my wife, who had readied a big dinner and a pint glass of Jim Beam. She knows me so well. After I decompressed I would have to let my extended family know what was going on so it was not a surprise. Most of them knew I had an interview with my good friends at the government three years before, but we had all thought it was over and passed.

It was June so my kids were home from college for the summer. When I came in the door they were all waiting and gave me big bear hugs. Even the dog's tail was wagging. They all had their iPads and computers out on the table and started to name off the web sites that my articles had appeared in. Forbes, Wall Street Journal, Financial Times, even the New York Post for God's sake. My Dad would be so proud. He used to bring the New York Post home from New York every day and all eight kids used to read it. My favorite headline was when the guy escaped from the mental institution and molested a woman and then fled the country. The headline was "Nut screws and bolts." Coming up with that headline? Talent. Pure talent. My comment as I took a huge gulp of brown nectar was, "I am more famous than Kim Kardashian." The kids liked that. I will have humor to the bitter end. Get used to it.

At dinner I was peppered with questions about the day. What a blur it was. I was unbelievably relieved. Can you believe that? Uncertainty is always worse than reality. I was ready to fight.

I sent an email to my family that night alerting them to their now infamous brother. I got nothing but love and support back. I needed that. A few of my siblings immediately started digging on my lawyer to make sure I was represented well. They all gave their seal of approval after they researched. That was funny. My good friend Jim Beam was also very helpful that night and I slept sixteen hours. I was ready to start this fight the next day.

41

I SPENT HE NEXT WEEK DECOMPRESSING and reaching out to my friends and consoling people. I could not have been more energized by the response I got from people. It was then that I realized how much people dislike the government and how little trust they have in "public servants."

One of my big concerns was my legal bills. I'd rather go to jail than bankrupt my family paying legal bills. But there was no way in hell I was pleading guilty to a crime I did not commit. I was an officer of Deutsche Bank New York, which gave DB no choice legally but to cover my bills. However, the bank was not in great shape and there were rumblings that they were going to try to renege. I did not trust them and had it in my mind we would end up suing them. No one needed that hassle so I asked my lawyer to get assurance the bank would fulfill their obligations. While waiting for word, we came up with a plan B and I had my own plan C. Plan B was a bare bones defense that I would begrudgingly pay for myself. Plan C was to blow the whole fucking process up and turn it into a circus by defending myself. Fuck everyone. Sorry, I digress. So we waited.

A week later my lawyer called me as I was playing golf and told me that the guy (XX) who used to work for me in New York had secretly pled guilty ten days before. That was certainly not a surprise to us. My lawyer had an inkling that was already happening the first time we had spoken. That's the way it works. When I got home and read his guilty plea I actually laughed. I was not laughing at XX. I felt sorry for him. He is a good guy who allowed himself to be caught up in DB's craziness. I laughed at the details of the guilty plea versus the facts as I knew them. I guess it really is true what they say about the government. They never let the facts stand in the way of their story. Ah, games and manipulation. Just like I am back at Deutsche Bank.

That night I got to thinking. Thinking about the timing of it all. Chills ran up my spine when it hit me. I booked my trip to Cancun in February. The government alerts me I was "trending to target" in late April. Of course they have access to flight manifests and know I had planned on taking a family trip. They set up a secret plea deal with the guy who used to work for me on the day I am leaving for my trip. Holy shit! I don't believe in coincidences. They were looking to get free press by sensationalizing my arrest and having me spend two days in jail! How fucking creepy is that? That is just my opinion but you can do that math yourself.

Here is some more math you can do. XX worked at DB until 2012, four years after I left. My body wasn't even cold yet when his reporting line changed to the Gunslinger in London and he got promoted to Managing Director and made himself rich. The facts are the facts and the government damn well knows this.

Well, let's look at the bright side. At least I got out of this with no pictures in the papers. Not so fast, kimosabee. I was expecting to not have to attend my court date in September. Most times for these dates, it's optional for the defendant to attend. In August I got a call from my lawyer that the government was adding another of the same type of charge to my indictment. It's called a superseding indictment. I don't really care. Until he tells me that the judge is going to make me come in for the court date to plead not guilty.

Ah, I immediately know what's happening. They want my picture! OK, so Kenny will get his picture in the papers after all. The good news is that I got two of my suits taken in so I don't have to wear my belt around my manboobs to keep my pants up. Always a silver lining. By that time we still have no assurance from Deutsche Bank and their financial condition is precarious. I really need an answer from them. I have very few skills in general but I can damn sure look at a balance sheet and figure out whether a bank is solvent or not and how its liquidity and finances look. I was not worried about DB from that perspective. They had plenty of cash and although I thought the weakness in the stock price was warranted, the credit quality for senior debt and creditors looked pretty solid. After all, I was now a creditor.

My next court date was not until late September, not much to do until then besides play some golf and keep checking in with pre-trial services every Tuesday. My family and I were starting to simmer down and get back into a groove as my court date approached. One Saturday in early September, a FedEx delivery guy rang our doorbell. I thought, wow, my wife is getting her shopping mojo back and ordering Christmas presents for the kids already. Excellent. Two envelopes arrived and I signed for them. Don't look like presents to me, I wonder what this is? Surprise, Surprise. A letter for my wife and me from Charles Schwab & Co. That is where most of my "fuck you" money resided, sitting in nice, safe bond investments which we were trying to live off. Apparently they could shut our account at any time and were giving us thirty days to either liquidate our account or move it somewhere else. If we did nothing after thirty days, they threatened to liquidate it themselves and send us a check. Wow, this was quite a blow. I guess I could understand a place not letting me open a new account, but shutting down a quiet, existing account for no reason? That's fucked up. I thought we believed innocent until proven guilty in this country. That's what my Mom always told me. Panic and anxiety now set in. I called Schwab & Co. and they told me the decision was irreversible. No options. So I started calling around to see if I could open a new account somewhere for the transfer, but that was not happening. So I had to come up with a plan B.

I had an investment account with Merrill Lynch/Bank of America. It had a bond fund sitting in it that I had bought six years previously, as well as my kids' college accounts. I had opened it up as I was leaving Deutsche Bank and the advisor was someone I knew from our town. I figured a good plan B was calling him and transferring this quiet bond portfolio to my existing account. No problem, right? Problem. When I called and asked he gave me the bad news. He told me he was sorry but that a week or two earlier he had gotten notice from Merrill that they were shutting my account down. He tried but he could not get the order reversed. They liquidated my bond fund on their own and sent me a check. They also sent me paperwork to fill out to close my kids' college 529 accounts that were still in use. I told him there was no fucking way I was filling out that paperwork to shut down accounts I don't want shut down. They do what they have to do but I'm not making life easy for them. I may even have thrown in, "and if they are taping this call and listening, you guys can GO FUCK YOURSELF!" That felt good but probably did me no favors with them. Apparently they could not liquidate those 529's without paperwork, which I was not providing. About a month later my advisor called me back with good news. He said his compliance department had agreed that if I took my name off the 529 accounts and just had it in my wife's name, that the accounts would be unaffected. That was a huge relief. The last thing I needed were the tax problems associated with the closing of those accounts before they were used for college expenses. They sent me the paperwork and I filled the forms out and sent it back. All good, right? Not so fast. A week later I signed in online and checked the balances for the kids' college accounts. Zero. I thought it was either a mistake or that the accounts were in transition from my name to my wife's. I'm paranoid so I called him to make sure. He said he was very sorry but that Merrill had unilaterally liquidated the accounts and was sending me checks. I was furious. Furious. Those un-American pricks had used my signatures on those forms to find a loophole and close my kid's accounts. He swore that was not the case but I told him I was going to find out and cause a huge legal problem if so. You can do the math. What do you think happened? I know what I think happened. Zero principle.

So leading up to my court date in September, we had a few balls in the air. Since I could not open any new accounts we would just use the fall-back of our Chase checking and savings accounts to dump our "fuck you" money in until all this got sorted out. The court date was pretty much as expected. No pictures on the way in so I was happy. My lawyer and the prosecution team discussed a few issues in the hallway outside the courtroom before it started. They do that so they can try to get on the same page so neither side looks bad in front of the judge. Judges seem to have little patience for squabbling. They bantered back and forth a bit and I only heard a few words so it was inconsequential to me. There was some jousting in court and I was growing tired of the bullshit. After I pled not guilty again court was over and I left the building after getting my phone back. On the steps of the courthouse I told my lawyer to find out once and for all whether Deutsche Bank would fulfill its legal obligations to me or if we would be filing suit in the next week. It was time for action and that made me smile. He agreed and we started down the building steps. Out from behind a hedge of bushes he pops, a dude with a camera the size of my forehead (big). He runs towards us and pops off about thirty pictures as he is walking backwards. Then he says "thank you" and scurries away. I had previously warned my lawyer that if I saw a photographer, I was going to pull down my pants and walk backwards, so he would not know which side to photograph. I was thinking about pulling that off as he clicked his pictures. You know damn well if I had time I may have done it. It was all good, just a matter of time anyway. So I got my picture on a few web sites. Bully for them.

I have no issues at all with the photographer. He was just doing his job and once I was charged it's just the way it is. If you're charged or if you are a fame whore, you get what you get. I feel bad for actors who are good at their art (acting) and are not fame whores, but who get paparazzied to death. And leave kids alone for goodness sakes.

On my way home, my wife and kids were inquiring how my court date went. I was driving but wanted to let them know it was fine and all was well. As I stopped at a red light I pecked out the following text and hit send to our group string: *Out of court, all good.* I wanted to allay their worries. As it turns out, in my rush to hit send before the light turned I unknowingly sent: *out of court, all goodbye.* Freakin' Autocorrect. I did not realize it but that text sent off a panic. I heard the texts whizzing back to me but never checked my text or their responses until I was parked in my garage. We had a good laugh that night at my stupidity.

A month after my court date the deadline for moving or liquidating my Charles Schwab & Co. bond account had come and gone. I checked daily to see if they liquidated my account as their letter stated they would. I wanted to know when the check was coming. A few weeks of no change after their deadline and I started to become optimistic that maybe they had a change of heart. I should have known better than to be optimistic. A few days later I went to log in to my account and it would not grant me access. Begrudgingly, I accepted that they were going to go through with what I felt was an un-American act and close my account. I decided to call their compliance department to see how long it would take. I got some douchebag on the phone who was probably a lawyer and he tells me the account will not be liquidated, it will be considered abandoned and will be sent to state probate court. "It will probably take years to get access back and it will cost you a percentage also." He said all bets were off and that I'd better get moving to transfer the account. He had my little raisins in a vice. Why did they have to lie? If your letter says you will liquidate it and send me a check, why lie and then do this. I ended the call by telling him he has a damn tough job if he does this to people every day for a living. So now I became desperate to get this sorted.

Thank goodness my bank accounts had stayed open. I had my checking and savings account with Chase as well as my credit cards. I had been a customer for over twenty-five years. I had accepted that it was legally possible for an investment account to be closed out of the blue for no reason, but certainly not bank accounts or credit cards, right? Wrong again, Matt. The letter came in late October as I was dealing with the Schwab transfer. Chase was closing my checking and savings account in thirty days and my credit cards in ninety days. That was a huge blow. What now? Scramble.

The worst part of Chase doing that was we had a long history and I had let them off the hook big-time twenty years previously. While banking in Chase at a downtown New York branch, one of their tellers defrauded our account. That employee took one of our supposedly closed overdraft accounts and maxed it out, putting the cash right in her pocket. The employee then changed the address to some P.O. box. She did this to a bunch of customers and then fled the country. All the bills for the overdrafts were going to a dead end post office box so we never had a clue. My wife and I found out because we started getting calls from collection agencies regarding a debt we did not know about. It also totally trashed our credit score. It was concerning because we were still very young and had not even started our family yet. I was too cheap to get my own lawyer so I talked to one where I worked, JP Morgan. When I found out we were defrauded, the JPM lawyer was sure they would be willing to settle for $20,000 to us just to keep it quiet.

The next week, Chase folks asked me to come down to the branch. I entered an office with about ten officers of the bank. They explained the whole fraud to me and exactly what happened. The group apologized profusely and said they wanted to "rectify" the situation. This was my chance to go for my $20,000. You know what I did? I told them, instead, to sort my account and fix my credit score. We'd call it even. Everyone makes mistakes. What an idiot.

For some reason I expected some good karma from that, especially from Chase. Nope. No good deed goes unpunished. As much as I see examples of that, I will never give up hope in humanity. Call me naive.

With my luck we would be moving money around because all of our accounts are being closed and the government would turn around and accuse me of hiding money from them. That's all I need. I let my pre-trial services officer know of my situation, as well as the government. I don't trust it will matter. What a cynic I am becoming.

As 2017 started, I had one account left in my name. I was getting by and maybe one place had some scruples left and I'd be able to skate by. Nope. On the last day of January I got an email from CapitalOne that my accounts, as well as my kids' accounts, were being shut down. One day's notice. By the next morning I had lost access and so had my kids. By this time I didn't even bother calling to beg. I just hit "reply" to every email and wrote "UN-AMERICAN." Won't do a damn bit of good but it makes me feel better. We will figure it out. It's a minor inconvenience compared to the real problems people have in this world. We will always have that perspective.

So I now stand accountless. It's eleven months from my

trial date of 2/21/2018 and every day I chuckle inside and wonder what's coming next. It's been a crazy roller coaster ride for the last thirty years and it ain't over yet. I am ready for whatever comes next. For some bizarre reason I get stronger for every obstacle my family and I climb over. It has taken this for me to find total happiness and peace. Tough to believe, I know. I can't explain it myself. I have no idea how this will turn out and how it does for me is irrelevant. The fight, for me, is more important than the result. Until the bitter end, when I am surrounded...I will attack.

www.ingramcontent.com/pod-product-compliance
Lightning Source LLC
Chambersburg PA
CBHW020416010526
44118CB00010B/271